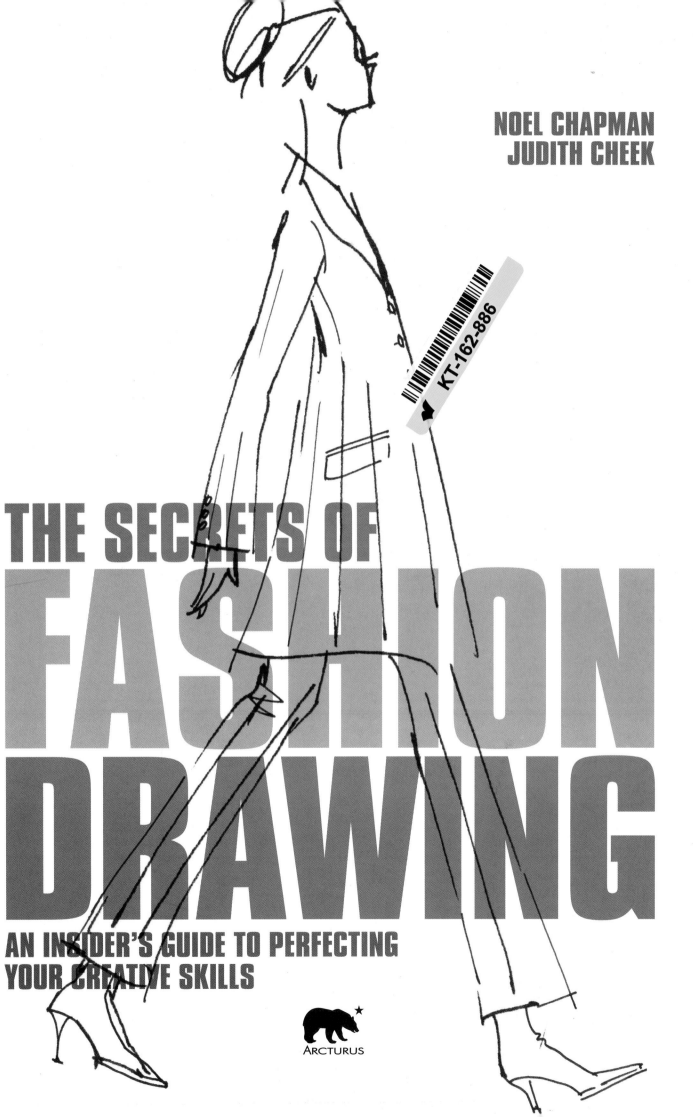

NOEL CHAPMAN
JUDITH CHEEK

KT-162-886

THE SECRETS OF
FASHION
DRAWING

AN INSIDER'S GUIDE TO PERFECTING
YOUR CREATIVE SKILLS

ARCTURUS

NOEL CHAPMAN trained in fashion and textiles at Liverpool John Moores University. He is a consultant designer specializing in knitwear, market and creative intelligence, who works with a wide range of clients throughout Europe, the USA and the Far East. Noel lectures in fashion, textiles and knitwear design and is a collector/dealer of vintage indigo textiles under the name Bleu Anglais. Previous books include *Careers in Art & Design* published by Kogan Page, *Careers in Fashion* published by Kogan Page and *Creative Fashion Drawing*, published by Arcturus, in collaboration with Judith Cheek. He is currently researching a book on Chinese folk textiles.
www.noelchapman.co.uk
www.bleuanglais.co.uk

JUDITH CHEEK trained in fashion design at St Martins School of Art before specializing in illustration. She works with a wide range of clients across all levels of the industry and her illustration work covers fashion, beauty, health and exercise, cookery and food. Previous books include *Creative Fashion Drawing*, published by Arcturus, in collaboration with Noel Chapman.
www.judithcheek.co.uk

We would like to thank everyone who has so generously given their time and their work to this book, and would like to say a very special thanks to Yvonne Deacon for her huge contribution, for freely sharing her thoughts and ideas, for her artwork and her tutorials. We would also like to thank Ashley Gray at Gray Modern & Contemporary Art for allowing us to use some of their wonderful collection of vintage fashion illustrations. Without everyone's generosity, this book would never have happened.

ARCTURUS

This edition published in 2014 by
Arcturus Publishing Limited
26/27 Bickels Yard, 151–153 Bermondsey Street,
London SE1 3HA

ISBN: 978-1-78212-641-6
AD003875UK

Printed in China

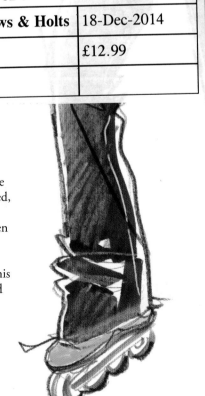

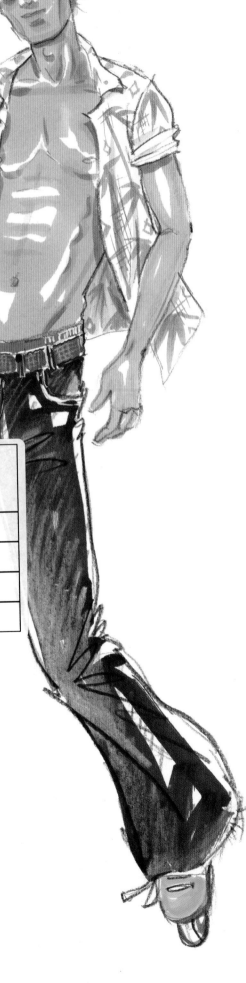

CONTENTS

INTRODUCTION

This book looks at the role which drawing and illustration plays in fashion – in designing, manufacturing and in the communication and promotion of fashion, fashion ideas and concepts. It explores the continuing importance of drawing in the creative process and shows how, despite the role electronic communication and the digital image plays at most levels of the industry today, drawing remains key. It is the primary skill of any designer worth their salt – whether it is drawing in the free, individualistic style associated with designers at the more creative end of the business, or in the everyday habits and processes of the working designer, or in the meticulous, digitally combined renditions now demanded by many areas of the industry.

This book helps you to build upon basic skills, knowledge and understanding and reveals many of the secrets of fashion drawing and illustration which underpin the industry. We begin by looking at materials, equipment and at ways of working; then we go on to address the language of fashion, its origins and uses. We answer some regularly asked questions, add a little insight into the rich and historic background to some of our most beloved clothes and fabrics, and correct a few misuses of names and phrases with a lively illustrated vocabulary. We make understanding colour a fun and fascinating study, unveiling some of its mysteries via clear diagrams and enlightening information. We discuss the importance and significance of colour in fashion and how it has spawned a whole industry on its own. We look at the importance of developing your own drawing style, at techniques for documenting and collecting

primary research and for recording and generating original ideas. Getting your ideas down on paper is often the first stage for many designers, whatever the exact end product or market positioning. This is followed by the important stage of refining, adapting and developing the ideas to achieve their best outcome, to best fulfil the aim of the assignment, whatever the specific brief.

Designer and university lecturer Yvonne Deacon takes us through the creative process of designing, from concept, research and development through to final line-ups. She also shares layout and presentation secrets in an enlightening visual tutorial.

Learning to adhere to a brief is key to the success of a design, and perhaps key to being commissioned for a specific job. We discuss how to follow a brief and how, after generating and developing ideas to a certain point, a designer or illustrator may be required to present ideas, or 'finished roughs', at an intermediate stage. It can be handy at this stage to think of drawings as proposals. There may be little point in taking your ideas through to beautifully crafted 'finished' drawings if there is an approval, selection or editing stage in the process. This is where the 'finished rough' is valid and useful. We look at how to develop a clear, readable style, with ideas documented and explained, because it is

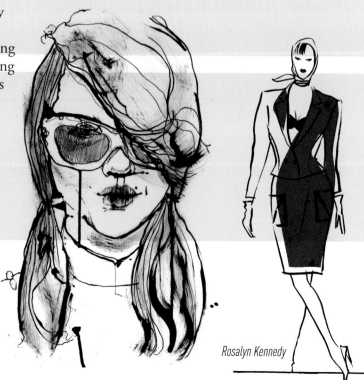

Patrick Morgan   *Patrick Morgan*   *Rosalyn Kennedy*

important to remember that your drawing often has to talk for you if you are not present at this stage.

We look at 'finished drawings' – what they are and when they are appropriate. We examine a range of drawing styles and presentation ideas, show the techniques involved, discuss their suitability and reveal some of the tricks designers and illustrators have developed to speed up jobs and produce better results. We explain when and where different styles of drawing are used and why they may be necessary, at how drawings need to be fit for purpose and what they indicate or suggest – silhouette, cut, detail and proportion, fabrication and colour, styling and outfit coordination, or the less tangible aspects.

We look at the supporting and collaborative roles illustration plays in the industry; at how a designer's sketches can be used to instruct the maker/factory, and how illustrators may need to draw existing garments for promotional purposes, for example.

We peek behind the scenes to discover how aspects of the industry work, as practising professionals reveal details of their careers, experiences, training, ambitions, planning and their often-serendipitous pathways through different aspects of the industry. Many share their skills, favoured materials, media and techniques and guide

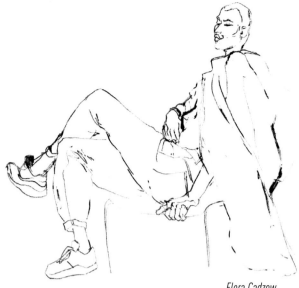

Flora Cadzow

us through the sequences and processes of their work where we learn the kind of valuable insights that can't be taught in the classroom alone.

The inclusion of vintage illustrations highlights an even broader range of styles and techniques while making the point that quality prevails, fashion is cyclical and the past always has something valid to offer the future.

The Secrets of Fashion Drawing is a down-to-earth yet inspiring and practical insight into aspects of drawing and illustration in the real world of fashion, with help from many of its key practitioners.

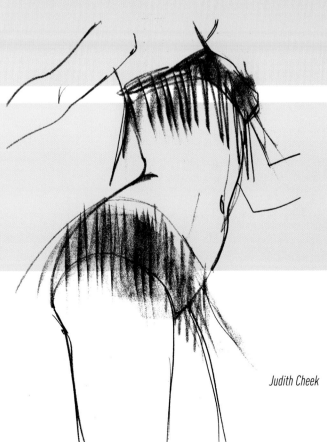

Judith Cheek

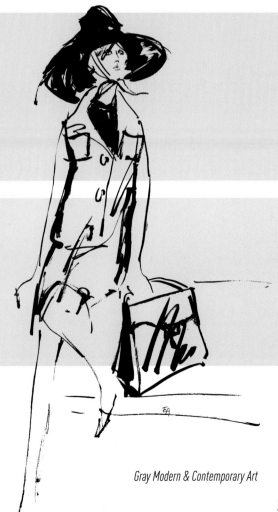

Gray Modern & Contemporary Art

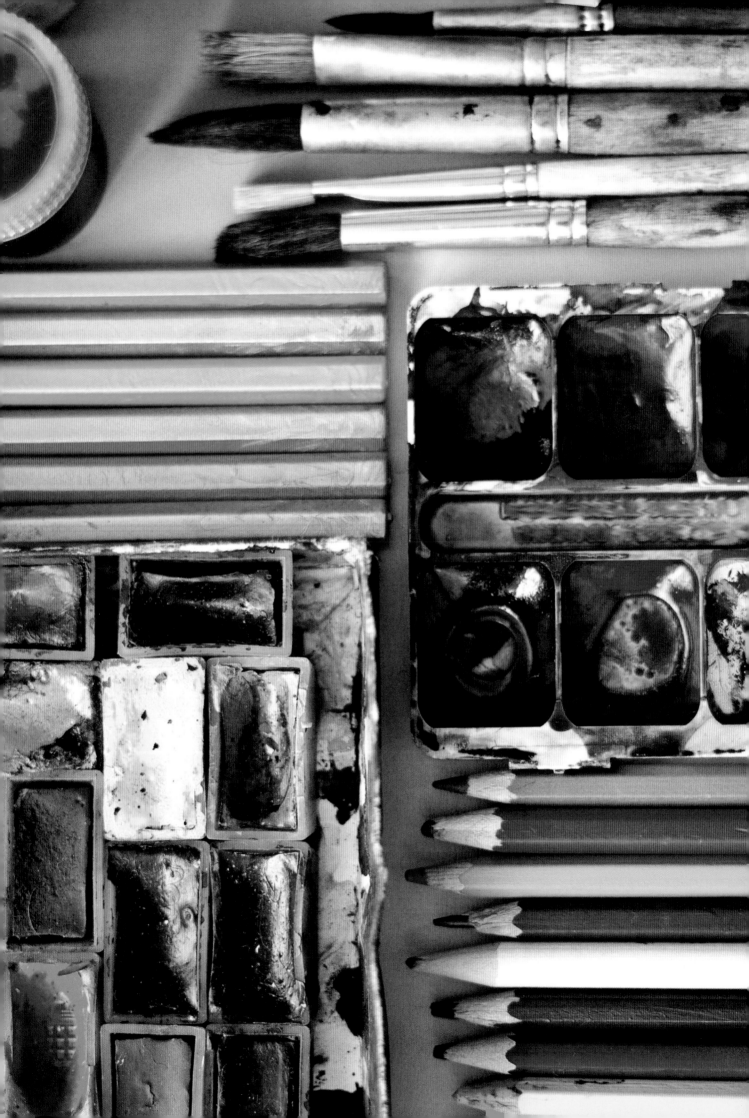

01 MATERIALS

For the contemporary designer or illustrator, the range and choice of materials and equipment can be bewildering. As well as all the traditional elements one can think of, there is an increasing amount of technical kit, though, to be fair, the technical stuff is getting progressively easier (and cheaper!) to use. Nevertheless, drawing in the traditional sense, with a pencil or pen and paper, is still the most fundamental and valuable skill of the designer and illustrator. Everything else is just a more or less sophisticated bit of additional equipment. As with all techniques, proficiency and expertise in fashion drawing result from practice and experimentation.

Larger and more costly equipment should be bought on the basis of what you need and when you need it; this may also be governed by the requirements of the job in hand, and the end purpose. For recording and generating ideas, the need is immediate and little more than a half-decent sketchbook, a few pencils, basic pens and some crayons for colour are a great start. For a more professional job that involves some level of presentation, a slightly bigger investment may be necessary (we will discuss following project briefs in detail later in this book). Further considerations should include whether the presentation is to be made as physical/hard copy or in a digital format.

THE LIFESPAN OF AN ARTWORK
Another related factor may concern the longevity of the work itself. For hard copy work it's not usually essential to think about the lifespan of the artwork; most work is relatively short-term – the real finished piece being perhaps printed. Or, as is the case with a designer's drawings, they are probably for one season only. But in some instances longevity may be a consideration. With time, most papers age and turn yellow and pigments in pens, paints and crayons can fade or change colour. So, for certain projects, more expensive archival materials such as acid-free paper, stable pigments and so forth may need to be a choice. Some of these considerations may also apply when you come to storing your old work or records of your work. Photocopies and some print-outs will fade after a few years (or less in bright sunlight) and some pigments will migrate, so drawing sheets may need to be interleaved to stop colour bleeding through stacks. In a portfolio, photocopies and some pigments may in time stick to the clear plastic pockets, which means you won't be able to remove them. Adhesive sprays and sticking tapes can dry out in hot conditions or lose their 'sticky' in humid ones. Other glues and sticky tapes will eventually 'ghost' through papers or fabric swatches. So in some instances you may want to store your work digitally. Digital records and archives should be backed-up on a separate hard drive and clearly labelled.

Few designers work solely digitally, as the very process of designing requires the physical immediacy of the hand-drawn process to record, generate, manipulate, develop and problem-solve ideas. However, digital processes are used increasingly for presentation and secondary development, colourways and the presentation and communication of more finalized ideas.

While many designers and illustrators use a combination of hand drawn and digital processes, some illustrators work exclusively digitally, as their task is to present an idea or concept that has already been developed. Rather than having to go through exactly the same creative processes as the designer, the illustrators' problems and considerations are somewhat different and some find they can work them all out on screen.

ORGANIZING YOUR WORKSPACE

Wherever you work, however small your workspace, it is important to be organized. Whether you are lucky enough to have a lovely modern studio or are working from home in a cosy corner, it is important to have a designated area no matter how limited the space. You can make yourself feel more positive about it by adopting the language of estate agents and thinking of it not as 'small', but as 'bijou and compact'! There is an argument that it's actually easier to be more organized and efficient in a small space than it is in a large one. Maybe this comes from someone talking up their own situation, but certainly it's good to have the stuff you need and use most regularly within arm's reach and often on view. There is, after all, often a great aesthetic to functional and traditional tools, equipment and materials.

As all those space people on TV shows and in magazines keep reminding us, 'good storage is the key to good organizing'. But good storage doesn't have to be expensive or even permanent, and options range from specialist to utilitarian and even novelty systems. All manner of boxes, crates and trays can hold papers, materials and equipment. Pots, tins and vintage finds can hold pencils and pens in readiness.

BELOW: *Desk plan for a right-handed person*

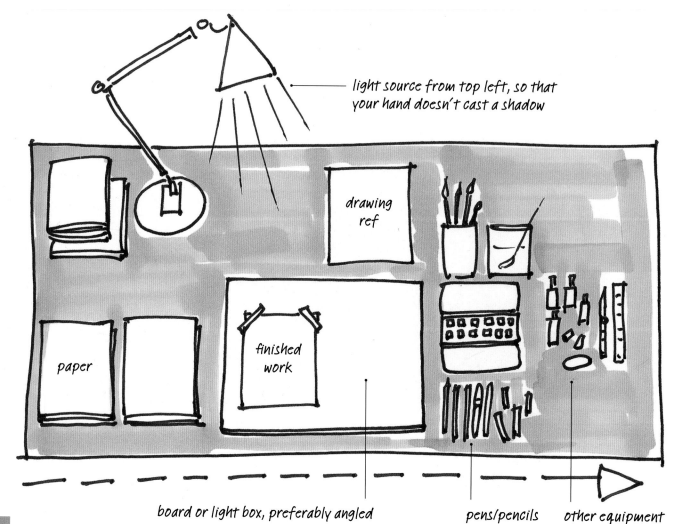

light source from top left, so that your hand doesn't cast a shadow

drawing ref

paper

finished work

board or light box, preferably angled

pens/pencils

other equipment

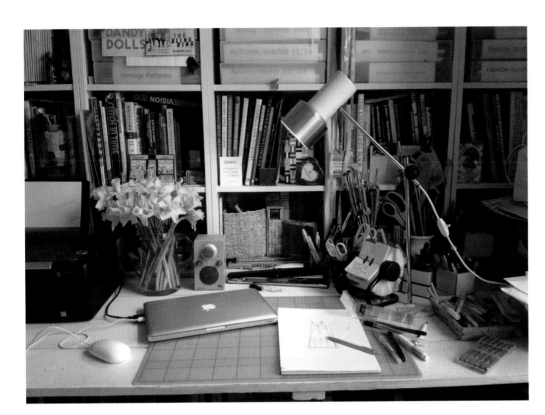

CHOOSING WHERE TO WORK

If you are a freelance or self-employed designer, your workspace will most likely be decided by budget at the beginning. Most cities have areas where space is a little cheaper; somewhere downtown maybe, a redevelopment area, or a place that other designers and creative folk have already found. Perhaps an area long established or a new one, rediscovered, which creatives have started to colonize and regenerate. Working in such an area can be great; it means you have like-minded neighbours and, ideally, services and suppliers too.

When looking for studio/workspace it's worth making yourself a checklist of what you need within reasonable distance. And don't forget the distance and travelling time from home, which may change throughout the year if the area has a seasonal tourist trade, for instance. Your checklist may include; an art supplies shop, a printer or photocopying bureau, a post office or courier service (if you are regularly going to have to send off 'physical' work). A nearby café or coffee shop might be a big plus too – for daily sustenance and as somewhere you can go to escape your own space for a while, do your emails using their wifi, or just to chat to other people – if you work on your own all day, you can go a bit cabin crazy!

Similar criteria and needs apply if you work from home, which has the advantage of saving you the expense and time of commuting to and fro. Many suppliers and services can be ordered over the telephone or online and delivered (often free) to your studio or home address. One of the possible disadvantages of working from home – though usually well compensated for by the advantages – is that you may feel that you never quite finish work.

*'For a number of years I had a work area in the corner of my sitting room; it worked well, utilizing an old dining table I'd found in the street, painted up as a desk, the extending leaves proving most useful from time to time. I would sometimes throw a cloth over my desk or stand a vintage screen in front to make sure it stayed undisturbed – even by well meaning but curiously enquiring visiting friends wanting to know what I was up to! – at other times just to hide it from myself, to enable me to **finish** work! Now I am lucky enough to have a small workroom at home – even though it gets pressed into service from time to time as a spare room for a guest – it is a great satisfaction to be able, especially at the end of a long extended day, finally to be able to walk out and close the door. A significant and symbolic gesture to myself that I've finished work and that everything will be as I left it, in the morning.'*

Noel Chapman

Wherever you work, it is important to be able to call the space your own, to personalize it to some extent, if possible, and to be able to get up from your desk and leave your work *just so* and undisturbed to come back to later, tomorrow, or after a weekend away.

PAPER

Paper is something we all take for granted, knowing little about its history and failing fully to grasp the range of its uses and possibilities: from the legal documents that control and facilitate our lives, to the products we use and purchase every day and even to the money with which we make those purchases. As creative people, where would we be without it? But even though we may consume great quantities of the stuff, we often under-explore its range and potentials.

The name paper derives from the Ancient Greek *Cyperus papyrus*, a plant from which the Ancient Egyptians created, by lamination, a paper-like material. In the 2nd century BCE, the Chinese invented paper more or less as we know it today, through a process of macerating plant fibres. Hemp and mulberry (a by-product of sericulture) were the chief fibre sources for these early papers. Paper spread slowly westwards from China along the Silk Road, through Samarkand, and by the 10th century had reached Morocco and the Iberian peninsular. Production continued to expand through Europe, where the invention of the printing press in Germany in the 15th century created something of a revolution and paper was its key protagonist. During the Industrial Revolution, mechanization facilitated paper's transition from luxury handmade

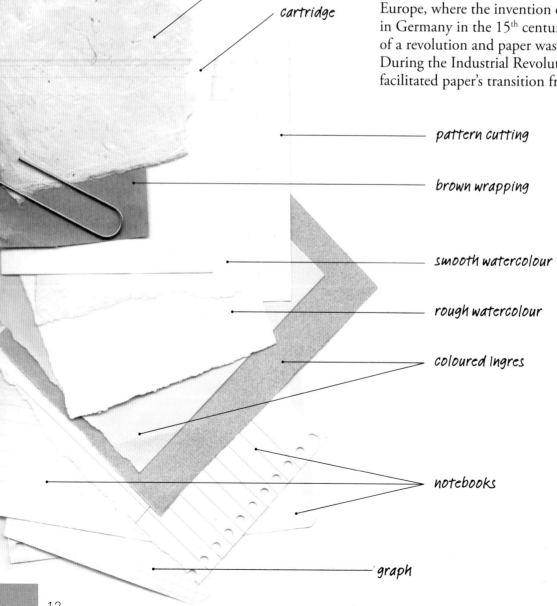

rough hand-made

cartridge

pattern cutting

brown wrapping

smooth watercolour

rough watercolour

coloured Ingres

notebooks

graph

craft material to ubiquitous, even commonplace, item. To the artist, designer and illustrator it remains an invaluable essential, despite the challenges of our digital age.

The following list offers information about paper's forms, availability and uses. For specialist jobs it's worth doing in-depth research. Some prized types of paper include *lokta* from Nepal and *kozo*, a mulberry-fibre paper from Japan. When travelling you may find local speciality paper sellers or, in little local shops and supermarkets, notebooks and pads of unusual grades and tones.

- Sketch books (various sizes and weights of paper): a small pocket notebook (A5 or such) is good for ideas on the go.
- Basic bulk paper for working out ideas: A4 and A3 size printer paper, weight around 80gsm (grams per square metre). Best bought in ream packs (500 sheets) from office suppliers, etc.
- Layout paper: this is finer than the bulk type (about 45gsm–55gsm) and semi-transparent. You can work through a series of roughs – amending, changing and redrawing, just by putting another sheet on top, until you get your 'finished rough'.

A good way of doing this is to buy the paper as a pad and begin at the back, working forward. It's worth remembering that spirit pens and fibre tips will bleed through to the underneath sheet.

- Cartridge paper: a good heavyweight paper that can take various media; an economical choice if you want to experiment with various ways of putting down colour.
- Bleedproof paper: around 70gsm, for use with spirit-based pens (marker pens). It allows you to put down flat colour with a clean edge. In the US there is a heavier weight type called 'Paris' bleedproof paper; in the UK an alternative is Bristol Board (see rag paper below), about 250gsm, a smooth paper, double faced, which can be used either side. Bleedproof paper is excellent for 'air brush' techniques. It is good to use heavier weight paper if the finished drawing is for your portfolio, as thinner paper starts to look shabby quite quickly but is all right for artwork going to print.
- Watercolour paper: for watercolour paints and coloured inks. It comes in two forms: 'cold press' (called NOT), has a rough, textured surface and is good for transparent washes and inks; 'hot press' (HP) gives a smoother finish, which is good for opaque paints such as gouache. All watercolour paper comes in various textures and weights, from fairly lightweight 90gsm to around 300gsm.
- Ingres/coloured papers for pastel work, gouache or collage: this is a beautiful laid paper taking its name from the neoclassical French painter who favoured it. Characterized by its subtle but distinctive lines, produced during milling and available in a wide range of attractively soft colours.
- Rag paper: perhaps one of the oldest examples of recycling, originally made from old clothes – hence its name. More specific versions are linen and cotton paper which are used to make banknotes more durable. Bristol and Somerset are both rag papers whose fibre composition remains the same as when they were first manufactured in the late 19th century. Somerset® is a world leading traditional printmaking paper, mould-made from 100% cotton to high archival standards.
- 'Found' paper: in addition to paper you can buy, you can use scraps torn from magazines, packaging paper and other interesting coloured and textured papers as good stock for drawing and collage work. These make an ideal media mix for fashion illustrations and can be used directly or scanned and used digitally.

ESSENTIAL AND BASIC KIT

The definition of essential equipment depends on whether you are more illustrator than designer, or a little of both. One of the first considerations is what size you should work at. US paper sizes differ from European ones, where standard sizes are formatted from A1 down. This affects whether your work will fit a standard portfolio case and whether you need to scan or copy it for your own records, and also how it will print out in the country you may be sending it to electronically. Most professional European portfolios are A3 maximum, but designers often also have a second smaller A4 version as well as digital files. While a smart digital presentation from an iPad is hugely convenient and can be impressive, for many people technology is no substitute for the touchy-feely experience and accurate colour of a physical portfolio.

The following lists offer guidance to essential and basic kit requirements; you may already own or have easy access to many of these items. Some of what is considered essential depends on individual choice and the type of work you do and includes considerations such as the use of roller and ballpoint pens to facilitate quick mark making and convenience. While the 'Must Have' list contains essentials, the 'Favourites' list is more personal and dependent on the type of work you do. Our 'On the Go' list consists of those few essentials you probably want to have with you always, and the 'Wish' list suggests some of the bigger stuff to save up for – one day. . . . Of course, you can add to or edit these lists to meet your own particular needs and preferences.

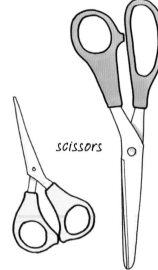

scissors

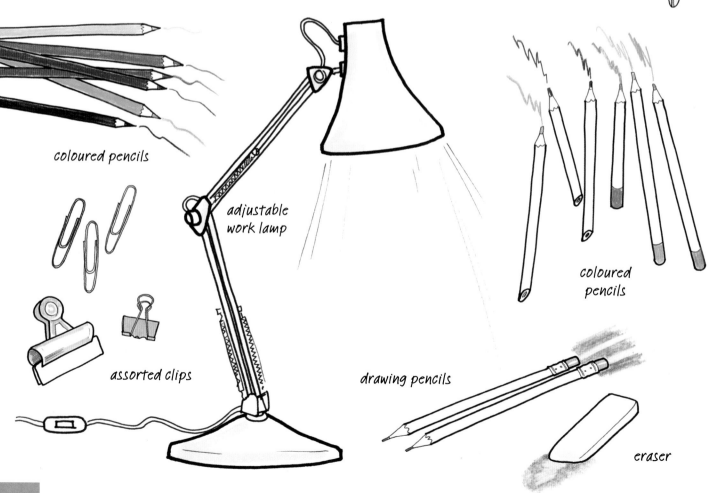

coloured pencils

adjustable work lamp

coloured pencils

assorted clips

drawing pencils

eraser

MUST HAVE LIST

- Adjustable work lamp with a daylight bulb for colour accuracy
- Comfy chair
- Selection of drawing pencils – graded hard to soft
- Pencil sharpener
- Eraser and eraser 'pencil' for finer work
- Coloured pencils
- Ballpoint and rollerball pens
- Scissors
- Assorted clips
- Dip pen and ink
- Fine fibre-tipped pens 0.05 to 0.8
- Brush pen
- Marker pens – perhaps the designer's most useful medium for adding colour speadily and cleanly
- Cutting mat – also good as a drawing surface and to help define a working area on a crowded desk
- Craft knife and blades
- Steel rule – for cutting and measuring
- Perspex rule – for measuring and drawing against
- Corrector pen
- Drawing curve
- Set square
- Masking tape
- Clear sticky tape – for 'ordinary' jobs
- Clear 'magic' removable sticky tape – for specific tasks
- Glue stick
- Sticky notes for notes to self and as positioning guides

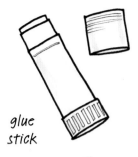

glue stick

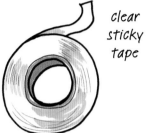

clear sticky tape

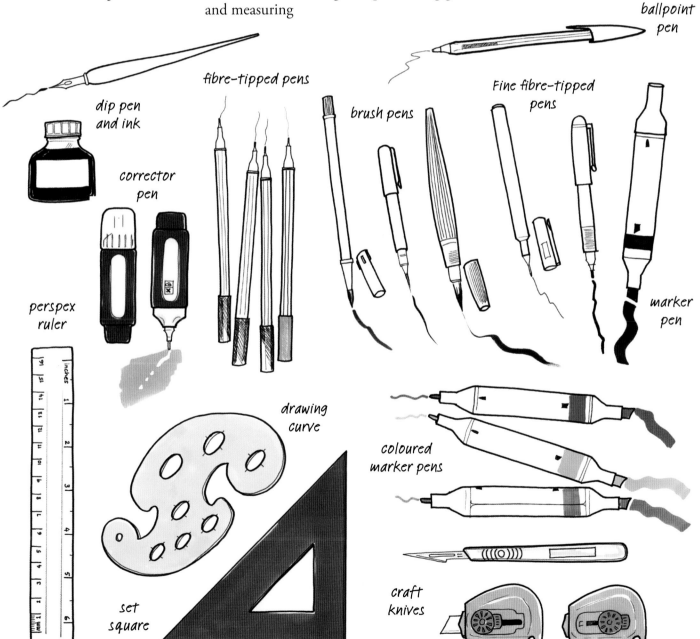

ballpoint pen

fibre-tipped pens

dip pen and ink

corrector pen

brush pens

Fine fibre-tipped pens

marker pen

perspex ruler

drawing curve

coloured marker pens

set square

craft knives

MUST HAVE LIST, CONTINUED

- Layout pad – 50gsm A4 or A3, according to preference
- Laptop or desktop personal computer
- A4 printer/scanner
- Inexpensive printer paper – 60/80gsm for roughs, etc.
- Desk-ready sketchbook
- Higher quality printer paper – 80/90/100gsm, for colour and finished work
- Selection of lined and graph papers – as drawing guides for checks, plaids and stripes, etc. Can be downloaded for free (see pages 156–9 for websites)
- Small stapler
- Long-arm stapler
- Pin board – or somewhere you can post important information and reminders to yourself along with inspirational images that will help personalize your workspace

ON THE GO LIST

- Pencil case with your favourite drawing materials – we love automatic pencils because they are sharp, clean and quick!
- Handy size sketchbook – A5 is great for your pocket or bag and can be used as a notebook
- Mobile telephone, for handy camera reference, record-making and notes

FAVOURITES LIST

- Graphite pencil
- Chinagraph pencil
- Conté pencils
- Charcoal pencil
- Chalk pastels
- Oil pastels
- Watercolours
- Acrylics
- Paint brushes for watercolours, acrylics and gouache
- Coloured inks
- Designers' gouache paints
- Soft sponge and roller
- Fixative spray
- Adhesive spray

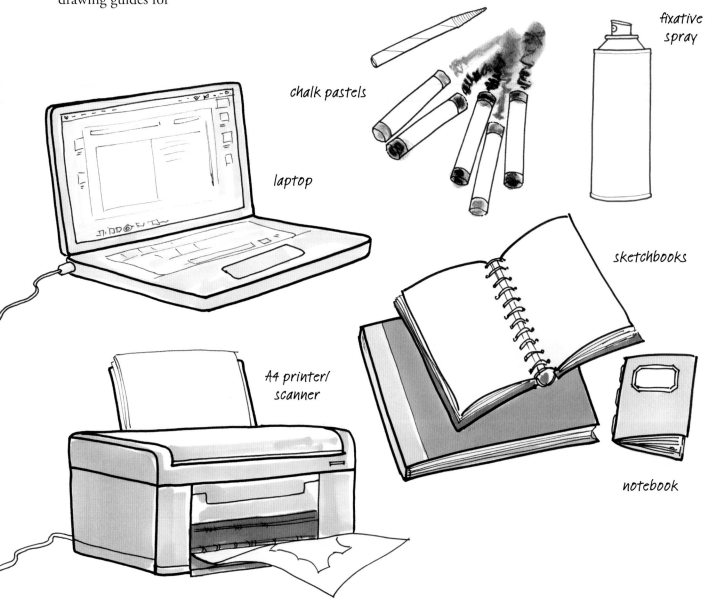

chalk pastels

fixative spray

laptop

sketchbooks

A4 printer/ scanner

notebook

WISH LIST
- A3 printer/scanner
- Light box – for tracing and copying drawings
- Desktop pencil sharpener
- Photoshop program
- Adobe Illustrator (industry preferred) or similar program
- Tablet for drawing and photography
- Professional camera

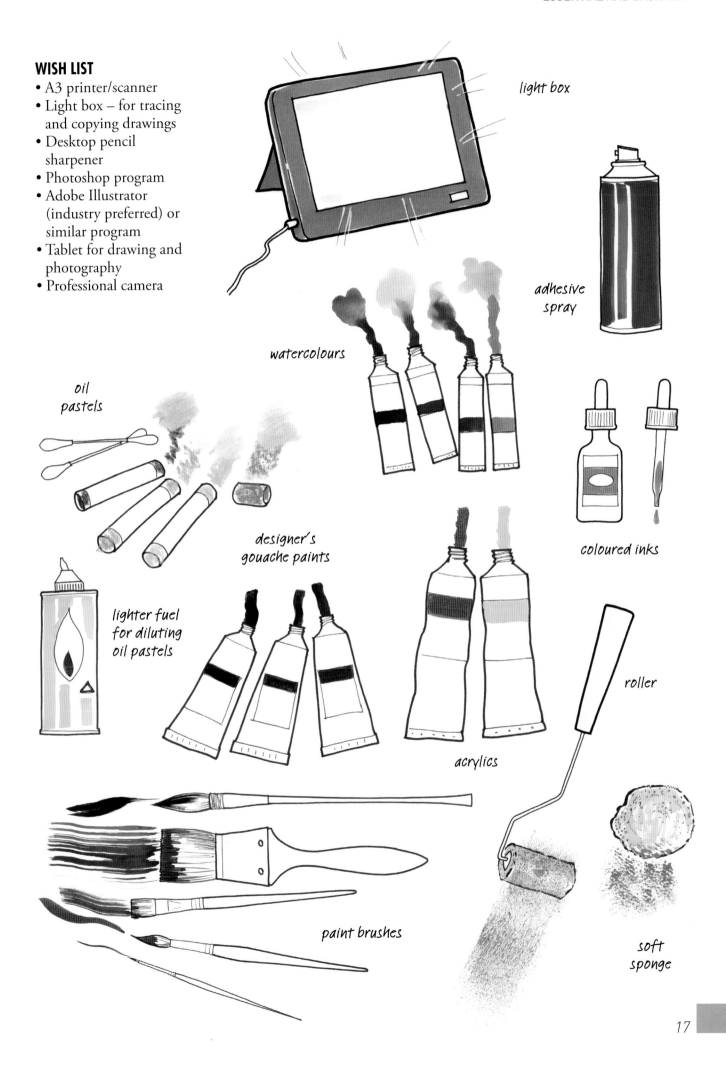

light box

adhesive spray

watercolours

oil pastels

coloured inks

designer's gouache paints

lighter fuel for diluting oil pastels

acrylics

roller

paint brushes

soft sponge

BASIC SKILLS

Fashion drawing requires the ability to draw accurately and symmetrically. Drawing involves the strict coordination of hand and eye. The page or drawing surface must be full-square to the drawer, as having the page at an odd angle or writing diagonally results in distorted hand positions and will spoil your work. It is worth remembering that professional designers may be required to draw all day, for days on end. The tensions that build up in the hand and arm can prove detrimental to long-term health and wellbeing; but they can largely be avoided by correct posture and hand positioning. This is equally as important as a good chair and proper sitting position are for the care of your back.

HOW TO HOLD A PENCIL CORRECTLY

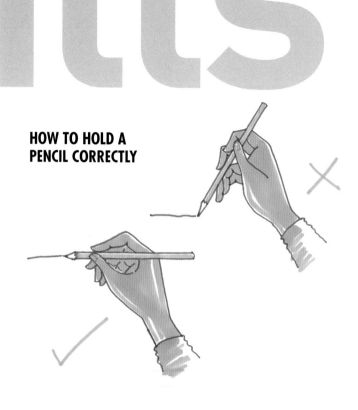

DRAWING CURVES AND CIRCLES

Following the movements shown here will make drawing easier, simpler and ultimately more successful. They can be broken down into steps – using fingers, hand and arm – and are particularly useful when drawing curves and circles, which can be tricky. There are four key movements, depending on the scale of drawing and size of curve:

- Fingers – for small curves, drawings and details, using the simple manipulation of the fingers
- Wrist and hand – for larger curves, using the basic 'hinge' movement of the wrist back and forth
- Elbow and forearm – for large curves and arcs; the elbow needs to lift off the drawing surface to facilitate freer movement
- Whole arm – for very large drawings, using the swing of the arm and even full body movements.

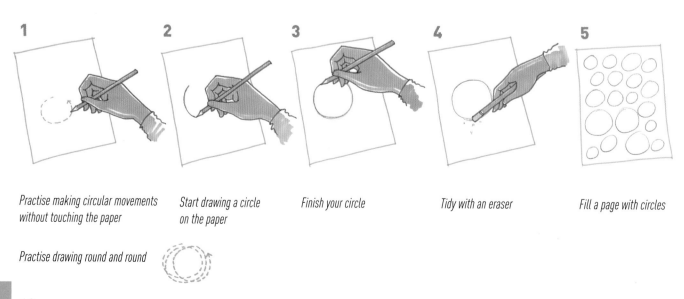

1 Practise making circular movements without touching the paper

Practise drawing round and round

2 Start drawing a circle on the paper

3 Finish your circle

4 Tidy with an eraser

5 Fill a page with circles

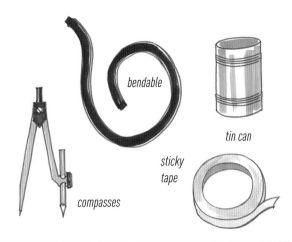

You can use found objects to draw round – the inside of your roll of sticky tape, a lid or tin can, and not forgetting traditional compasses like the ones you used at school. There are also clever bendable guides you can buy specially for the purpose.

bendable

tin can

sticky tape

compasses

To help understand the range and limitations of these movements it's best to practise a few of them with a small range of equipment and media; pencil, pen, brush, ink and paint, etc. The best, most successful curves are generally drawn in one stroke, from inside the curve – following the body's natural movement – and with a certain amount of speed to keep the stroke fluid. This may be an instance where turning the page can produce a better result. When drawing small curves – a neckline on a garment, for example – there is a point at which, in the action of drawing, the pen changes from being dragged to being pushed. It is at this point that a bump or wobble occurs, so it is important to recognize and if necessary to compensate by moving or turning your drawing page. Of course it may not always be possible to turn your drawing round, you may have to move your body instead. If you are doing a large drawing and want to draw a nice, continuous sweeping curve not only do you need the physical space to work in, you also need suitable media. You've already chosen your paper or board and considered whether it takes wet or dry materials well but if, for example, you are using paint or ink, your brush needs to be large enough to hold enough paint or ink to travel the length of the line.

Of course it's not essential to achieve perfection; sometimes the inaccuracies in a drawing become part of its appeal and character. With practice and growing self-awareness you will be able to judge what adds to and what detracts from the success of a drawing in the context of its end use.

DRAWING CIRCLES USING LITTLE FINGER AS COMPASS

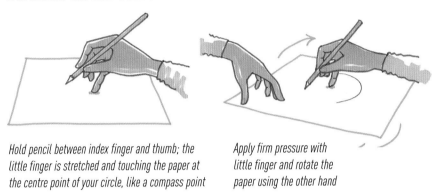

Hold pencil between index finger and thumb; the little finger is stretched and touching the paper at the centre point of your circle, like a compass point

Apply firm pressure with little finger and rotate the paper using the other hand

DRAWING CIRCLES USING WRIST

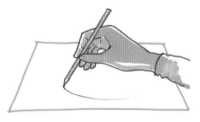
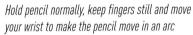
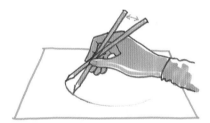

Hold pencil normally, keep fingers still and move your wrist to make the pencil move in an arc

Use lots of little movements to make a large circle and fewer to make a small one, turning the page as necessary

DRAWING CIRCLES USING FOREARM

DRAWING CIRCLES USING WHOLE ARM

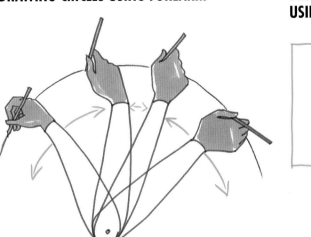
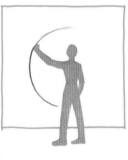

To create large circles, move from the elbow to make wide sweeps in either direction

DESIGN LINE-UP

The start of a new drawing or illustration assignment is influenced by personal choice and the nature of the specific job. We used standard cartridge paper for this line-up of drawings – a good all-rounder suitable for the wide choice of media to be deployed. We used a fine fibre-tip pen for the outlines and main details of the drawings and gave considerable thought to the nature and qualities of the fabrics of the various garments, and the suitability of different media for successful rendering.

1 *Magic marker pens were used for areas of flat colour, together with soft chalk pastels blended with a twisted paper pastel blender. Watercolour paints and a fine brush were used to add further texture and highlights.*

2 *Magic marker pens were again used for the flat base colour; dip pen and white ink were used for the pinstripes; and pencil crayons were used for shading and highlights.*

3 *Designers' gouache paints were used for the flat opaque ground with details picked out in fibre tip pen; shadows and highlights were created using pencil crayons.*

4 *Famous for its qualities of good coverage, acrylic paint was applied with a small sponge roller. When the paint was completely dry, shadows and highlights were added with pencil crayons.*

5 *A swatch of 'mock-croc' was used for rubbing over with conté crayon and pencil crayons to create the appropriate textured effect. Finally the drawing was stabilized with spray fixative.*

HEALTH AND SAFETY NOTE
Spray glues and fixatives should ideally be used in an approved fan-assisted spray booth or at least in a well-ventilated room. Remember to wear a protective face mask – available from good art shops or DIY stores.

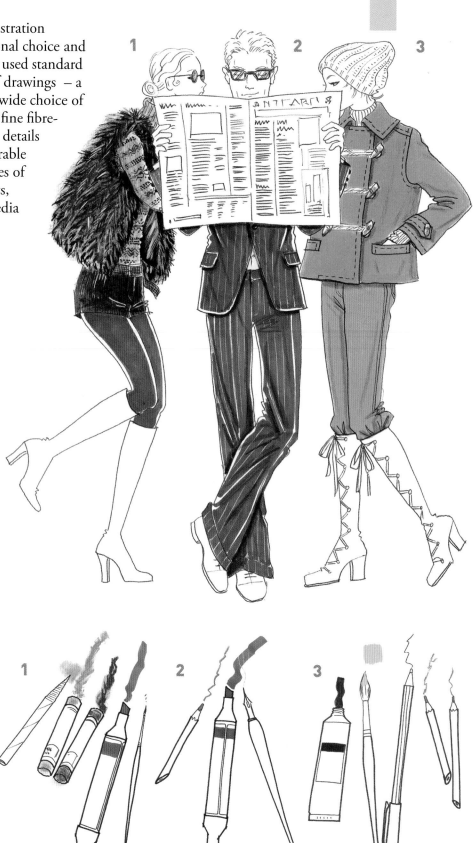

6 *Details of the sweater were coloured with oil pastels blended using cotton buds and a petroleum-based solvent such as lighter fuel, turpentine or white spirit (in a well-ventilated room). For the skirt, scanned fabrics were cut out and collaged using pencil crayons for highlights, definitions and shadows. Finally oil pastels were applied to make the tweed flecks.*

7 *Bold watercolour stroked washes were applied as a base then stippled through a paper doily to create the effect of lace. Pencil crayons were used to add definition; highlights were produced using white ink and dip pen.*

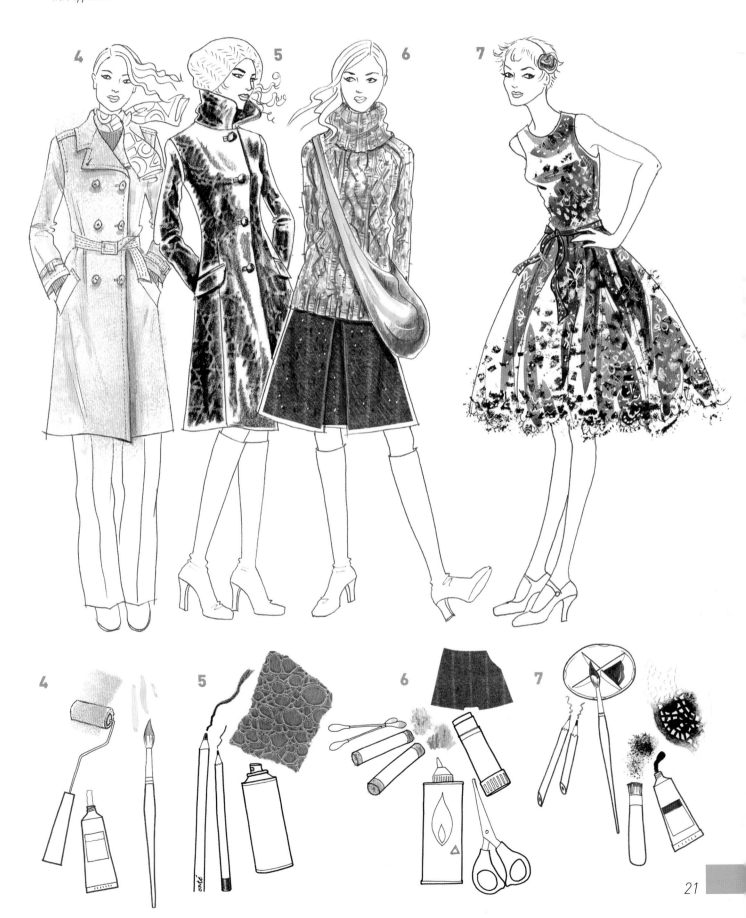

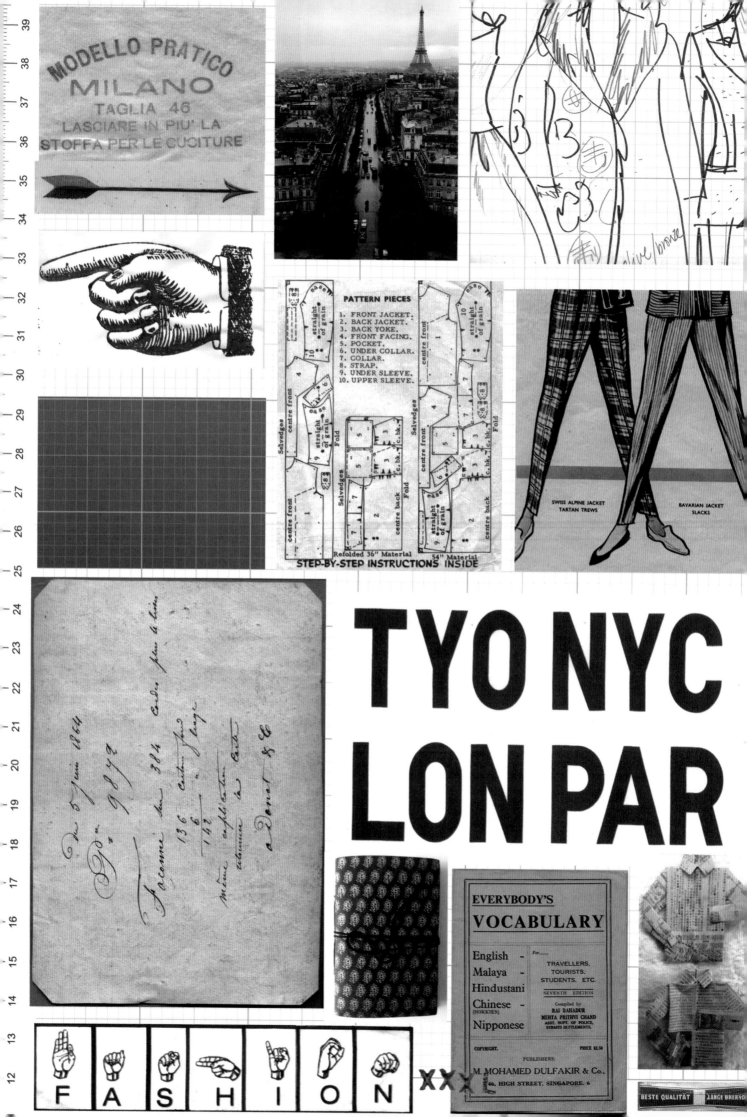

MODELLO PRATICO
MILANO
TAGLIA 46
LASCIARE IN PIU' LA
STOFFA PER LE CUCITURE

PATTERN PIECES

1. FRONT JACKET.
2. BACK JACKET.
3. BACK YOKE.
4. FRONT FACING.
5. POCKET.
6. UNDER COLLAR.
7. COLLAR.
8. STRAP.
9. UNDER SLEEVE.
10. UPPER SLEEVE.

Refolded 36" Material   54" Material
STEP-BY-STEP INSTRUCTIONS INSIDE

SWISS ALPINE JACKET
TARTAN TREWS

BAVARIAN JACKET
SLACKS

TYO NYC
LON PAR

EVERYBODY'S
VOCABULARY

English —
Malaya —
Hindustani —
Chinese —
(HOKKIEN)
Nipponese

For
TRAVELLERS,
TOURISTS,
STUDENTS, ETC.

SEVENTH EDITION

Compiled by
RAI BAHADUR
MEHTA PRITHVI CHAND
ASST. SUPT. OF POLICE,
STRAITS SETTLEMENTS.

COPYRIGHT.   PRICE $2.50

PUBLISHERS:
M. MOHAMED DULFAKIR & Co.,
46, HIGH STREET, SINGAPORE. 6

F A S H I O N   XXX

BESTE QUALITÄT   LANGE BRENND

02 HOW TO SPEAK FASHION

To be successful in any sphere, it is important to be familiar with its terminology and language. This is no less important for fashion designers and illustrators than it is for other professionals, and anyone interested in the fashion trade will benefit from knowing something of its history and traditions and the derivation of specific terms associated with it. Traditional techniques and skills still inform and enhance even the most contemporary and avant garde aspects of the fashion industry, while new phrases and language continue to be imported and taken up as standard.

The importance of learning the correct and universally accepted vocabulary – for your notes, research, understanding of briefs and international communication – is fundamental to any successful career. The aim of this section is, with the inclusion of a little fun, to help inform and inspire you to further study and investigation; to provoke curiosity to discover more; and to encourage you to be diligent and even pedantic about the use of accurate terminology. Your own fashion drawing and design will improve as you gain a sounder knowledge, understanding and appreciation of fashion's crafts and heritage.

We don't attempt to, and cannot be fully comprehensive within the confines of this book, but we hope to explain – along with many established words and regularly used expressions – a few misunderstood ones, to correct a few sloppy ones, and perhaps to revive a few of our favourites which we'd be sad to see disappear. Read on to learn how to speak the language of fashion . . .

INDUSTRY & TECHNICAL TERMS

BESPOKE a custom-made piece of tailoring (particularly menswear); bespoke is also used to refer to custom-made shirts, shoes and boots. Though historically women went to their dressmaker for most of their wardrobe and trousseau, their riding habits and other country attire would often be made *bespoken for*, in the same way as a gentleman's. This service is made to measure and to clients' specific requirements and includes accessories, jewellery and luggage (see also **haute couture**, opposite).

COLLECTION a range of garments which a designer creates for a specific season or label/brand. The term is used increasingly to upgrade and add fashion cachet to all sorts of ranges of products. See also **line-up**, opposite.

COLOURCARD a presentation showing a range of colours for a collection.

COLOUR COMBO an American term for **colour combination**, popularly adopted across the industry.

COLOUR EFFECTS **iridescence** (also known as **goniochromism**, **pearlescence** or, in France, *changeant*), a phenomenon caused by the angle of light on certain surfaces which gives the appearance of colour changes (typically butterfly wings, soap bubbles and sea shells). It is frequently emulated in fabrics, beads and sequins. Fabrics with these qualities are traditionally known as 'shot', which describes the way a contrasting weft colour, sometimes shiny and light-reflecting, is shot through the warp on the shuttle as it is woven. See also **weave/woven**, page 30.

COLOUR PALETTE a selected range of colours, perhaps focussed on a specific season or range of goods.

COLOUR PIGMENTS see **dyeing & dyes**, page 31.

CROQUIS a template for drawing fashion figures. From the French *croquer*, meaning to draw or sketch quickly, though textile designers also use this phrase for a finished painted or drawn textile design.

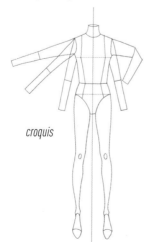

croquis

DANDY generally, a man who dresses flamboyantly with extreme attention to detail. The most famous early dandy was Beau Brummell; others included Lord Byron and Oscar Wilde. Similar terms include **beau**, **gallant** and, perjoratively, **fop**, **coxcomb** and **popinjay**. The end of the 18th century saw the height of dandyism. By the early decades of the 19th century the fashion had acquired some women followers, known as **dandizettes**.

dandy

DATA SHADOW not strictly a fashion term, but used generally and increasingly by fashion companies to describe a person's online shopping and browsing habits that are analysed by marketing companies and used to target their customers for new sales and products.

DELUXE from the French *de luxe* (of luxury) and originally from Latin *luxus* meaning excess.

FASHION the great British designer **Jean Muir**, never too grand to call herself a dressmaker, liked to use the word as a verb – to fashion/to make – to reinforce the notion of the craft of fashion design.

FASHIONISTA a light-heartedly derogatory colloquial term for people in the fashion business or industry.

FLATS drawings of garments as if laid flat, clearly showing all seams, design and construction details, but without the visual complications of fabric pattern, colour or styling.

FLOATS similar to flats, but less rigid, drawn as if animated by an invisible model/wearer.

LAB DIP a swatch of fabric test dyed to specific colour instructions by the factory for approval by the designer.

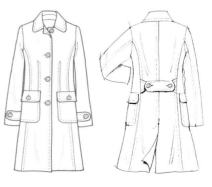

flat   *float*

HAUTE COUTURE literally meaning *high sewing*, this phrase can be traced back to the reign of Louis XVI of France and his 19-year-old queen Marie Antoinette whose love of extravagance and exquisite fashion immortalized the name of her dressmaker, Rose Bertin (1747–1813). Charles Worth, an Englishman working in Paris, is often heralded as the first couturier. Worth opened his atelier in 1858 and, to regulate the craft of haute couture, he founded the Chambre Syndicale de la Couture in 1868. The couturier (only latterly described as the designer, as the emphasis was always placed on craftsmanship rather than simply the design) will make a small selection of garments (models) which are presented to his or her clients. A client chooses a garment which is then specially made, with amendments to suit. An atelier would seldom make more than six costumes of a particular model. Today there are officially 23 designers on the official Chambre Syndicale de la Haute Couture Parisienne calendar. Gowns can take over 800 hours of work and involve the world's most skilled pattern cutters, dressmakers, tailors, embroiderers and beaders. Consequently, daywear starts at around £8,000 ($13,000) – for the rest, the sky is the limit. After the golden age of haute couture in the 1940s and 1950s, the number of customers decreased drastically; but thanks to developing economies it is now estimated that there are 4,000 women worldwide who patronize true couture, an increase of 20–30%, though only a few hundred are regular customers. See also **bespoke**, opposite.

HOMAGE a convenient let-out phrase used when a designer is inspired by or blatantly copies ideas and stylistic characteristics closely identified with another designer.

LINE-UP a row of drawings showing a garment range or collection, or part of one, as if the models were on a runway or catwalk.

LOOK BOOK a book, booklet, pamphlet or such that presents images of a seasonal range or collection, usually given to customers as promotional material. Generally, a look book is also presented online.

NEW LOOK in February 1947, as Paris and the rest of Europe struggled to recover from seven years of war, Christian Dior opened the House of Dior and launched his first collection, entitled Corolle, for the following winter. Most famous was the Bar Suit, a neo-Victorian silhouette with narrow shoulders and a tiny corseted waistline emphasized by padded hips with skirts so full that many of them took up to 20 yards of fabric. It was seen simultaneously as a step backwards for women's emancipation, a return to an image of femininity not seen for 30 years or so, a boost to the ailing textile industries and a blatant extravagance in a Europe still blighted by rationing. Carmel Snow, editor-in-chief of *Harper's Bazaar*, echoed a phrase that was popular in the politics of the day, announcing to Dior that: 'Your dresses have such a New Look!' The rest, as they say, is history.

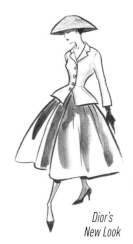

Dior's New Look

MOOD or **THEME BOARD** a small collection of images, that evoke the look, mood or theme of a season, trend, product or collection, without showing the actual product itself. Usually assembled early on in the design process as a way to focus.

PAPARAZZI the collective term for press photographers who pursue celebrities to get photographs of them. The name is an eponym from the 1960 Federico Fellini film *La Dolce Vita* in which one of the characters is a news photographer named Paparazzo.

PRÊT-À-PORTER literally meaning 'ready to wear', the name was first coined in 1966 when couturier Yves Saint Laurent offered a prêt-à-porter range from his shop in the Rue de Tournon, Paris, which he saw as a step towards the democratization of fashion.

RANGE PLAN a plan of a range or collection, showing all the component styles and pieces. Usually drawn as flats, with colour and fabric options. For selling and promotional use and often included as part of a **look book**, see left.

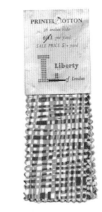

STRIKE OFF a small swatch of fabric printed by the factory for colour and pattern quality approval before the final seal is placed on the order.

SWATCH colour swatch, design swatch, sample swatch, tension swatch, test swatch . . . A sample of fabric, knit, embellishment or such, used for referencing, colour, fabrication, techniques, compatibility or embellishment, etc.

swatch

TEAR SHEET an interesting page or piece of reference cut from a magazine or such, also called a **swipe**.

TECH-PACKS/SPECS a tech-pack is what is sent to a factory to instruct them to make a sample. It includes a spec (specification), which is a flat drawing with measurements, details and swatches of fabric or materials, colour reference, yarn, etc., plus special construction information, including specified threads and stitches, tension and finishing information, such as washing, pressing, etc.

TREND FORECASTING part of the designer's role is to anticipate coming moods and directions, informed by research and awareness, finely tuned antennae and confidence in his/her own instincts. For a few people this is a career in its own right; professionals in this field are called **cool hunters**.

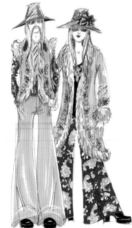

UNISEX a phrase first coined in relation to fashion in the 1960s – fashion's reaction to the sexual identity questioning of the times. A number of designers presented identical clothing on male and female models on the runway, and on the streets hippie couples swapped clothes.

unisex

VINTAGE a catch-all phrase that came into fashion use in the late 1990s and borrowed directly from the wine industry; 'vintage' implies something is rare and has improved with age – not always strictly true for fashion items! Used to describe and simultaneously upgrade what were previously described unceremoniously as 'old' or 'secondhand' clothes. There is apparently a guideline that recommends pieces should be at least 30 years old to be classified as vintage, but this is frequently only loosely adhered to. The media quickly latched on to this value-laden phrase and it is now applied to anything of non-specific age, from homeware and ephemera to music, food and recipes from a past era, and often without merit.

XXXL a hugely expanding market

ZEITGEIST the mood of the moment, as defined and indicated by the creative, intellectual and fashionable ideas and thoughts of the particular time.

FIBRES, FABRICS, YARNS, DYEING & DYES

Fundamentally, there are three types of fibre – natural, man-made and synthetic.

NATURAL FIBRES (ANIMAL)

ALPACA a long, silky, luxury fibre from the fleece of this South American relative of the llama.
ANGORA from angora rabbits, ethical production involves brushing the hair from the animal rather than plucking or stripping, which injures and eventually kills it.
CAMEL both the coarser outer-hair and the softer under-hair are used.
CASHMERE misleadingly for a luxury wool-like fibre, this comes from angora goats.
LLAMA a similar fibre to alpaca.
MOHAIR we'd like to tell you about a tiny, shy, elusive creature called a Mo, living high up in deepest . . . but no, mohair comes from the angora goat (which may be slightly misleading too, so you had better also read about **angora**, above!)

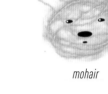

mohair

QIVUIT the soft, downy, waterproof, hypoallergenic wool of the muskox, a rare luxury fibre much prized by the people of Greenland and used to make traditional smokerings (nachaqs) and accessories.
SILK silk fibres are released by dissolving the glue around the cocoon spun by the silk worm, which lives on a particular species of mulberry tree. The whole process is known as **sericulture**.

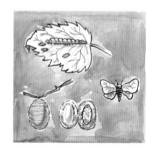

lifecycle of the silk worm

WOOL/LAMBSWOOL/MERINO/WORSTED sheep are sheared to obtain the wool fibre. Young sheep produce a softer fibre known as lambswool. **Merino** is a luxury longer-fibre wool produced mainly in Australia. **Worsted** is a process of spinning wool with longer fibres, keeping them parallel to produce a smoother, tighter yarn and cloth. Woollen spinning produces a looser, fuzzier yarn and cloth.
VICUNA a small animal, similar to the llama and native to the Andes, the vicuna provides the aristocrat of animal fibres, fine and softer than any wool. Forty fleeces are needed to make enough cloth for one coat-length of cloth.

NOBLE FIBRE the collective noun for rare and high quality fibres such as **alpaca**, **cashmere**, **mohair**, **silk**, **vicuna**, etc.

NATURAL FIBRES (VEGETABLE)

cotton

COTTON/ORGANIC COTTON derived from the seed head of the cotton plant, this is the world's most widely grown and used fibre. Vast quantities of chemicals and water are involved in its growth and mass production. As awareness grows of the impact of cotton production on the environment, there are an increasing number of schemes for producing organic cotton.

FLAX/LINEN a **bast** fibre obtained from the fibrous stems of the flax plant.

HEMP a bast fibre similar to coarse **linen**, obtained from *Cannabis sativa*, a relative of the marijuana plant.

JUTE a coarse bast fibre used in a similar way to **sisal**.

NETTLE a soft, delicate bast fibre that is gaining in popularity. The cultivation of nettles is

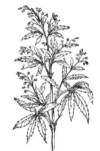

Cannabis sativa

more ecologically sound than that of most cotton. The hollow fibres give yarns and fabrics a natural insulation, warm in winter and cool in summer.

RAMI a bast fibre from the nettle family, somewhere between coarse cotton and linen, recently gaining popularity as a cheaper alternative.

SISAL a coarse fibre from the *Agave sisalana* plant, frequently confused with hemp, used principally for string, twine, scrim and sacking, etc.

MAN-MADE FIBRES manufactured fibres, as distinct from fibres that occur naturally, made from chemically processed natural vegetable or mineral based materials.

PROTEIN including milk and soya based fibres.

CELLULOSE rayon and viscose, produced largely from wood pulp.

MINERAL including glass fibre, steel, copper and other metals.

SYNTHETIC FIBRES manufactured fibres produced from polymers built up from chemical elements or compounds in contrast to fibres made from naturally occurring fibre-forming polymers. Produced largely via oil and fossil fuels.

ACRYLIC **polyester** and **polyamide**, and includes **nylon**, often added to blends for its hard-wearing and low-power stretch properties.

ACETATES part cellulose based and part synthetic fibres.

KEVLAR® the registered trademark for a para-aramid synthetic fibre used in personal armour for the military and other protective clothing, such as motorcycle wear.

LYCRA known for its extreme elasticity, this is a trade name for a synthetic form of latex. Known as **Elastane** in most of Europe and in North America as **Spandex** (an anagram of the word 'expands').

FABRICS

BATISTE a fine, sheer cotton or linen cloth, named after the linen weaver who created it, Jean Baptiste.

BOLT a flat, folded way of storing and selling fabrics, usually at the quality end of the market. There is no standard measurement, as loftier fabrics make larger more cumbersome bolts; average lengths may be between 50 and 100 yards. See also **waste** (page 30).

BONDED a composite of two fabrics produced using heat, adhesive or felting.

BOUCLÉ a fabric woven from looped or knotted yarns that create a curly, textured surface. Historically associated with **Coco Chanel** and her famous jackets (see also **yarn**, page 30).

BROCADE taking its name from the French word for 'ornament' – a rich jacquard weave with a raised design, traditionally floral or figurative in origin.

BRODERIE ANGLAISE sometimes called Swiss embroidery, a fine eyelet-embroidered cotton.

CALENDER a mechanized process involving heat and heavy rollers to finish fabrics with a smooth, sometimes lustrous surface.

CALICO a simple plain woven cotton used in various weights for toile making (named after Calicut on India's Malabar coast, from where it originates).

CHAMBRAY a soft cotton fabric where the vertical (warp) threads are coloured and the horizontal (weft) threads are white. Named after Cambrai in northern France.

CHENILLE a tufted pile fabric named after the French word for 'caterpillar'.

CHINO a twill-woven cotton that has been mercerized to increase its strength and lustre. Created for summer uniforms for American armed forces, so lending the name to the casual trousers.

CIRÉ from the French word for 'wax', used to describe fine, showerproof fabrics of a waxy appearance.

CORDUROY a hardworking, ribbed cotton pile fabric originally used to make livery worn by the servants of French kings (*cor du Roi*). Fine versions are **needlecord** or **babycord**. As in knitting, the ribs in the cord are called **wales**, and the cloth is often categorized by the number of wales per inch.

COVERT a twill weave medium or lightweight overcoating fabric with a lightly flecked appearance from the grandrelle yarns made of worsted wool. Its dense surface was thorn proof and made it suitable for hunting clothes. The name derives from the covert or shelter that the animals sought.

CREPE yarns are twisted to create a dry, wrinkled surface – available in many fabric variations.

CROMBIE a soft overcoating with a raised pile finish. Associated with a classic style of overcoat made of this fabric, 'Crombie' is the registered trade name of J.&J. Crombie Ltd, founded in 1805.

DENIM a robust twill weave (serge) cotton originating from Nîmes in France, *Serge de Nîmes*. Traditionally denim is made from blue vertical warp threads woven with white horizontal weft threads. See **weave/woven**, page 30, and **indigo**, page 31.

DOBBY a fabric featuring all over woven repeats, which can take the form of a texture or a coloured pattern. They are woven using a special heddle (header) on a jacquard-type loom.

DOUBLE FACE **face** or **face-side** – the right side of the fabric. **Double face** means fabric that is double sided, sometimes with contrasting colours or pattern with plain. Plated knitwear or knitted fabrics can be similarly created using a technique that feeds a particular yarn only to the back of the stitch.

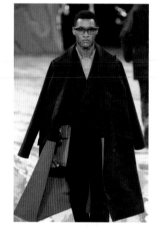

double face

EMBELLISHED/EMBELLISHMENT somewhat all-encompassing words for fabrics enhanced with one or more techniques or processes, including **beads** and **sequins** (also called spangles or by the French *paillettes*), studs or eyelets. **Appliqué:** a method whereby additional motifs, fabrics and materials are applied with stitches, heat or other techniques. **Embossed:** a technique of producing pattern in relief by applying heat and pressure with an engraved roller or plate on to fabric in a process similar to **calendering**.

EMBROIDERY an array of decorative stitch-based techniques applied to pre-existing ground fabrics by hand or machine.

EMBROIDERY LACE a lace construction created by stitching on to a pre-existing ground of tulle, net or dissolvable net to produce a decorative effect (see **lace**, page 29).

FELT non-woven felt is created by applying heat, moisture, friction and pressure to layers of primarily woollen fibres until they matt together. **Woven felt** is created similarly by applying moisture, friction and pressure to loosely woven primarily woollen fabric until the surface becomes dense and matted.

FERRANDINE a luxury silk and wool fine blend cloth.

FINE the correct description for quality, delicate or micro-gauge fabrics (rather than 'thin'). See also **noble fibre**, page 27.

FLANNEL a light twill weave woollen or worsted fabric, slightly napped on one side. The name originates from the Welsh word *gwlamen* meaning 'allied to wool'.

FLOAT a term used in both knitting and weaving where secondary colours are traversed across the back of the fabric surface.

FUR many volatile arguments exist in favour of and against fur. Undoubtedly, many animals bred for fur have a miserable existence even before meeting their end. In Scandinavia, a method is being developed which avoids killing animals; the moult of mink and foxes is collected and processed to produce single and 2-ply yarns which is then woven into fabrics.

GABARDINE originating in Spain in the Middle Ages (the Spanish word *gabardinia* means 'protection from the elements'). A fine twill woven cotton or wool cloth; a later version in waterproof Egyptian cotton was adopted by a certain London tailor, Thomas Burberry.

GINGHAM from the Malayan word *gingan*, a simple cotton fabric with even checks of colour, usually plus white. Frequently associated with school and nurses' uniforms.

GRAIN the direction of the warp and weft of the fabric; when garment patterns are cut down the grain they are cut parallel to the **warp**; when cut across the grain they are cut parallel to the **weft**.

GUIPURE strictly speaking, an embroidery with no visible background, with bars and threads joining the motifs. The name derives from the French word *guipe*, a cord around which silk is rolled.

HABOTAI one of the very many types of silk fabrics; soft and downy, it takes colour excellently.

HANDFEEL how the fabric feels to the hand, an inaccurate but widely used way of assessing the success or appeal of a fabric.

IKAT a pattern made by binding areas of the warp before dyeing; a certain amount of bleeding, capillary action and discrepancy means that, when woven, the pattern has an attractive blurred and smudged definition.

INKLE a linen thread or tape for making laces (not many people know this, but we think they should – it's such a good name!).

JACQUARD an elaborate loom invented in 1802 by Joseph Marie Jacquard to mechanize the production of brocade and damask patterned fabrics. Since its invention, any pattern-woven fabric or ribbon is generally referred to as a 'jacquard'. See also **knitwear** (page 36).

JERSEY see **jerseywear & knitwear** (page 36).

LACE a fine, open-work fabric with a background of net or mesh with patterns worked simultaneously or applied later by looping or twisting. Made by hand with bobbins, needles or by machinery. Lace-type fabrics can be created by knitting, crochet, tatting, darning, embroidering, macramé and weaving.

LAMÉ a fabric in which either the warp or weft threads are metallic in appearance. From the French verb *laminer*, 'to flatten', from the days when real metals were used to create such fabrics.

LOFTY the trade term for bulky, but light and springy fabrics.

LUREX the registered brand name of a type of metallic-look yarn. Fabrics made of this yarn are frequently similarly called **lurex fabric**.

MADRAS from the Indian city, more or less a jolly multicolour version of **gingham**.

MERCERIZED of cotton thread that has been treated with sodium hydroxide to increase its lustre and affinity for dye – also known as 'pearl cotton'. The process was invented by John Mercer in 1844 and improved by H.A. Lowe in 1980.

MOIRÉ from the French verb *moirer*, 'to water'; wavy watermark type patterns characterize this lightly ribbed, taffeta-like fabric.

MOUSSELINE or **MOUSSELINE DE SOIE** a sheer or semi-sheer fabric, like chiffon, but crisper and paper-like.

MULL similar to **calico** (see page 27), these days mull is almost solely used for **toile** making; its Indian name means 'soft and pliable'.

NAP any pile to the surface of a fabric.

NEP when a garment has nep, it means that the fabric has been woven in such a way that some of the fibres protrude from the main surface.

OTTOMAN a heavy, corded silk-type fabric with crosswise ribs. **Grosgrain** and **petersham** are similar in ribbon form, used for waistbands, trims and finishes.

OXFORD a heavy cotton used largely for shirts or summer suiting.

PAISLEY a curved, pine-cone shaped motif named a *boteh*, originating in India. When the British East India Company imported patterned shawls from Kashmir, the craze drove manufacturers to produce their own versions printed on to fine wool challis. The Scottish town of Paisley became a specialist, producing printed versions of these shawls and the name was forever linked.

PINSTRIPE a finely striped fabric that can be interpreted in almost any fibre combination. Wider striped versions are sometimes called **chalk stripe**, particularly in woollen versions where the stripe becomes broken-up somewhat.

POPLIN a plain, medium weight woven cotton.

QUILTING a way of increasing the loft of fabrics by sandwiching a filling between and stitching them together. Used for warm linings or as design feature in its own right.

RASCHEL a warp knitted lacy fabric made on a machine of the same name. Very popular in the 1920s and 1930s; subsequently revived by the Italian company Missoni in the 1970s.

SATIN a **silk, rayon/viscose** or such fabric characterized by a smooth, shiny face and a dull back. Excellent draping qualities are part of its appeal, though it is tricky to handle because of its slipperiness.

SEERSUCKER a rippled, striped, textured fabric taking its name from an old Persian word meaning 'milk and sugar'.

SELVEDGE a selvedge on either side of a woven material is general, but not invariable. *Solve* is the Scandinavian name for a heddle (part of a loom). The name means the end or the edge of the material. The threads at the edges are threaded double to make the edge stronger. The selvedge is always threaded plain, the real pattern beginning after the selvedge. Some cloths will have the name of the mill woven through the selvedge as a guarantee of authenticity and endorsement of quality.

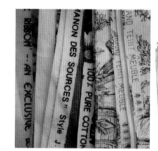

printed selvedge

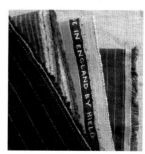

woven selvedge

SHODDY along with linen paper, perhaps one of the earliest examples of recycling – a generally inferior yarn or cloth made from the shredded fibres of waste woollen cloth and clippings (also sometimes known as **mungo**).

SUITING usually taken to refer to fine **worsted** cloths, traditionally used for tailored suits.

TARTAN AND PLAID the traditional woven woollen clan fabrics of Scotland. **Hunting plaids** are more subtly coloured than dress plaids. The square repeats of the plaid are known as **setts**.

TOILE DE JOUY famous printed cotton fabrics from Jouy in France, which first appeared in the 18th century. Usually one colour – Madder red, French or China blue, Olive green or, occasionally, black – all on white or ecru ground. The designs feature flowers or pictoral landscapes with figures.

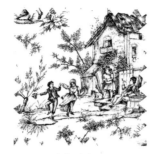

toile de jouy

TWEED an all-encompassing name for a vast array of traditional woven cloths, including **estate tweeds**, a family of traditional tweed cloths originally woven for countrywear on the great estates of England and Scotland and including all the great classics; **gunclub**, **hound's tooth**, **shepherds**, **Glenurquhart**, **Rothiemurchus**, **Wyvis** etc. **Prince of Wales check**: a varient of Glenurquhart check much favoured and popularized by HRH Prince Edward Prince of Wales (later the Duke of Windsor) in the 1920s and 1930s. **Harris tweed** has been spun, dyed and woven in the Scottish islands of Harris and Lewis for over 300 years. It has been much favoured by Vivienne Westwood and other designers and is now a registered trademark. **Donegal**: a tweed fabric originally hand-woven in County Donegal, Ireland. Characterized by a speckled, neppy surface. See also **nep**, page 29. **Hound's tooth**: a two-colour, broken-check cloth; also called **dog's tooth**. Smaller versions frequently informally called **puppy tooth**.

TWILL a diagonal rib or grain achieved as part of the weaving sequence.

VELVET a short, thick pile fabric, usually woven double. The fabric is cut apart to create the pile. With **cut velvet**, the pattern is a raised brocaded surface on a plain ground. With **façonne velvet/devoré**, the pile is eaten away (devoured) via a printing process to create a pile/non-pile design, sometimes with a sheer chiffon-like ground.

VENETIAN a luxury worsted wool satin-like fabric with a soft polished surface.

WARP AND WEFT the warp is the length threaded upon the weaving loom; the weft is the thread woven across the warp (across the width of the loom). When warp and weft stripes are combined, a check or plaid is produced.

WASTE Cabbage: the fabric a garment manufacturer has left over after production is complete. The manufacturer may illegally make additional identical garments or simply use the fabric to make alternative garments for sale covertly. **Fents**: a length of fabric sold by the mill, usually at a mill shop, sometimes in a trial colourway that never went into production or with unusual colour changes throughout the length which occurred during trialling. Usually sold by weight. **Remnant**: a length of fabric sold by a fabric merchant from what is left at the end of a roll or bolt. It is sold by the piece, take it or leave it.

WEAVE/WOVEN fabrics are woven on a weaving **loom**. A few traditional fabrics are still hand-woven. Weave designers generally still hand-weave their first samples. Hand-woven fabrics can be described as **hand-loomed**.

WOOLLEN SPUN generally loose, fuzzier finished yarn and fabrics made with shorter fibre wool.

WEIGHT cloth quality is calculated by the weight in grams per square metre and written as GSM or $gm/^2$. Some traditional fabrics are still sold in imperial measurements – oz/yd^2 = ounces per yard squared.

ZEBRA an eternally popular monochrome pattern, successfully interpreted by a huge range of designers, including Coco Chanel, Bridget Riley, Mary Quant and Roberto Cavalli.

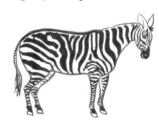

YARN

YARN & FABRIC COUNT yarn count is calculated by thickness of the yarn end and the number of twists. Fabric is the number of ends to the inch.

BALL/ BOBBIN/ CHEESE /CONE/ HANK/ REEL/SHUTTLE/ SKEIN/ SPOOL different ways of buying and using yarn and thread.

BOUCLÉ a looped or knotted decorative yarn. See also **bouclé fabric**, page 27.

CHINE a French word meaning 'speckled'; two threads (ends) of contrasting colours or tones are twisted together.

GIMP a helically wrapped and spun yarn which has a crimped, irregular texture.

GRANDRELLE a 2-ply twisted yarn of two colours, or two tone, sometimes one yarn having a lustre to create a matt and shine contrast.

JASPE similar to chine, usually jaspe yarns have one end black and the other end colour.

MAL-FLAMME literally 'badly spun', an uneven, slubbed or rustic-looking yarn.

MÉLANGE the French word for 'mixture', yarns are comprised of mixed tones.

PLY the number of ends twisted together to make a yarn – 2-ply, 3-ply, etc.

ROVING YARN unspun or loosely spun yarns.
TWIST the way ends of yarns are spun together.

DYEING & DYES

BLUE WOOL SCALE this measures and calibrates the permanence and light-fastness of dyes.
GARMENT DYE a process where garments are made in un-dyed cloth and dyed as whole garments, begun so that garments could be dyed closer to the season in fashionable colours, but now frequently used purely for its soft, washed/aged look.
PIECE DYE a similar process for knitwear, in which the garment parts (pieces) are dyed and then assembled by linking.
OVER DYE [*ton sur ton*] a process whereby base colours or patterns are dyed over to produce tone-on-tone effects in garments or fabrics.
TIE DYE a process where the garment or fabric is tied tightly in areas so that when dyed, areas and patterns are not exposed to the dye and remain undyed.
YARN DYE a knitwear phrase which describes using yarn that is already dyed (see **piece dye**, above).

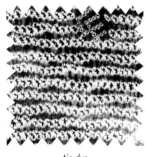

tie dye

OMBRE derived from the French for shade or shadow – a colour effect achieved in dyed or woven fabrics so that they change gradually from dark to light or from one colour to another (also known as **dégradé**).
MADDER an evergreen plant native to Asia and the Old World, the roots of which produce beautiful pink/red colours and dyes, known as madder and sometimes as Turkey Red.
INDIGO a blue pigment extracted from the leaves of the *Indigofera tinctoria* plant. One of the oldest and most treasured dyes it used to be known as 'blue gold'. Still valued above its synthetic rivals, indigo is responsible for our ongoing love affair with denim and its connotations of authenticity and democracy.
KHAKI legend has it that during a safari, a hunter dressed in customary white leant upon a cashew tree and the gum permanently stained his jacket. It was realized that this was a most suitable camouflage colour. The cashew has been a natural source of khaki dye ever since.

CUT & CONSTRUCTION

ASYMMETRIC/SYMMETRIC most garments, like most people, are more or less symmetrical, or even, on both sides. Double-breasted features make a nod towards asymmetry, but true asymmetry has a deliberate absence of balance. Garments may typically have one shoulder, one sleeve, or be a combination of fitted and flare. Japanese designers Rei Kawakuba for Commes des Garçons and Junya Watanabe, in particular, have recently pushed the limits of asymmetry to extremes with some extraordinary, challenging, but exciting collections exploring this oeuvre.

BIAS to cut fabric crosswise to the grain of the cloth (at 45 degrees). A technique pioneered by Mme Madeleine Vionnet in the 1920s which utilizes the natural stretch of the cloth to create a gentle cling and drape rather than a straight/free-hanging silhouette. The technique, all but forgotten and neglected, was revived and further explored by John Galliano in the early 1980s and has since gained popularity thanks to much improved production techniques.

BIAS BINDING a narrow tape cut from cloth at a 45 degree angle. Used for binding seams and sometimes appropriate for finishing hems, necklines and tricky curved edges, etc.

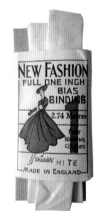

bias binding

BLIND HEM/BLIND STITCH a method of hemming that is almost invisible. When sewing, only a single thread of the outer fabric is caught.

BLOCK or **BODY BLOCK** the standard basis of a pattern, not strictly a garment in itself, it is cut according to a standard size or to the fit of an individual for following garments pattern or design (see also **toiles**, page 33).

BUTTONHOLES these are traditionally hand finished, but now more usually machine stitched. Tailored and heavier fabric garments traditionally have **keyhole** buttonholes to facilitate functioning. Fabric or bound buttonholes, sometimes called **jet** or **jetted** buttonholes, can be made using self or contrasting fabric, sometimes used on the bias.

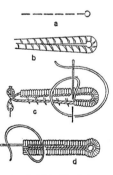

hand-stitched keyhole buttonhole

jet or jetted buttonhole

CONSTRUCTION the way in which a garment is made, referring to methods, techniques, etc.

CUT the way in which a garment is cut, the fabric grain, silhouette and line. See **silhouette & line** (page 33) and **grain** (page 28).

DECONSTRUCTED the ideas first appeared in fashion in the late 1980s, the term 'deconstructed' applied a few years later and borrowed from theories on architecture that had been evolving throughout the 1960s and 1970s. Ideas were apparently simultaneously explored by a handful of designers across the globe, including avant garde Japanese designers Rei Kawakuba for Commes des Garçons and Yohji Yamamoto, the Belgian designer Anne Demuelemeester (one of the Antwerp Six), and Parisian Anne Valerie Hash. This disparate group of rebellious spirits were united in trying to challenge the set traditions of construction and the accepted standards of making and finishing of garments. Seams exposed and edges left raw, unfinished and un-hemmed, were just some of the characteristics. Aspects of tailoring normally hidden internally, but involving great skill and craftsmanship, were proudly exposed and transferred to the outside of garments to be enthusiastically admired by the sympathetic cognoscenti.

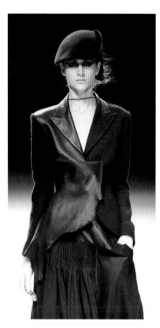

deconstructed

FIT/FITTING/FIT MODEL the toile or first sample garment is usually examined for fit as well as aesthetic interpretation compared to the design drawing. The garment is usually tried on a model whose measurements are perfectly standard size (a **fit model**). During the fitting process, alterations may be drawn and written on the toile, or pinned on the garment and meticulously

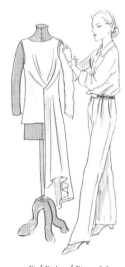

fit / fitting / fit model

noted for amendment. More recently, digital photographs have also become part of this procedure.

GRADING & SIZING once perfected and sold, garment patterns are graded up and down according to standard international size grades. Quality garments are refitted again in each of the sizes to make sure the fit is correct.

HEMLINES shaped, handkerchief, asymmetric, shirt-tail, hi-lo. See also **blind hem**, page 31. The circumference of the hemline is known as the **sweep**.

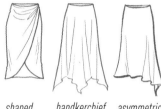

shaped   handkerchief   asymmetric

INTERFACING a layer of woven or non-woven fabric layered on a garment to support and facilitate shaping. Sometimes stitched, otherwise fused with heat (fusable interlining).

LINE often used to describe the simplified cut, defining outline or silhouette of a single garment or the common denominator which unifies a collection. A number of silhouettes have evolved along various lines that have since become standard references. We can probably thank the Empress Josephine (1763-1814) for popularizing the high-waisted empire line, also known as Directoire after the French Directoire period 1795–9. See also **line-up**, page 25.

PATTERN MAKING
PATTERN BLOCK/SEWING PATTERN/LAY the **pattern block** is usually the first version of the pattern, perfecting the basic silhouette. The pieces and panels that make up the garment design are known as the **garment pattern** or domestically as the **sewing pattern**. The arrangement of pattern pieces on the fabric, correct to grain, match and nap and for best, most economic use of the fabric, is called the **lay**.

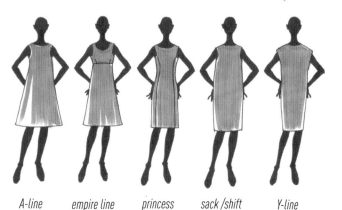

A-line   empire line   princess   sack /shift   Y-line

SCISSORS different types include dressmaking, embroidery, paper, pinking, tailor's shears, snips.

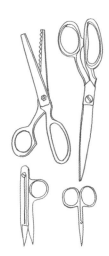

SILHOUETTE & LINE in 1760, Etienne de Silhouette (1709–67) was the unsuccessful French minister of finance to King Louis XV. So brief was his tenure that it led to public ridicule and he became associated with anything penny-pinching and cheap (*à la Silhouette*). At the same time there was a fashion for simple portraits cut in outline, like a shadow, from black paper. It was not long before the name Silhouette was linked to this inexpensive alternative to portrait painting.

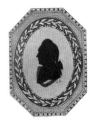

silhouette

STAND/DRESS STAND/ MANNEQUIN/ DRESS FORM a stuffed, modelled facsimile of the human torso, accurately made to standard sizes or custom made. Sometimes also unfortunately called a 'dummy'.

TOILES the series of mock-up garments made in calico (sometimes called muslin) to develop, refine and perfect a design before using the final fabric. Every detail should be fully trialled and resolved at this stage, being aware that the choices of weights of calico should be appropriately matched as closely as possible to the end fabric's characteristics. Jersey garments are similarly toiled in substitute jersey fabric. A designer may work on several toiles to develop the perfect version of his or her design, beginning by working solely on the silhouette. This may then be used as a block for future design variations and garments. This creates continuity and a strong identity within a range or collection.

GARMENTS & ACCESSORIES, JERSEYWEAR & KNITWEAR

GARMENTS
BODICE a garment for the upper body, neck to waist, or the top or upper section of a complete dress or coat.

Derived from earlier times when the bodice of a dress was separate from the skirt.

BUSTIER originally a form-fitting garment worn as part of underwear, more recently worn as outerwear.

CORSET a body-shaping, smooth-fitting garment, usually extending from under the bust to the waist or hips. Originally boned, with metal, wood or whalebone, later substituted with plastics and Lycra to enforce a silhouette. Modern versions are more fetish than foundation.

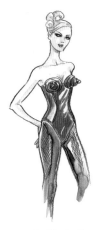

Gaultier bustier

CROWN not just for royalty, but also the top part of a hat or sleeve.

CULOTTES short knee breeches worn throughout Europe from the late Middle Ages to the early 19th century. During the French Revolution (1789–99), working-class rebels were known as the *sans-culottes* (without culottes) – those who rejected aristocratic dress. Today the term is applied to almost any short or cropped trousers, sometimes a close relative of the split skirt.

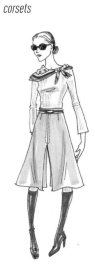

corsets

FROCK originally a loose, long garment with wide sleeves worn by monks and priests – hence the word 'de-frock' for when they left the clergy. By the 16th century a frock had evolved to become a women's dress or gown, unfitted and comfortable for wear in the house. By the 17th century it was a loose working garment for men and women, sometimes called a smock frock and sometimes buttoning all the way down the front.

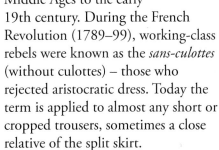

culottes

GAUCHO traditional wear of the South American cowboy; wide-hemmed, mid-calf-length trousers, similar to a split skirt.

KAFTAN sometimes **caftan** or **qaftan** – traceable back to biblical times and the Middle East. A long, loose, open-sleeved tunic, displaying the under garment sleeves and split at the sides.

SHIRT/BLOUSE traditionally we consider

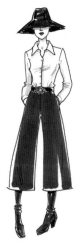

gaucho

shirt to be male and blouse to be feminine, but originally a blouse was a peasant garment worn by both sexes. The shirt was underwear for men only, not intended to be seen. As men's clothes became more sober throughout the 19th century, the shirt with collar and cuffs that we recognize today became accepted formal attire. The blouse became accepted office wear towards the end of the 19th century for the growing number of working women, a look popularized by the Gibson Girls drawn by Charles Dana Gibson.

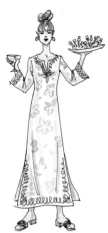

kaftan

SHIRTWAISTER the style probably first appeared in the 1940s. Later versions became little more than extended or oversized shirts, frequently worn belted or cinched.

SINGLET/VEST originally an undergarment only, now worn as outerwear and active sportswear. In North America a vest is a waistcoat and a singlet, curiously, is a **wife beater**.

SMOCK traditionally worn by rural workers and closely related to the shirt and peasant blouse. Associated with artists and craftspeople, particularly in the 19th century. A strict pull-on version became the traditional workwear of Cornish fishermen and was immortalized in the paintings of the Newlyn School of artists in the 19th and 20th centuries.

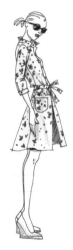

shirtwaister

TANK a simple, sleeveless garment with wide, built-up shoulders and no opening or fastening. Usually made in jersey or knit fabrics. Originating in the USA, from the one-piece bathing suits of the 1920s worn in tanks (swimming pools). **Tank dress** – an extended form.

TOP a word to be avoided at almost any cost (please!) – there are far better and more accurately descriptive names you can use.

TROUSERS to put it grandly, a bifurcated garment worn by both sexes. Styles, silhouettes, cuts and variants are

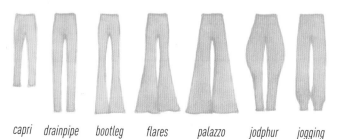

capri   drainpipe   bootleg   flares   palazzo   jodphur   jogging

many and include **bootleg, drainpipe, harem, jodphur, loons, Oxford bags, sailor, slacks, track, trews, palazzo** and **zouaves**.

WRAP in 1974, a little-known New York designer, Diane von Furstenberg, encouraged by the famous editor of US *Vogue*, Diana Vreeland, launched her jersey wrap dress. It was an immediate success. By 1976, she had sold over 1,000,000 of them. Relaunched in 1997, the famous wrap dress is now considered a perennial and classic design.

ZOOT SUIT a big trend look associated with black musicians of the 1930s and 1940s, most famously the Cotton Club's top-billing Cab Calloway. Typified by an oversized, long, wide-shouldered jacket, baggy and exaggeratedly tapered trousers, often light or flamboyantly coloured, and accessorized. In the 1980s, the look was successfully revived, along with elements of the musical genre, by Kid Creole.

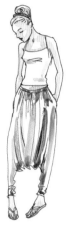

zouaves

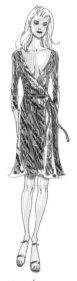

wrap dress

COATS & JACKETS

ANORAK a waterproof hooded jacket fastening with a zipper, with a drawstring at the bottom. It became popular during World War 2, when warm, quilted or fur-lined versions were worn by pilots. The name is thought to derive from similar Eskimo garments from which the anorak may be traced. See also **cagoule**, below.

BIKER JACKET a motorbike jacket of black leather, with zip fasteners and stud closures; a perennial fashion favourite since the youthquake days of the 1950s. Famously worn by Marlon Brando for his iconic role in *The Wild One* (1953).

BLOUSON a loose blouse-type jacket, gathered or reduced at the waist to create the characteristic silhouette.

CABAN a short warm coat, similar to a **reefer jacket** (see facing page), worn by Breton fishermen for centuries. Originally white – *kap gween* means 'white cloth' in Breton – it changed to navy blue during the early 19th century.

CAGOULE/CAGOUL/KAGOULE/ KAGOOL a short, waterproof, hooded jacket; many versions

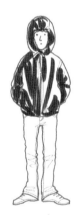

anorak

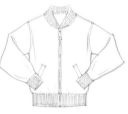

blouson

pull on over the head rather than opening completely. Otherwise almost indistinguishable from an anorak, taking its name from the French *cagoule*, meaning 'hood'. Some well-designed versions fold away into their own chest pocket or small sack.

CAPE from *Batman* to *Dracula* and *Miss Marple* by way of Courrèges, there are endless variations from grand and tailored country classics to sci-fi fantasy. A sleeveless garment worn around the shoulders, open or fastened at the front; sometimes with openings for hands or arms.

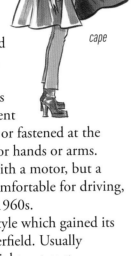
cape

CAR COAT no, not a hybrid coat with a motor, but a short, hip-length tailored coat, comfortable for driving, which first appeared in the early 1960s.

CHESTERFIELD a classic overcoat style which gained its name from the 4th Earl of Chesterfield. Usually a fly-fronted, single-breasted, straight-cut coat, characteristically with a velvet top collar. Variations include double-breasted and more fitted versions.

CROMBIE see **fabrics**, page 28.

DUFFEL/DUFFLE COAT the Belgian town of Duffel gave its name to a heavy, woollen woven cloth and subsequently to the warm protective coats for the military and navy. Traditionally vent-less, with a double layered yoke, large collar or a hood and fastening with wooden or horn toggles.

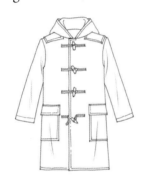
duffle coat

ENGINEER'S JACKET a boxy cotton drill or denim utility jacket, with breast and hip pockets and close-fastening cuffs as a safeguard for engineers using machinery.

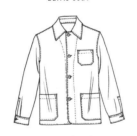
engineer's jacket

FLYING or **AVIATOR JACKET** a short usually leather jacket with utility pockets, maybe a double closure of zip and buttoned flap, tight knitted rib cuffs and waist and often a mouton collar, typically worn by pioneer aviators and World War 2 pilots.

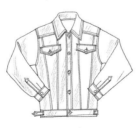
jeans jacket

JEANS JACKET a short, shirt-style, usually close-fitting denim utility jacket.

INVERNESS a tweed overcoat with a deep cape attached, as typically worn by Sherlock Holmes.

JERKIN/GILET/BODY WARMER a sleeveless jacket, waist- or hip-length; padded and down versions have revived the look.

GREATCOAT originally a voluminous, extra-heavy fur-lined coat, belted and reaching mid-calf or longer, worn by British soldiers. Officers wore a shorter version, known affectionately as a **British Warm**.

HARRINGTON a short, zip-up casual jacket with a band collar, first made in the 1930s by British companies Grenfell of Burnley and Baracuta of Stockport. Frank Sinatra and Steve McQueen apparently both wore the Baracuta G9 jacket, as did Elvis Presley in his 1958 film *King Creole*. But when Ryan O'Neal wore one in the cult 1960s soap opera *Peyton Place*, his character Rodney Harrington gave the jacket its popular name.

MACKINTOSH a waterproof coat named after the Scottish chemist Sir Charles Mackintosh who invented a rubberized cotton fabric in 1823.

REEFER JACKET (also known as a **PEA COAT**) a warm coat with wide revers, double-breasted, short hip length, similar to a **caban**, see opposite, worn by the American Navy in the early 18th century and later by Navvies. The name can be traced back to 1846, when the pilot schooner USS *Reefer* famously led task forces in the Mexican–American War.

TRENCHCOAT a long, belted rain or showerproof coat worn by officers in the trenches in World War I. Typified by a short, caped-yoke back and storm flaps at the front. Versions with a deep inverted pleat from back waist to hem were for riding, similar to those still worn by British mounted police today.

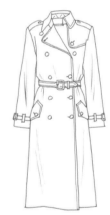
trenchcoat

ACCESSORIES

COWL a tall funnel-like collar, sometimes a completely separate entity, worn like a scarf. Versions with an inbuilt twist follow the principle of a Mobius band. Often mistakenly called a snood, which is a net for the hair. There is an Eskimo (Inuit-Yupik) version of the cowl called a smokering (nachaqs).

FASCINATOR little more than an alice band with pretensions – a poor excuse for a proper hat.

MUFF a tube of fur or warm cloth

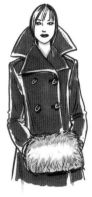
muff

into which the hands are inserted for warmth.

MUFFLER a long scarf.

SCARF a square or rectangle of cloth usually worn at the neck or on the head.

TIPPET a scarf worn draped round the neck by ecclesiastics or a separate fur collar worn as a warm accessory around the neck.

SHOES/HEELS see illustration of some different types below.

SNOOD traditionally a close-fitting cloth hood, more often made of net or mesh-like fabric, last popular in the 1940s. See also **cowl**, page 35.

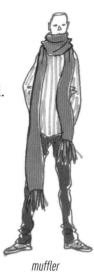

muffler

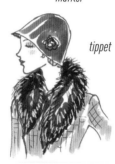

tippet

JERSEYWEAR & KNITWEAR

JERSEY the name of the island that gave us the particular style of sweater now more commonly known by the name of its neighbouring island, Guernsey. Jersey has subsequently given its name to all knitted structures and to fabric sold by the metre, as other fabric, and cut, sewn and constructed in more-or-less similar ways to woven fabric. Jersey garments made in this way are often referred to as **cut & sew** garments.

ARAN a style of fisherman's sweater traditionally knitted in ecru wool. Typified by a rich mix of cable patterns and textured stitches.

CABLE a crossover knitted stitch resembling ropes, typically found in traditional folk knitwear such as Aran sweaters.

FAIR ISLE a traditional style of knitwear pattern from the Fair Isles off the coast of Scotland, typified by multiple small-scale geometric patterns combined in many subtle colours.

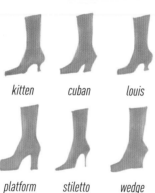

kitten	*cuban*	*louis*
platform	*stiletto*	*wedge*

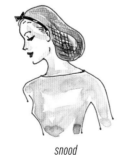

snood

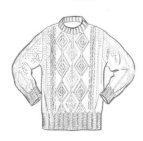

Aran sweater

GUERNSEY a style of fisherman's sweater, more or less square and loosely based on a smock, originating centuries ago on the island of Guernsey in the English Channel. Yorkshire fishermen have long called their navy blue sweaters **guernseys** or **ganseys**.

GAUGE in much the same way that in hand-knitting different yarns are knitted on thicker or thinner needles depending on the thickness of the yarn, in machine knitwear it is the number of needles across the needle bed that dictates the gauge. The higher the gauge number, the finer the knit.

KNITWEAR a knitted garment, a **sweater**, but no longer called a **pullover** or a **jumper**.

MATELOT the French word for sailor, used to describe the perennially popular navy-and-white striped sweaters and T-shirts originally worn by sailors and first brought into the fashion arena by Coco Chanel.

INTARSIA a technique for knitting large-scale patterns without using floats.

JACQUARD patterns created in knitwear with floats; the name borrowed from a woven pattern system.

SINGLE JERSEY a plain knit structure producing a right (jersey) and wrong (reverse) side.

DOUBLE JERSEY a generic term for a range of weft knitted fabrics made on a rib or interlock basis.

WEFT KNITTING machine-knitted fabric or garments made on a flat bed or circular bed machine.

CROCHET related to knit in that it is a system of interconnecting loops, but using a single needle to create fabrics and trims. There is no machine version, crochet can only be handmade.

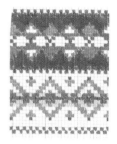

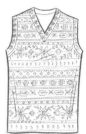

fair isle

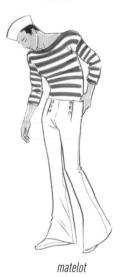

matelot

GARMENT DETAILS & PARTICULARS

COLLARS

COLLAR generally consisting of three parts, the stand, where it is joined to the neckline, the top and the under collar.

SPREAD the distance between the points of a collar.

CUTAWAY as the name suggests, a widely spread collar with the front edges cut away.

FUNNEL a tall, upstanding collar.

COWL a soft draped neckline, created by cutting the bodice with fullness and on the bias.

HIGHWAYMAN an historic feature, with a tall or extended stand.

MOUTON a sheepskin or shearling top collar.

PETER PAN a flat turned-down collar, named after the J.M. Barrie character.

SAILOR as typified by the traditional sailors' uniform, a flat collar, large and square at the back, forming a V at the centre front. Sometimes called a **middy** collar, from midshipman.

TURTLE a shallow, standaway collar reminiscent of its namesake.

WING a formal collar with turned-down corners resembling wings. An earlier form, with curved or rounded corners, is known as a **butterfly collar**.

LAPELS, REVERS, ETC.

Lapel: the front, turned part of a jacket collar. **Rever**: a large lapel. **Notch**: the V-shape cut out where the lapel meets the collar. **Gorge seam**: the visible turned-back part of the join. A **peaked rever** is a stylistic variation.

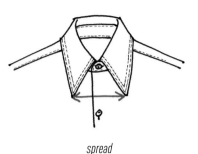

spread

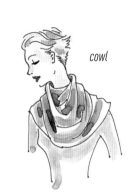

cowl

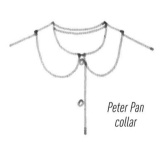

Peter Pan collar

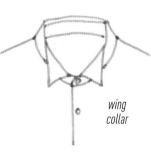

wing collar

gorge seam

NECKLINES

BATEAU French for 'boat' – a more glamorous way of describing this attractive, shallow, wide neckline.

CREW NECK a high, close-fitting round neckline usually finished with a trim, as in T-shirts.

DÉCOLLETÉ/DÉCOLLETAGE a very low neckline, popular in Directoire times and various periods in history, particularly for evening-wear, often displaying the cleavage.

HALTER a strap from the garment front or built-up bodice which passes round the back of the neck to support the garment.

JEWEL a wider, lower version of a crew neckline that can display neck jewellery.

POLO NECK / POLO COLLAR confusion always here! In Europe, a **polo neck** is a high, close-fitting turned-down collar; in the US this is called a **roll neck**. A **polo collar** is a simple, square-cut collar typically found on **polo shirts**.

SWEETHEART a low-ish neckline, cut in two more-or-less semicircular curves, so that the bodice resembles a heart shape.

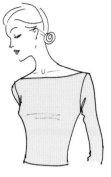

bateau

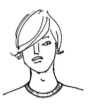

crew neck

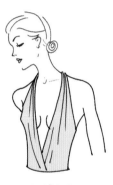

décolleté/décolletage

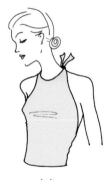

halter

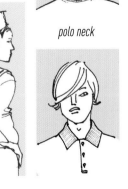

sailor

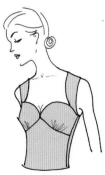

polo neck

polo collar

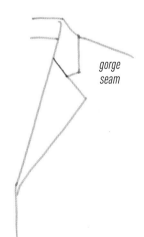

sweetheart

DART a shaped tuck, pointed at one or both ends, created to control excess material and develop fit. Similarly, pintuck, smocking and ruching are all ways of controlling and creating volume and shape. See **pleat**, below.

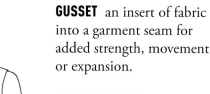

dart

DRAPE the way in which fabric falls and hangs. Used also to describe a way of developing a style directly on the dress stand, known as **modelling**.

EPAULETTE from the French word *epaule*, meaning 'shoulder'. A largely decorative ornament or strap at the shoulder, originally on the naval or military uniforms of officers, later used to display rank at all levels and widely adopted as a fashion detail.

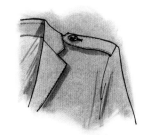

drape

FROG FASTENING a decorative fastening consisting of a looped braid and knotted button, versions of which are loosely based on Chinese and oriental costume.

GALLOON metallic braid, lace or other trimming as used on dress military uniforms.

GODET a usually triangular-shaped fabric inset, often stitched into a hemline to create fullness.

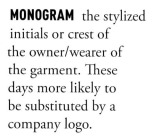

epaulette

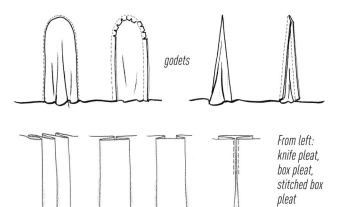

godets

From left: knife pleat, box pleat, stitched box pleat

GUSSET an insert of fabric into a garment seam for added strength, movement or expansion.

HABERDASHERY sometimes called **notions**, in North America **findings**, a range of delightful phrases that encompass all the bits and pieces of the sewing and fashion workroom, from pins and needles, threads and buttons to linings, interfacings and a myriad of things besides.

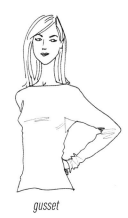

gusset

MITRE the name of a bishop's or archbishop's hat; in fashion it is more commonly encountered as square-cut collar profile or as a way of finishing right-angled corners.

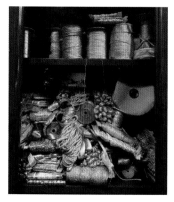

haberdashery

MONOGRAM the stylized initials or crest of the owner/wearer of the garment. These days more likely to be substituted by a company logo.

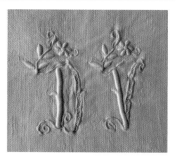

monogram

MOTHER OF PEARL/NACRE a natural organic material from the inside of shells; the term is also used to describe the luminous colour effects recreated in plastics and synthetics for fabrics, sequins, etc.

PLEAT a fold of fabric, to control fullness; popular variations include **knife**, **box**, **sunray** and **crystal**. *Plisse*, the French word for pleat, is used specifically to describe a narrow, sometimes uneven or puckered pleat.

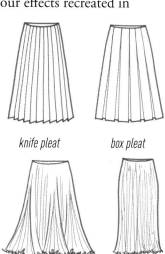

knife pleat

box pleat

sunray

crystal

POCKETS there are numerous variations, including bellows, flap, bound, jetted, smile, frontier, accordion, patch and welt.

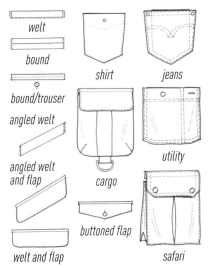

welt

bound

shirt

jeans

bound/trouser

angled welt

angled welt and flap

cargo

utility

buttoned flap

welt and flap

safari

RISE the depth of the crotch seam from the top of the leg to the waist or top of the garment.

SHOULDERS, SLEEVES & ARMHOLES

SADDLE the sleeve has an extension along the top of the shoulder into the neckline.

SET IN a standard or regular sleeve, set in to the body of the garment.

MAGYAR taking its name from the traditional costumes of the Magyar people of the Urals, the term is used to describe a deep sleeve cut all in one piece with the body. Very deep versions, where the sleeve comes from near the waist, are often called **batwing** sleeves – for obvious reasons.

DOLMAN traditionally a long loose Turkish robe dating back to the 16th century, open at the front with wide sleeves, now generally used to describe a deep-set, wide, loose sleeve.

saddle shoulder

set in sleeve

magyar (batwing)

dolman / magyar / kimono

raglan sleeve

RAGLAN sometimes also called raglan shoulder, named after Lord Raglan (1788–1855), a British commander in the Crimean War. The sleeve is extended more or less diagonally across the body from underarm to collarbone. Sometimes the name is also used to describe a type of overcoat.

STORM FLAP typically the shaped flap at the shoulder or neckline that covers the neck opening on a trenchcoat as a double closure.

TAB the fabric strap at a cuff, neckline or sleeve that facilitates closure or holds rolled up sleeves in place, etc. Also the opening placket on shirt cuffs.

VENT from the old French word for 'to let out air' and from the Latin for 'wind', a vent is a split at the sides or centre back of a coat or jacket.

WELT the finishing band at a hemline or pocket top. In knitwear this may be the ribbed hemline or pocket trims.

YOKE a panel or section, sometimes shaped and usually of double fabric, at the shoulder usually of a shirt or jacket that supports the rest of the garment. The classic **cowboy shirt** presents a fine example.

ZIP the history of the zip fastener or zipper is long and convoluted. First versions date back to the mid-19th century, but in its crude early forms its potential uses were undervalued. Later developments, patent issues, production problems and rights were not resolved until the early 1920s. But the zipper was largely overlooked by the fashion industry for another decade or so. It was only after a financial deal between the Canadian division of the Lightning Fastener Company and the Italian couturier Elsa Schiaparelli that she used zips in her winter 1935–6 collection, characteristically shocking buyers by using them exposed as unexpected design features, that they made their slow but eventual acceptance into high fashion.

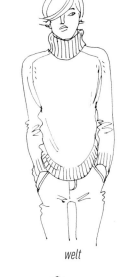

welt

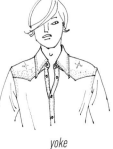

yoke

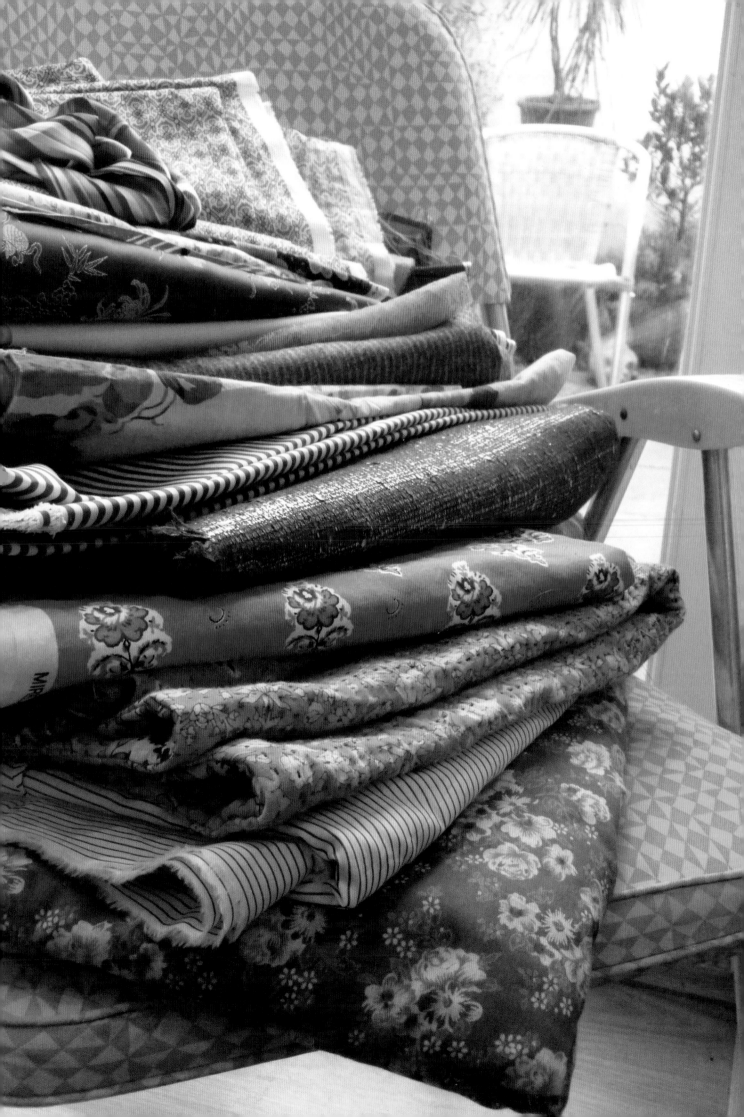

03 COLOUR

'Colour is the place where our brain and the universe meet.' PAUL KLEE

We live in a world of colour. It is a stimulus for our creativity, a trigger for our memory and emotions, a major influence on us all. Almost everyone has some opinion on the subject: a favourite colour, for example, or one they dislike – hate, even. Such are the passions which colour can evoke.

From antiquity, tradition and beliefs have influenced our colour understanding and perceptions. The Ancient Greeks understood the antithesis between black and white and developed a theory of black, white and red as the primary colours. Colour confused even Aristotle, who proposed the opposition of light and dark to be the origin of the intermediate colours. Hippocrates later arrived at the four-colour theory: black, white, red and yellow. It is perhaps surprising, if not extraordinary for a country so deeply associated in our minds with idyllic azure seas and skies, that the Ancient Greeks had no word for the colour blue.

Since these early times there have been many developments in our knowledge and understanding of colour. For anyone wanting to study the science of colour in depth there are libraries devoted to this fascinating subject. However, it is important at this stage to have a basic grasp of what colour is and the way in which we see it.

There are two factors in our perception of colour – light and the human eye – for light is what creates colour in our eyes. The magnetic rays we know as light sit at a frequency somewhere between radio waves at one end of the spectrum and gamma rays at the other, and they include microwaves, infrared, ultraviolet and x-rays. The average human eye can detect only a tiny portion of this vast range, known as 'visible light', and humans can distinguish about ten million variations within it.

In this chapter we look at the fun and fascinating world of colour, and unveil some of its mysteries.

'The purest and most thoughtful minds are those which love colour the most.'

JOHN RUSKIN

UNDERSTANDING COLOUR

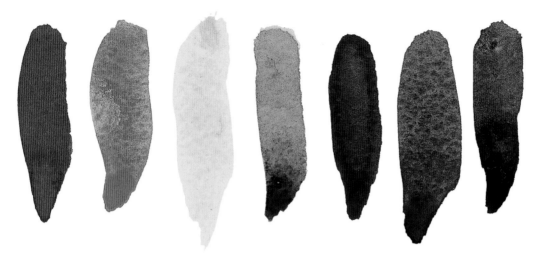

In 1666, English physicist and mathematician Isaac Newton discovered that by using prisms of glass he could refract light and split it into colours. He also found that there was a strict sequence to the colours, which pertained to the angle at which the light was split. The sequence was always the same. You can see this with a rainbow, where light filtered through water droplets produces a pattern of colours identical to those seen using the glass prism.

RODS AND CONES

When our eyes see the whole range of visible light together, they read it as 'white'. When some of the wavelengths are missing, they see it as coloured. The ability to see is what we call vision, and it is achieved by rods and cones in the delicate and complex mechanism of our eyes. Rods recognize black and white and facilitate the most basic part of our vision – black/grey/white. Cones recognize and capture colour and they develop in two stages during early infancy. At first, the baby develops the ability to recognize blue and yellow; next, he or she grows to recognize red and green. What we call colour blindness occurs when the cones fail to develop properly, usually at the second stage of cone development. Cones work best in strong light, which means that our colour vision at night hardly exists. In daylight, as visible (full spectrum) light falls

on an object, the physical and chemical properties of its surface allow it to absorb much of the light. The light that is not absorbed is reflected and bounced back as the colour we see. It is sometimes said that an object is 'doing colour' rather than 'being colour'.

Our eyes see about 80 percent of the colour range. A small percentage of what we see goes on in our head – it is neurological – and this hints at some of the more emotive aspects of colour.

With a pair of red shoes, for example, the colour atoms of the object behave in such a way that, when light falls on them, they absorb most of the blue and yellow and reflect the red. Paradoxically red shoes contain every wavelength of light – except red.

In 1810, the German writer, dramatist, poet, philosopher and scientist Johann Wolfgang von Goethe published his *Theory of Colours*. Much of this proved later to be scientifically inaccurate, but it was perhaps the poet in him that led him to study systematically the physiological effects of colour. Michael Eugene Chevreal, a chemist who was director of the dye works at the Manufacture des Gobelins in Paris, observed how colours looked differently depending upon the colours they were used next to; this discovery led to his theory of 'simultaneous contrast', which states that context influences the colours we see.

'The learned compute that seven hundred and seven millions of vibrations have to penetrate the eye before the eye can distinguish the tints of a violet.'

EDWARD G. BULWER-LYTTON

'Any white and opaque surface will be partially coloured by reflections from surrounding objects.'

LEONARDO DA VINCI, *THE NOTEBOOKS*, VOL. 1

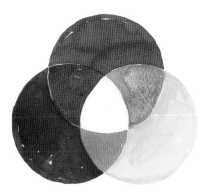

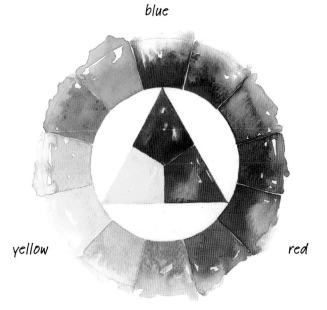

blue

yellow   red

In the early 20th century our understanding of the way colour works was developed by theorists such as Wilhelm Ostwald, a Baltic Latvian chemist who developed the colour wheel as we recognize it today. Albert Munsell, an American painter and art teacher, further developed these ideas and was the first to separate hue (colour), value (lightness) and chroma (purity or shade, sometimes called saturation) into a system that could be illustrated and calibrated. In the language of colour theorists, a tint is the mix of a colour with white, which increases its lightness. Adding black to a colour reduces its lightness and produces a shade. A tone is produced when a colour is mixed with black and white or (in simpler terms) with grey. When a colour is mixed with black, white or grey this reduces its colourfulness, or chroma, though the hue remains the same. However, we tend to use the word shade to mean any variant of a colour, whether it be hue, tint or tone.

COLOUR HARMONY
Colour harmony is when colours are combined in a way that pleases the eye. The simplest colour harmony is analogous, when neighbouring colours are used from the colour wheel, such as yellow-green, yellow and yellow-orange. When directly oppositional colours are combined, such as red and green, blue and orange or yellow and purple, they are known as complementary colours. A third type, known as triadic colour harmony, combines colours evenly spaced around the colour wheel.

'I love colour. I feel it inside me. It gives me a buzz.'

DAMIEN HIRST

METAMERISM
Metamerism is science's way of describing why colours change, appear differently or fail to match in different lights – the cool light of morning or from the north, the warm light of evening and the south, daylight, artificial light, filament, tungsten, fluorescent, and so on. Basically, different materials and surfaces, when combined with different dyes and colourants, will absorb and reflect light differently and appear differently in different lights. We hope you're not confused!

'"Yes!" I answered you last night;
"No!" this morning, Sir, I say!
Colours, seen by candle-light,
Will not look the same by day.'

ELIZABETH BARRETT BROWNING

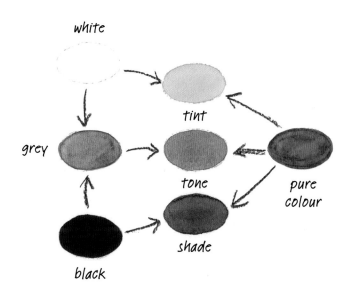

white

grey   tint

tone   pure colour

black   shade

BLACK

The browner tinged blacks were originally achieved using extracts from alder and oak trees, the bluer tinged blacks used woad. Thanks in part to improved dying methods, black made its transition into dress as the pious middle classes of the Reformation adopted it as a stance against excess. Its widespread use for this purpose is exemplified in the portraits of Van Dyck and Frans Hals. Today black is still generally associated with restrained good taste.

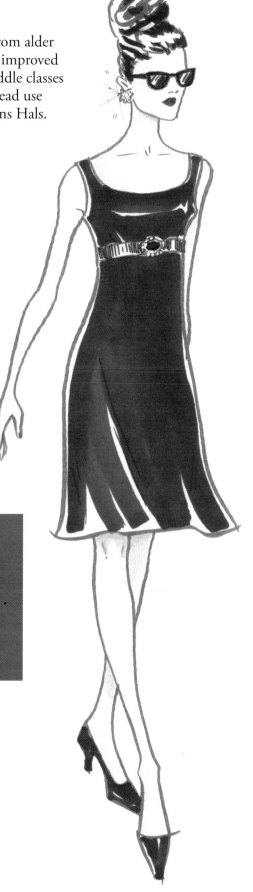

'One is never over- or under-dressed with a little black dress.'
KARL LAGERFELD

'I fell in love with black; it contained no colour. It wasn't a negation of colour . . . Black is the most aristocratic colour of all . . . you can be quiet, and it contains the whole thing.'
LOUISE NEVELSON

'I've been 40 years discovering that the queen of colours was black.'
PIERRE-AUGUSTE RENOIR

'[The] fashion world and designers can jump through hoops with all their prints and their colours and it doesn't mean a damn! Look at the women in Paris during Fashion Week – they're all in black. Of course, look at the black . . . There isn't a dumb black dress . . . it's such a fashion force.'
BILL CUNNINGHAM, *THE NEW YORK TIMES*

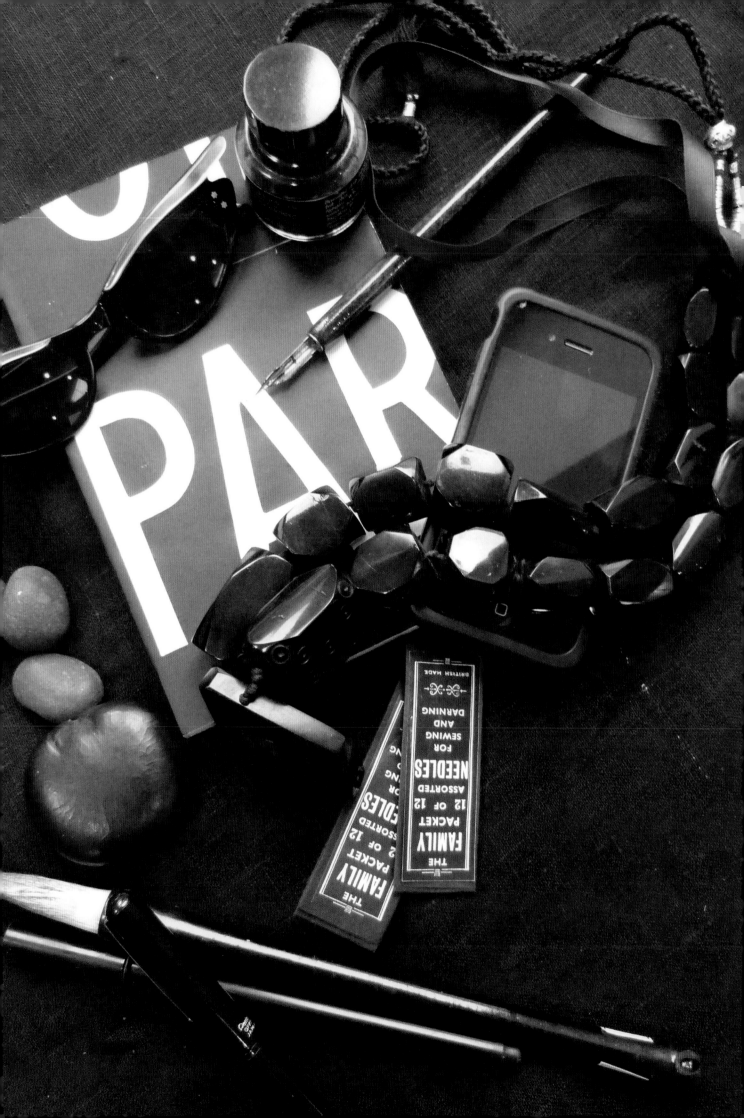

WHITE

Ever since the Catholic Church adopted white in the 12th century as symbolic of purity and divinity – replacing imperial purple inherited from the Romans – the West has favoured white for everything it wishes to appear pure and unsullied, from brides and babies to the Pope. But in the East white is associated with sickness and death and in India widows don white and disassociate themselves from the vibrancy of life.

'Working in white makes people look into it. White is ethereal. There is purity to it, it makes things look elevated in a way. There's a whole palette of white.'

JONATHAN MILNE

'White is not a mere absence of colour; it is a shining and affirmative thing, as fierce as red, as definite as black.'

G.K. CHESTERTON

'There is no colour like white, madam – it's so lasting, so genteel.'

GEORGE BORROW, *ROMANY RYE*

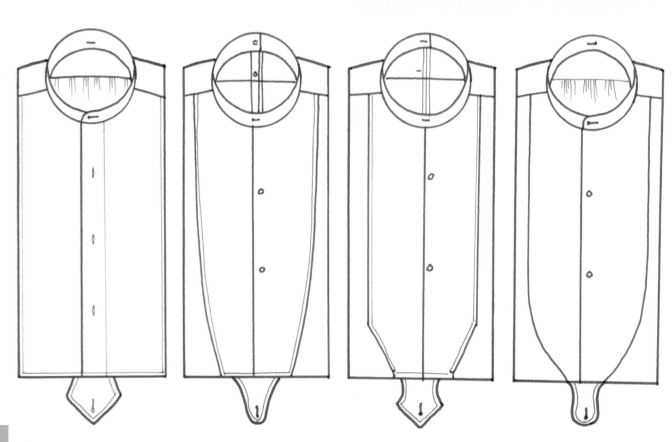

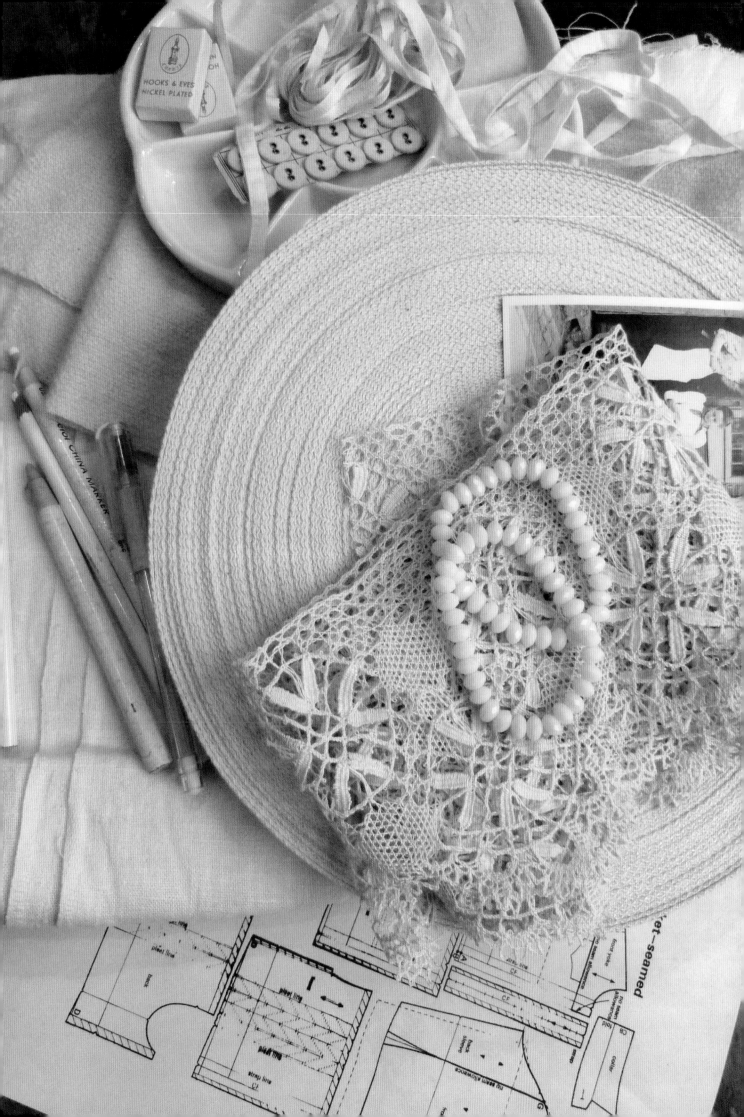

GREY

Known as the Velvet Gentleman, the dapper French composer Erik Satie was an innovative presence in the artistic and intellectual circles of Montmartre in the decades around the turn of the 19th century. In 1895, in an effort to streamline his life to enable him to focus more on his work while still maintaining his reputation for his immaculate appearance, he ordered from his tailor seven identical grey suits, one of which he wore every day until the end of his life in 1925.

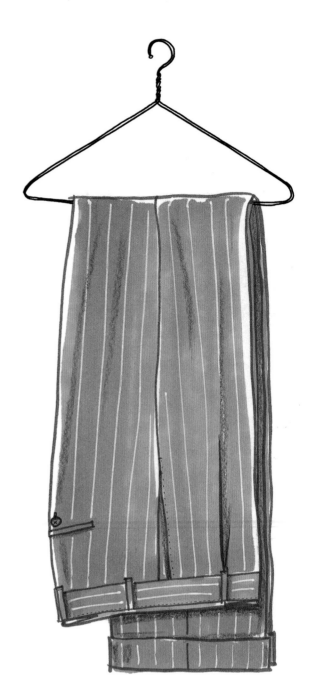

'Better grey than garishness.'

JEAN-AUGUSTE-DOMINIQUE INGRES

'Speed kills colour . . . the gyroscope, when turning at full speed, shows up grey.'

PAUL MORAND

'The colour of truth is grey.'

ANDRÉ GIDE

'Grey. It makes no statement whatever; it evokes neither feelings nor associations: it is really neither visible nor invisible. Its inconspicuousness gives it the capacity to mediate. . . . It has the capacity that no other colour has, to make "nothing" visible.'

GERHARD RICHTER

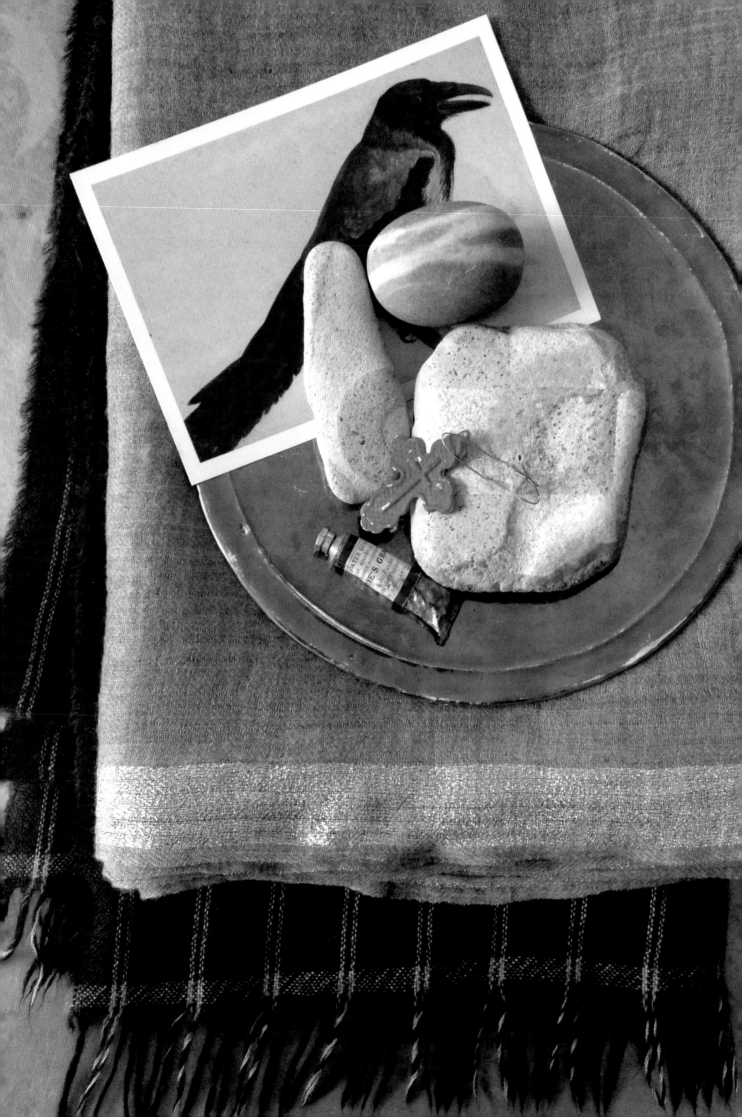

RED

Madder is one of a number of natural red pigments. Extracted from the root of the Rubia tree, it was this wonderful warm red that made Venice and Florence the most renowned centres for dying fine wool and silks in the 14th century and subsequently became deeply associated with the Italian Renaissance. Also known as vantia (from garance or garanza) and related to quality, it eventually gave us our word 'guarantee'.

'You cannot go wrong with the use of red; every painting should have red in it.'
GEORGE DE GROAT

'In Russian, the words "red" and "beautiful" are drawn from the same adjective.'
ANON

'Red, of course, is the colour of the interior of our bodies. In a way it's inside out, red.'
ANISH KAPOOR

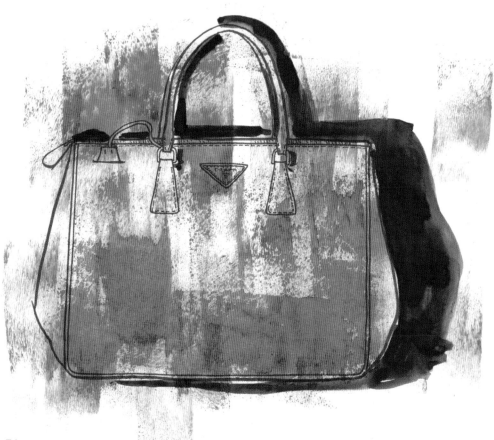

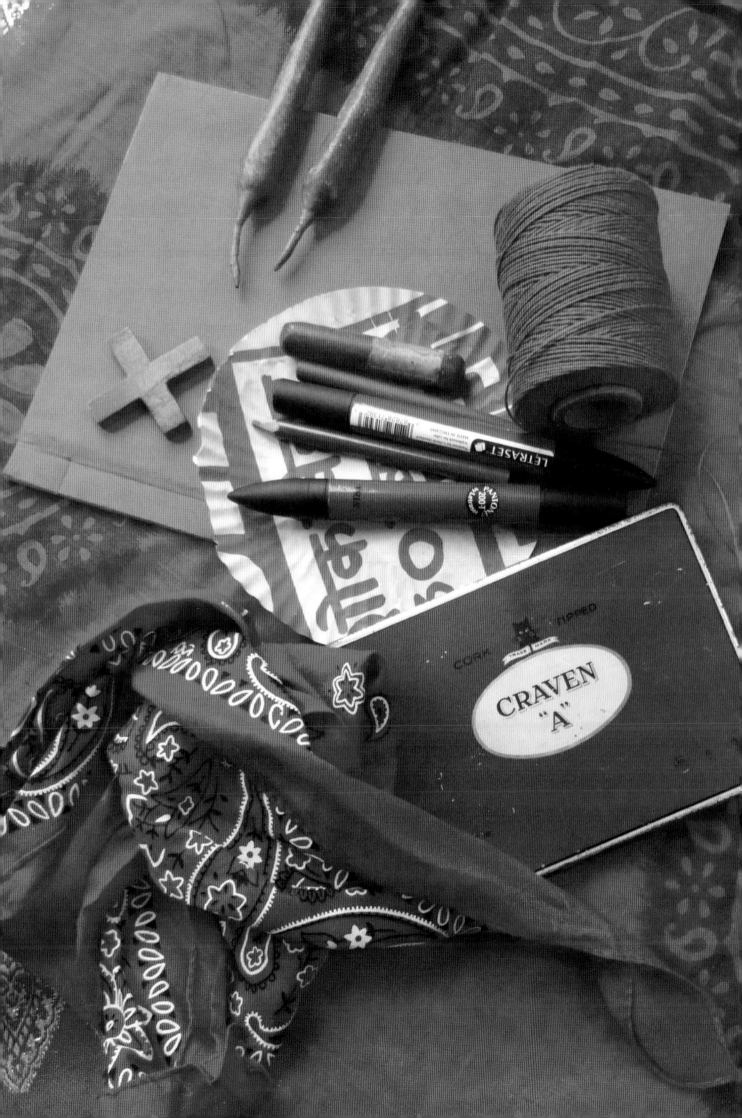

PINK

Not until the late 19th century did baby clothes begin to change from centuries of all white to pastels. But the 'pink for a girl and blue for a boy' doctrine was only cemented as a result of heavy American marketing ploys in the 1940s. In the 1920s, Jay Gatsby's pastel pink suit was regarded with suspicion by Tom Buchanan in F. Scott Fitzgerald's memorable novel *The Great Gatsby*.

'I adore that pink! It's the navy blue of India.'

DIANA VREELAND

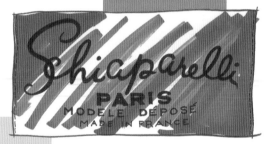

'Pink to make the boys wink.'

ANON

'Pink, though one of the most beautiful colours in combination, is not easy to use as a flat tint even over moderate spaces; the more orangey shades of it are the most useful, a cold pink being a colour much to be avoided.'

WILLIAM MORRIS, *HOPES AND FEARS FOR ART*

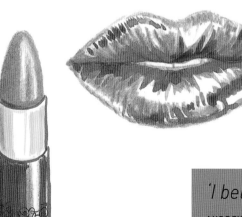

'I believe in pink.'

AUDREY HEPBURN

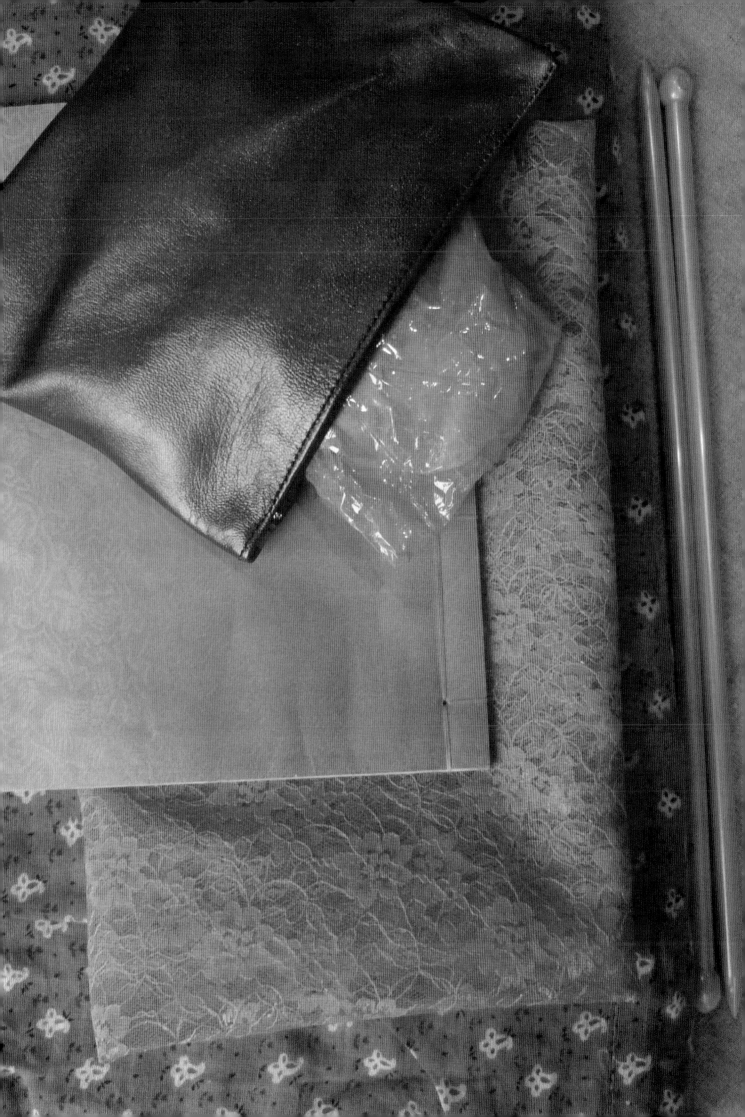

ORANGE

Orange is deeply associated with Buddhism, and many believe that wearing this powerful, positive colour can help to balance the emotions during times of stress or shock. The United Nations Secretary General's campaign to end violence against women and girls celebrates and raises awareness, and promotes its cause with Orange Day every year.

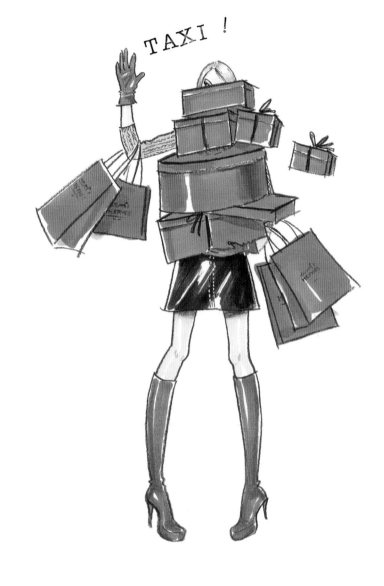

TAXI !

'Orange's note is that of a church bell, a strong contralto voice, or the largo of an old violin.'
WASSILY KANDINSKY

'Where yellow dives into red, the ripples are orange.'
DEREK JARMAN

'The first recorded use of the word "orange" as the name of a colour in English was in 1512, and it will probably come as no surprise that it is actually named after the fruit. Seems they're inseparable. Before 1512 it was known as geoluread (yellow red).'
VICTORIA ALEXANDER, *COLOUR: A JOURNEY*

'Orange is red brought nearer to humanity by yellow.'
WASSILY KANDINSKY

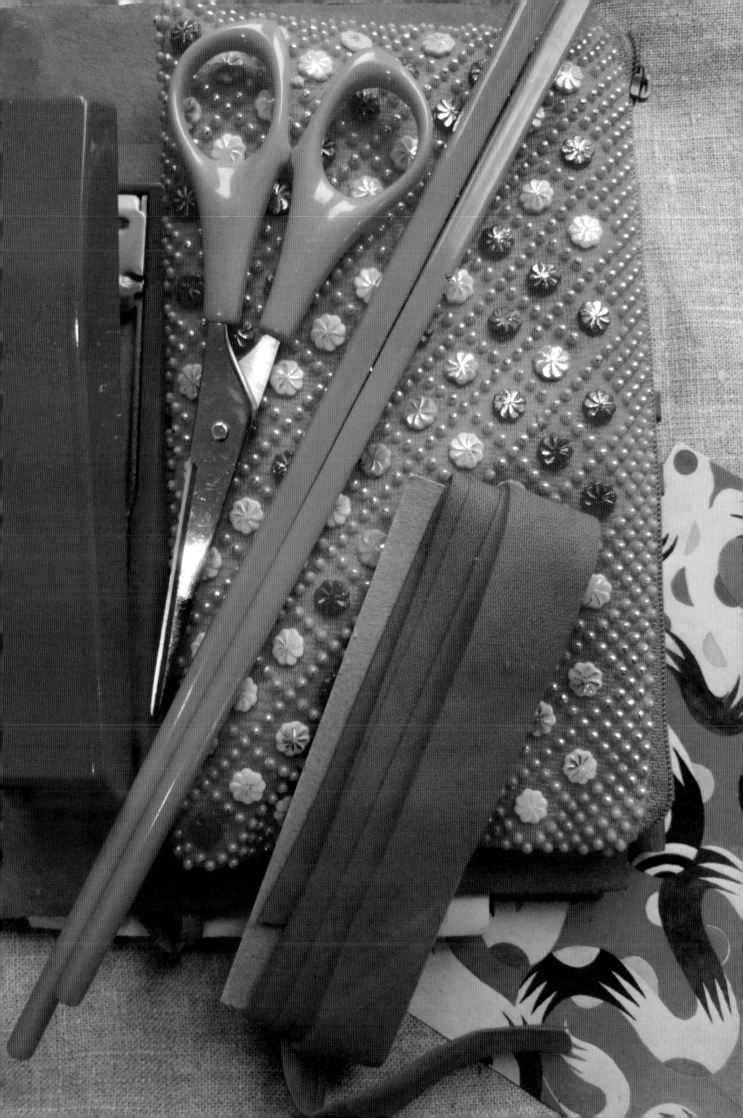

YELLOW

In China, from the 6th century and for many centuries afterwards, yellow was the imperial colour, associated with rebirth and reserved for the emperor and princes of the blood. Saffron is probably the world's best known and most expensive natural yellow pigment. It takes the stigmas of about 700,000 crocus flowers, picked by hand, to make 500 grams of saffron, which costs around US$1,000.

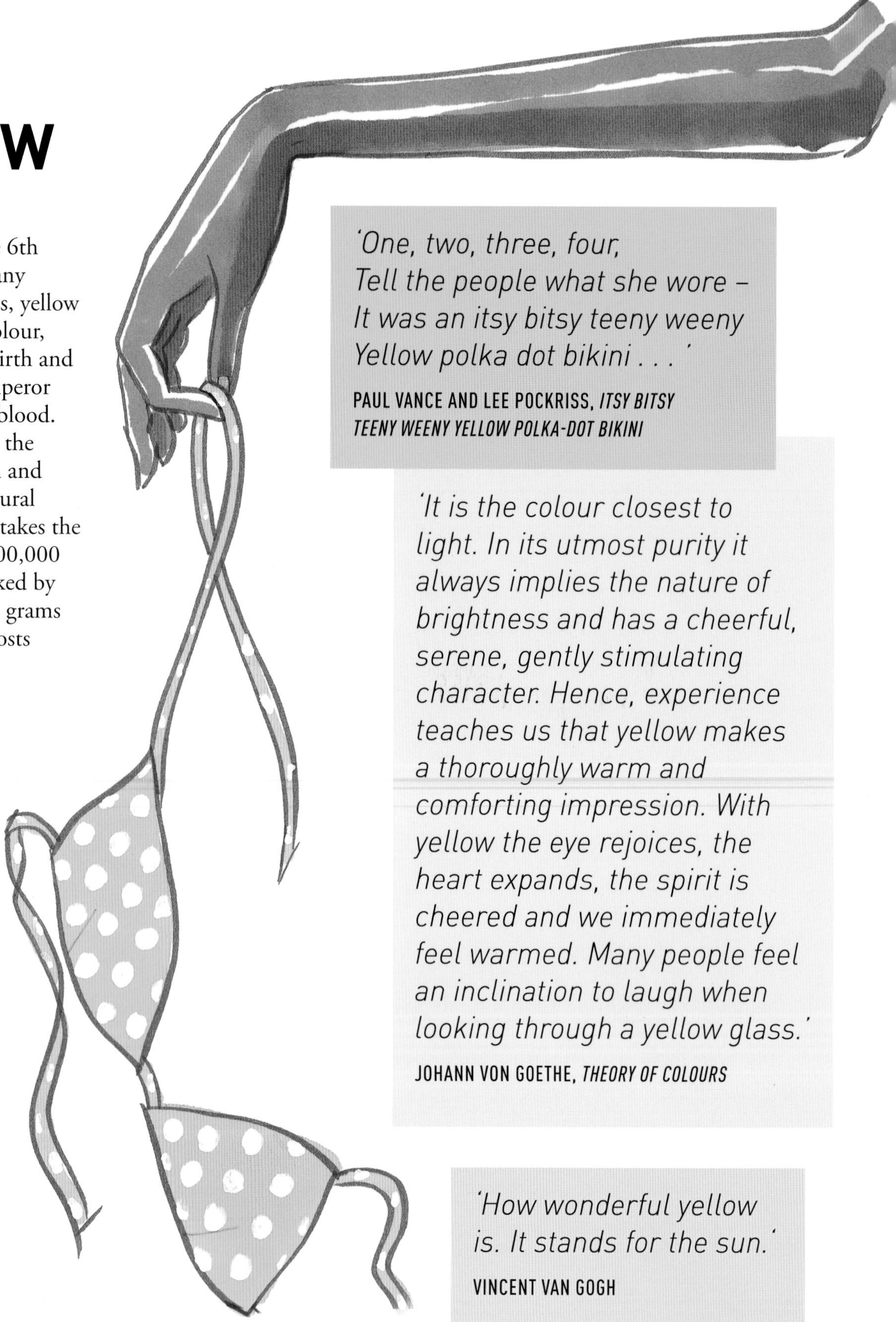

'One, two, three, four,
Tell the people what she wore –
It was an itsy bitsy teeny weeny
Yellow polka dot bikini . . .'

PAUL VANCE AND LEE POCKRISS, *ITSY BITSY TEENY WEENY YELLOW POLKA-DOT BIKINI*

'It is the colour closest to light. In its utmost purity it always implies the nature of brightness and has a cheerful, serene, gently stimulating character. Hence, experience teaches us that yellow makes a thoroughly warm and comforting impression. With yellow the eye rejoices, the heart expands, the spirit is cheered and we immediately feel warmed. Many people feel an inclination to laugh when looking through a yellow glass.'

JOHANN VON GOETHE, *THEORY OF COLOURS*

'How wonderful yellow is. It stands for the sun.'

VINCENT VAN GOGH

'Indian yellow, banned. Cows were poisoned with mango leaves and the colour was made from their urine. It is the bright yellow in Indian miniatures. Although yellow occupies one twentieth of the spectrum, it is the brightest colour.'

DEREK JARMAN

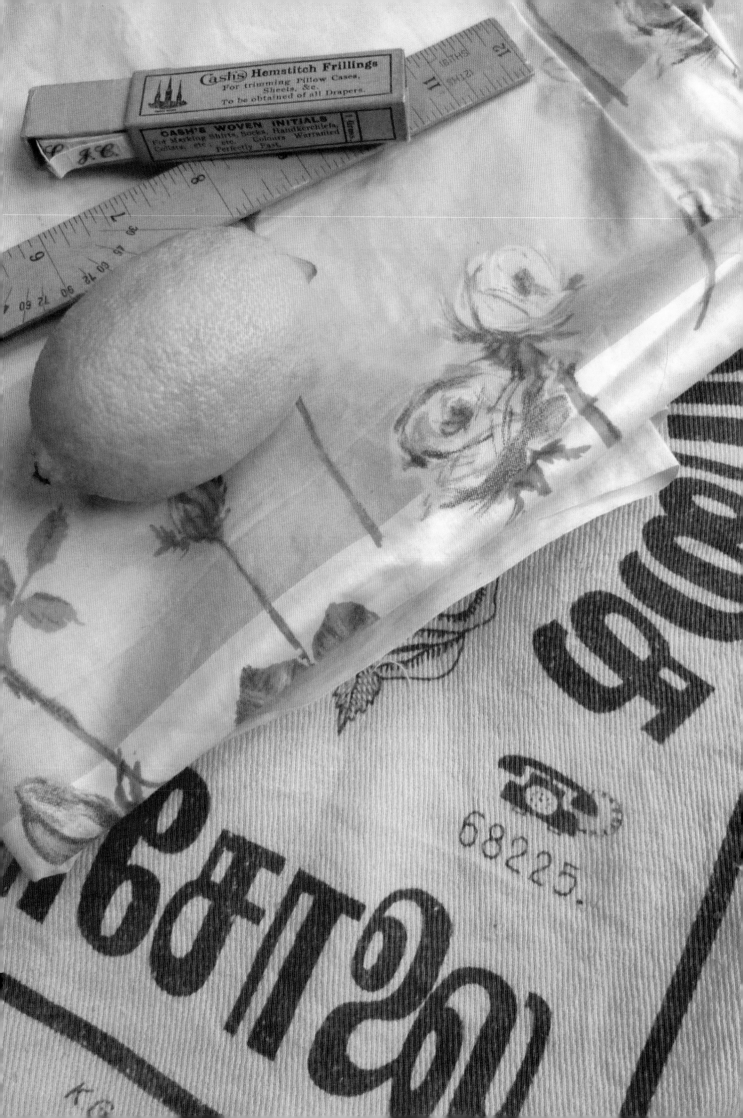

GREEN

A very popular colour with 19th century aesthetes and members of the pre-Raphaelite movement, who dressed themselves in 'green and yellow melancholy' (*Twelfth Night*, William Shakespeare). In China, 'wearing a green hat' is an expression used for a man who is being cheated on by his wife. It apparently dates back to the Yuan dynasty, when husbands of prostitutes were required to wear green hats in public!

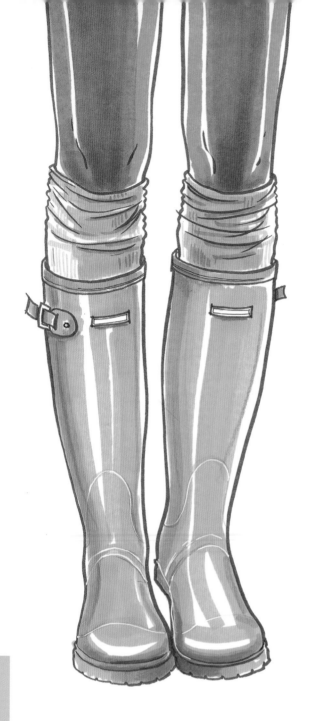

'We wear green clothes because it's the colour of the grass and the leaves, and when we sit down under a bush or lie in the grass they walk by without noticing us.'

JAMES STEPHENS,
THE CROCK OF GOLD

'He had that curious love of green, which in individuals is always the sign of a subtle artistic temperament, and in nations is said to denote a laxity, if not a decadence of morals.'

OSCAR WILDE

'Visit a green place to understand green. '

SUSAN EASTON BURNS

'It's not easy being green.'

KERMIT THE FROG

BLUE

Blue is the favourite colour of 50 per cent of people in the world, according to French scholar Michel Pastoureau. This colour is universally synonymous with manual work, giving us the term *bleu de travail* or 'workers' blue'.

First coined in 1924, the phrases 'blue collar jobs' and 'blue collar workers', to distinguish manual work from managerial (white collar) employment, are still commonplace today. Chambray work shirts, dungarees, coveralls, overalls, union suits, boiler suits and all manner of work clothes are traditionally blue.

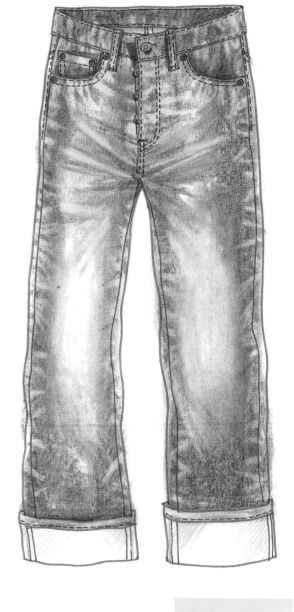

'I have often said that I wish I had invented blue jeans: the most spectacular, the most practical, the most relaxed and nonchalant. They have expression, modesty, sex appeal, simplicity – all I hope for in my clothes.'

YVES SAINT LAURENT

'What is blue? Blue is the invisible becoming visible . . . Blue has no dimensions. It is beyond the dimensions of which other colours partake. All colours arouse specific associative ideas . . . while blue suggests at most sea and sky, and they, after all, are in actual, visible nature what is most abstract.'

YVES KLEIN

'Blue is the only colour which maintains its own character in all its tones . . . it will always stay blue; whereas yellow is blackened in its shades, and fades away when lightened; red when darkened becomes brown, and diluted with white is no longer red, but another colour – pink.'

RAOUL DUFY

'What bliss there is in blueness. I never knew how blue blueness could be.'

VLADIMIR NABOKOV

60

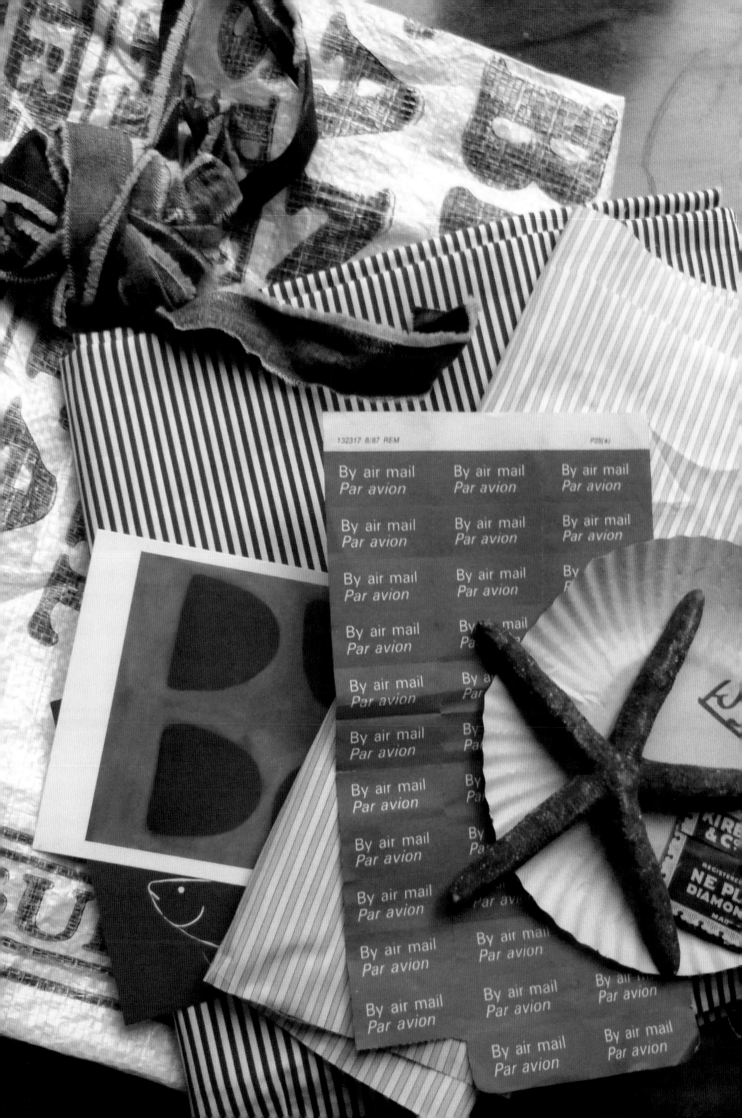

INDIGO

In the 18th century, indigo printed cloths were often known as 'China Blue' and in France as 'Bleu Anglais'. Originally from India, from where it gains its name, the plant family *Indigo fera tinctoria* has many genera around the world. The pigment is also found in woad. The invention of blue jeans, arguably accredited to Levi Strauss in the 1870s, has its roots in the traditional indigo blue sailors' trousers of Genoa (hence 'jeans').

'Indigo is the colour of clothes; cobalt of glass; ultramarine of painting.'

DEREK JARMAN

'Indigo has a purifying, stabilizing, cleansing effect when fear, repression, and obsessions have disturbed your mental body. Indigo food vibrations are: blackberries, blue plums, blueberries, purple broccoli, beetroot, and purple grapes.'

TAE YUN KIM, *THE FIRST ELEMENT: SECRETS TO MAXIMIZING YOUR ENERGY*

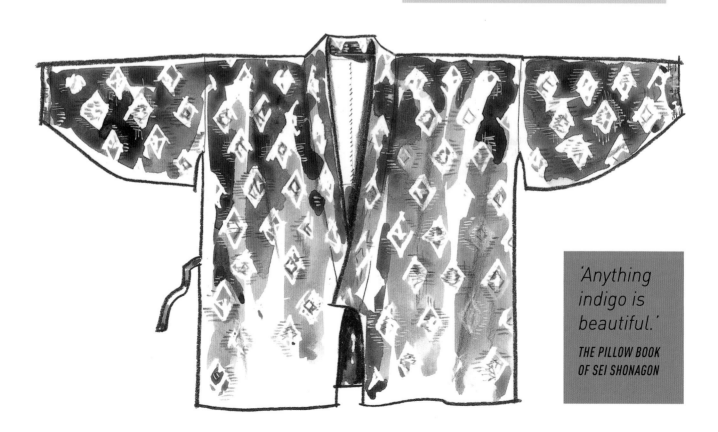

'Anything indigo is beautiful.'

THE PILLOW BOOK OF SEI SHONAGON

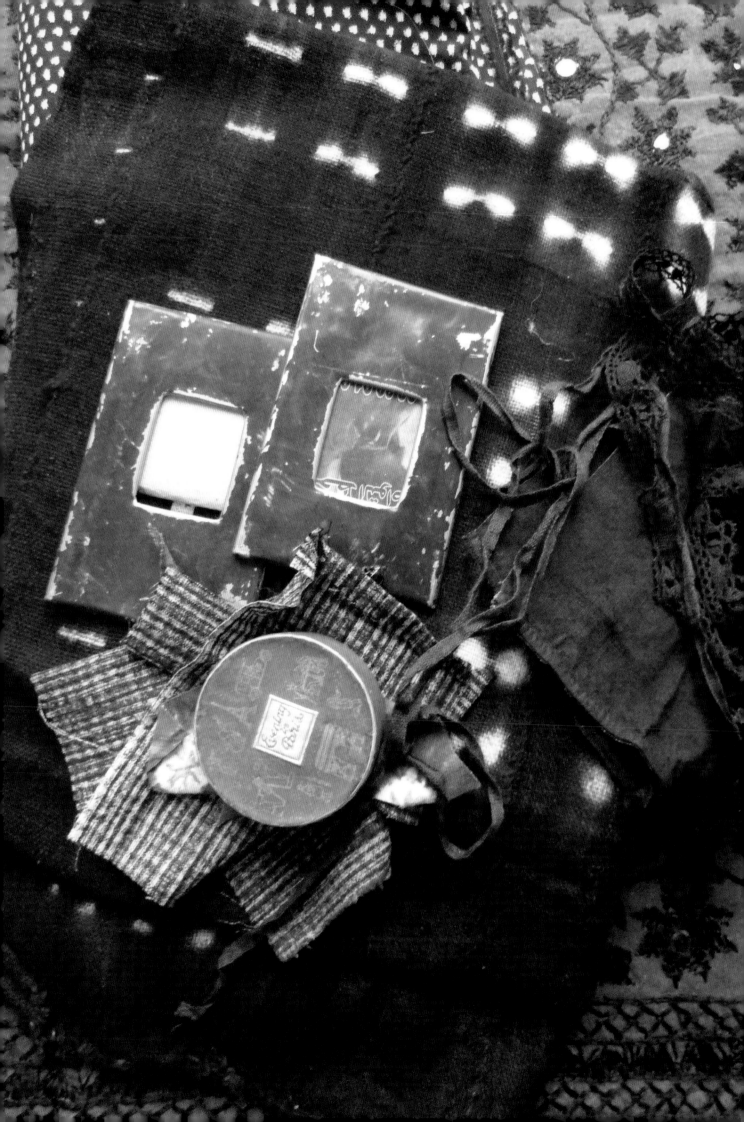

VIOLET

The earliest purple was Imperial Purple, known also as Tyrian Red or Tyrian Purple, obtained with difficulty from a Mediterranean sea snail first discovered by the Phoenicians in Tyre. It was so rare and so admired by the Romans that it became the *color officialis* of Rome – only permitted for emperors to wear. Purple remained the privilege of the rich and powerful, namely the Catholic Church, for centuries until the almost accidental discovery of Mauveine, the first synthetic purple dye by William Perkin in 1856, part of the synthetic dye revolution that subsequently democratized colour.

'Mauve? Mauve is just pink trying to be purple.'

JAMES ABBOTT MCNEILL WHISTLER

'She was wearing a purple T-shirt, with a skinny black dress over it that made you remember how much of a girl she was, and trashed black boots that made you forget.'

KAMI GARCIA, *BEAUTIFUL CREATURES*

'Violet has the shortest wavelength of the spectrum. Behind it, the invisible ultraviolet. Roses are red, violets are blue. Poor Violet, violated for rhyme.'

DEREK JARMAN

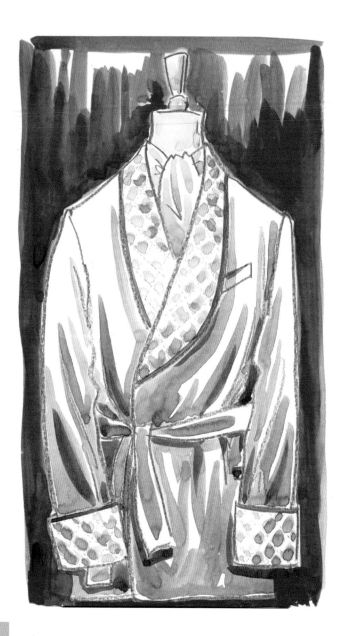

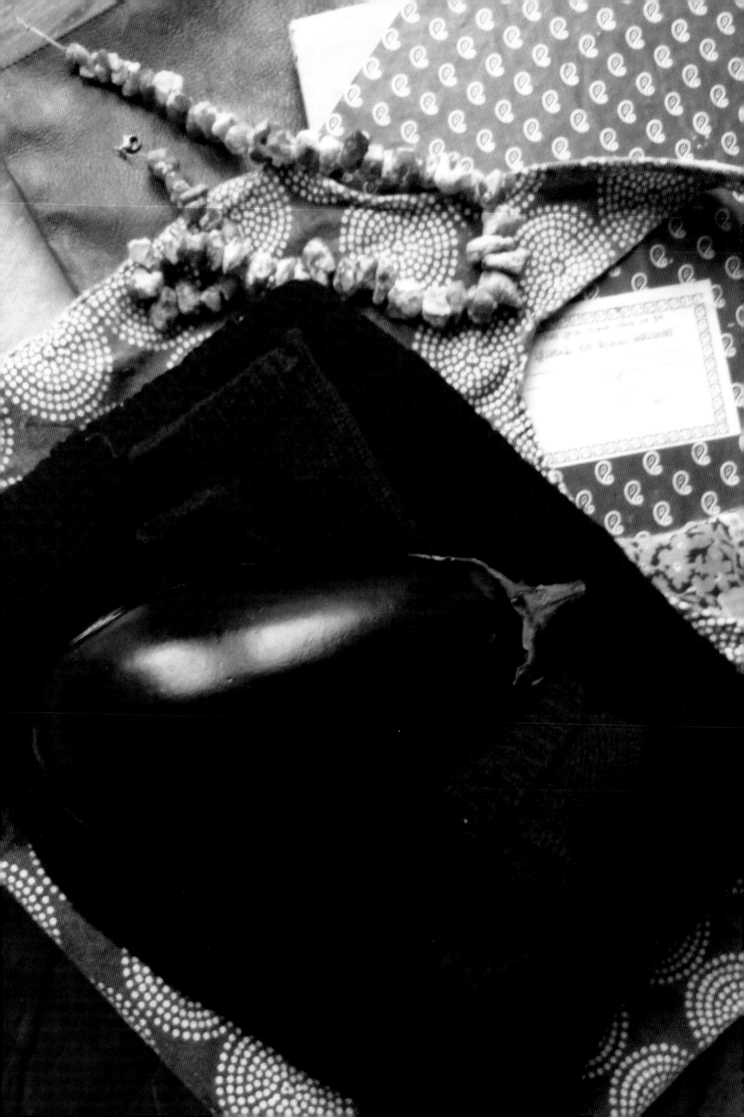

COLOUR & FASHION

In the world of fashion particularly – though this phenomenon is becoming widespread throughout all areas of commerce – colour has always been a major part of the newness offered by designers each season. We frequently hear how fashion has in-built obsolescence; in one season, out the next. Without going into too much depth at this juncture, this can partly be excused by the fact that some colours are perhaps more naturally suited to a particular season – though this appropriateness is more and more often challenged these days as season crossover and *fashion* tends now to influence everything. Colour is, though, the cheapest and easiest way to update anything and, in the interests of commerce, designers do exploit this, as we are well aware. The new colours are usually the main point of curiosity and interest each season.

Looking back in history we can see very definite trends in colours, many of them driven by economic, political and scientific developments and scenarios which as a subject would make for fascinating and enlightening research beyond the scope of this book. More recently we can easily associate colours such as purple with the late 1960s – orange, too. In the 1970s the darker purple and aubergine shades of Biba gave way to brown as part of a huge retro trend. In the 1980s Japanese designers, in particular Yohji Yamamoto, Issey Miyake and Rei Kawakubo with her label Comme des Garçons, converted almost the whole fashion world to black – an influence that still reverberates today.

SIGNATURE COLOURS

Most designers have their 'colour moment', when a colour they show or are associated with is particularly pertinent. Despite changing seasons and over-riding trends, some designers, however, are very much permanently associated with particular colours and in some instances they become ongoing – their signature colour(s) – if not because they regularly show part of their collection or accessories using those colours, then because of the significant colour of their branding and packaging.

In the evolution of fashion brands (as we now know them), designer Jeanne Lanvin was one of the first to be associated with a particular colour. Working in Paris in the early 20th century, Lanvin travelled to Florence where she saw a

Fra Angelico fresco and reputedly fell in love with the 'quattrocento blue'. She decorated her home with it and went on to use it extensively in her work. The shade became known as 'Lanvin blue' and, when the label was revived in 2001 with Alber Elbaz as artistic director, the colour became key to the identity through its packaging, branding and perennial inclusion in the ranges.

In 1926 a short, simple black dress by Coco Chanel was featured in American *Vogue* and heralded as the answer to many contemporary dressing dilemmas. As modern as the Model T Ford (which came only in black), elegant and chic, it was soon considered in its essence to be timeless. Chanel herself often broke the severity of black with simple white collar or cuff details, so black and white became the signature house colours until her demise. As she famously stated: 'Women think of all colours except the absence of colour. I have said that black has it all. White too. Their beauty is absolute. It is the perfect harmony.' The label was revived in 1983 under the creative directorship of Karl Lagerfeld. Since then, much has been made of the black and white theme and its contemporary marketing.

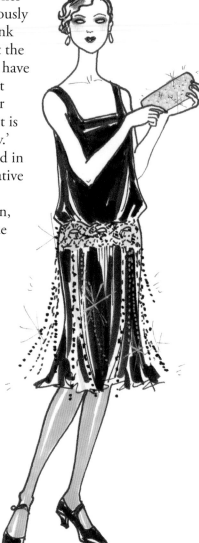

RIGHT: *Chanel's short, elegant little black dress was identified as the 'shape of the future' in 1926.*

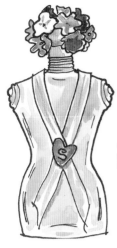

In the 1930s, another Parisian couturier, Elsa Schiaparelli, became synonymous with a particularly fierce shade of bright pink. When in 1937 she launched her perfume Shocking de Schiaparelli packaged in this shade, the colour became widely known as 'shocking pink' and is still known by this name today.

The French fashion house Hermès was originally a high-end equestrian outfitter and tack-maker, which gradually made the transition to fashion brand. It has maintained and capitalized on its bright orange packaging (reputed to be Pantone 17-1463 Tangerine Tango).

Another early 20th century luggage brand which made the transition to full fashion range is Milan-based Prada. Perhaps still more famous for its bags and accessories than its clothes, Prada has a reputation and association with red, using definitive shades that are never brash or flashy.

Italian designer Valentino has been known for his signature red evening dresses for at least two decades: 'Red is a colour that is not shy . . . ' he says. 'When I was young, I went to see the opera *Carmen* in Barcelona and the whole set was red – the flowers, the costumes – and l said to myself, "I want to keep this colour in my life." So I mixed a shade with the people who make fabrics – it contains a certain amount of orange – and Valentino Red became an official Pantone colour.'

Red also provides the signature colour for the soles of Christian Louboutin shoes, whatever the style, colour or fabric of the rest of the shoe.

With typical restraint, when Christian Dior opened his couture house on the Avenue Montaigne in Paris in 1946 it was decorated in soft grey Louis XVI style. The colour became the signature colour. When the nose François Demachy recently created a new fragrance in honour of the house and the heritage of the brand, he called it Gris Montaigne.

Yves Saint Laurent, perhaps the greatest of the late 20th century couturiers, was undoubtedly a great colourist. Frequently influenced by fine artists and by traditional costume and dress from exotic corners of the world, which frequently inspired flamboyant colour palettes, he was equally known for his restraint and could just as successfully make a statement in signature navy blue.

The great British designer Jean Muir, who sadly died in 2007, was known for her great confidence with colour on the runway, but was similarly a huge promoter of navy blue, for which she was widely known and adored. She personally wore only navy blue all her life and was widely feted for her clever little navy dresses.

The Italian brand Gucci began its revival and revamp in 1994, with the appointment of Tom Ford as creative director. The signature red and green stripe was revived and Ford changed all the packaging and branding to a chic dark brown, reviving this colour from its dreary 1970s associations and challenging the then ubiquitous black branding of almost all the other big name labels.

Parisian Jean Paul Gaultier has since his 1980s heyday been forever associated with navy and white matelot stripes.

'Colour is the language of poets.
It is astonishingly lovely.
To speak it is a privilege.'

KEITH CROWN

TALKING COLOUR

As we have mentioned, everyone sees colour slightly differently. Lighting and other factors affect how we see colour, so systems have evolved to recognize and standardize colours for industry. The most widely known and popularly used system is Pantone, first developed by Lawrence Herbert in the early 1960s to help an American printing company simplify their stock control.

The Pantone Matching System (PMS) allows designers, industry and manufacturers to colour match, regardless of location and without the need for direct contact with one another. The system is used across an increasingly wide range of industries including print, paint, plastics, yarn, fabric and, consequently, fashion. Pantone colours are identified by a unique serial number and letter suffix which denotes the medium; textile colours have the suffix TPX. New colours are added regularly, responding to fashion trends and innovations. Recent additions include metallics and fluorescents.

TREND FORECASTING

Fashion and colour crossovers aside, colour is a big and important business. Attempts at finding the right colour are the *raison d'être* of the numerous studios and bureaux specializing in trend forecasting, many of which target specific product areas and market levels. One of the biggest of these is the Colour Association, established in 1915. Its founding members were milliners, glove makers and hosiery suppliers who simply recognized that customers needed coordinated, fashionable accessories.

Today it is more complex, as the various influences on consumer tastes and values include economic, environmental and global factors – and fashion is bound up in all of this. When, perhaps rather foolishly, a *New York Times* journalist contacted the Paris office of Alber Elbaz, creative director at Lanvin to ask about fashion forecasts, the newspaper could only report: 'we think we can read "How to Become a Millionaire" or "Find a Gorgeous Husband in Three Weeks", but a book is a book is a book. We have to go with our intuition . . . ' Bureaux, studios and style agencies tend to take their lead from the runway shows of influential designers such as Elbaz, not the other way round. Fashion forecasts are for the mass market; for retailers and

manufacturers to ensure they have enough blue sweaters in stock next winter!

Pantone is linked into this circuit, not only supplying the means of accurately disseminating colour information, but also contributing to it. Each year, since 1999, Pantone has declared a 'Colour of the Year', chosen approximately one year in advance. The first of these – Cerulean Blue 15-4020 (chosen for its calming, Zen-like qualities) – was for 2000. The choice is discussed and debated by industry, media consultants and creatives and, according to Pantone, 'responds to and reflects the zeitgeist'. For example, the press release declaring Honeysuckle the colour of 2011 said: 'In times of stress, we need something to lift our spirits. Honeysuckle is a captivating, stimulating colour that gets the adrenaline going – perfect to ward off the blues.'

Chosen in the Spring of 2012, the colour for 2013 was Emerald 17-5641, described as: 'Lively. Radiant. Lush . . . A colour of elegance and beauty that enhances our sense of wellbeing, balance and harmony.' For 2014 the choice was Radiant Orchid 18-3224: 'an expressive, creative and embracing purple – one that draws you in with its beguiling charm. A captivating harmony of fuchsia, purple and pink undertones, Radiant Orchid emanates great joy, love and health.' The secrecy around the Colour of the Year is such that the Instagram promotional film for the 2014 colour was made in black and white! More detailed accounts of the colour meetings are published in *Pantone View*, a trade publication used by fashion designers, retailers, florists and other consumer-oriented companies to help inform their design choices and future product planning and coordination.

> 'Mere colour, unspoiled by meaning, and unallied with definite form, can speak to the soul in a thousand different ways.'
>
> OSCAR WILDE

COLOUR PALETTES

'I never met a colour I didn't like.'

DALE CHIHULY

Colour is an inspiration – it can create and evoke moods by planting ideas and atmospheres, otherwise intangible, firmly in our minds. A successful colour palette is essential for communicating and referencing colours. Although reference numbers are usually enough for technical purposes, that's not how most people remember colours; we tend to find a name far more evocative and easier to recall. An appropriately named colour can evoke the exact shade in the mind, even though the person may not have necessarily seen it. Once seen together, the connection between name and colour can stay with us forever. So it is worth considering carefully the names you give to your colours; they should be appropriate to your mood or theme and, in the interests of simplicity, be single words only. It is unnecessary, for example, to call a colour 'Rose Pink'; 'Rose' should be enough, and if it isn't you need to pick the appropriate pink flower or object to reference. In industry, many mistakes have been made when one or other of the colour names has been omitted or someone has understood there to be two colours rather than one.

Colours were originally called after their natural pigment names: Ochre, Raw Umber, etc. But colours also readily conjure up images of alchemy and science or historical, geographical and cultural routes; Cadmium Yellow, Prussian Blue, Vermillion, Cardinal, etc. To ponder Ultramarine is to evoke the bluest of oceans – there is magic in the words.

Names and places stimulate the senses, evoke atmospheres and similarly inspire colours themselves. A good colour name can be employed as a powerful communication tool. For example, name a colour Samarkand (you may even conjure up a specific colour as you read this) and it can evoke notions of ancient silk routes – of a mysterious land, part fairytale perhaps, somewhere between Europe, Asia and the Orient. The imagination conjures ikat weaving, exotic silks and even jewels. Find some good reference images and the rest of a wonderful palette falls into place with other colours named from your imaginary adventure. Colours have a volume and intensity that can be generated though themed palettes by balancing, contrasting and orchestrating shades to your own ends and uses.

BELOW: *This old postcard inspired a relaxed casual palette of soft midtones in warm and cool shades (Sunset, Dusk, Sky and Grass). Bank, a soft olive shade, and Sand, a yellow ochre, act as useful neutrals. Mallard and Terroir add richness, with Storm providing definition and sobriety. By giving colours appropriate and evocative names, the palette's identity is reinforced.*

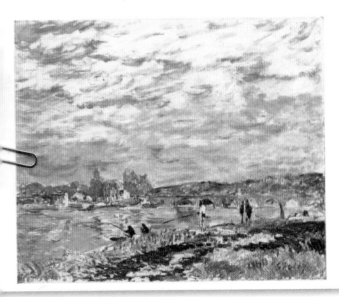

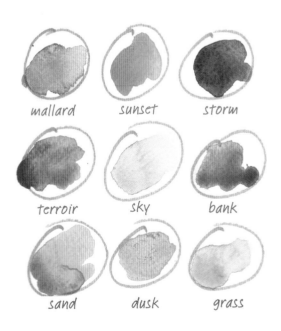

'Colours, like features, follow the changes of the emotions.' PABLO PICASSO

When designing a colour palette, it is important to think about how it is going to be used. If intended for garments – what season, what type, what market, what materials, even? As some colours will translate differently into different cloths, they may become dull/flat or, conversely, a bit flashy. If the colours are to be used for fabric prints or patterns, how might they be combined? Do you need some highlight or upbeat colours or do you want neutral/quiet colours to set others off to advantage? Maybe you need some darker or richer tones for depth and definition, as a single colour level can be monotonous.

Use the following quick, simple exercise to create a colour palette. Begin with an image you feel has a fashion relevance – a postcard of an artwork or a magazine tear that has a colour mood you like – and simply pick out the colours using windings of yarn, small snippets of fabric or coloured tape, etc. You can add small objects – a button, pebble, seashell or seed-head, a small plastic toy – anything that thematically relates and helps build towards the correct feeling and balance of colour.

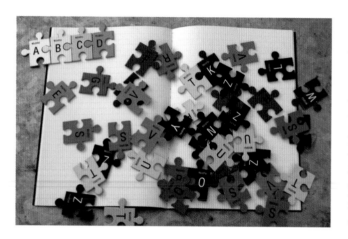

Here is a fun, novelty colour palette in the form of a jigsaw, running A–Z, from Italian spinning company Millefili Spa. It presents a large colour palette for their range of high-fashion quality knitting yarns. As a designer, rarely would you use more than ten colours in a professional fashion colour palette for a range, but you can cheat a little sometimes and have lighter and darker shades of the same colour – if really necessary! Generally, though, the tighter the palette, the more concise and positive your colour message. A clear, confident message in your work will in turn instil your client's confidence in you.

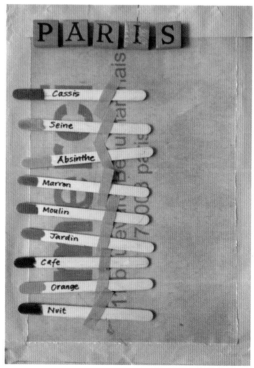

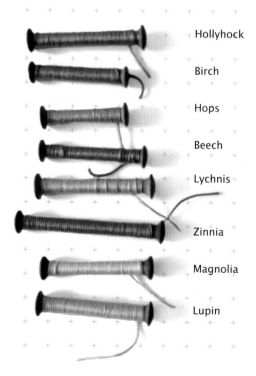

Hollyhock

Birch

Hops

Beech

Lychnis

Zinnia

Magnolia

Lupin

LEFT: *Using old wooden bobbins to wind embroidery threads as colour reference, this palette evokes a vintage needlework theme. It would need to be cross-referenced with Pantone shade numbers for accurate communication internationally.*

'The virtue of a small palette – the limitation stretches you to invent places where they can go.' BRIDGET RILEY

'Often an ugly colour is introduced such as a faded black or drab, to give counterpoint to colours that are sweet and clean.' JOHN FOWLER

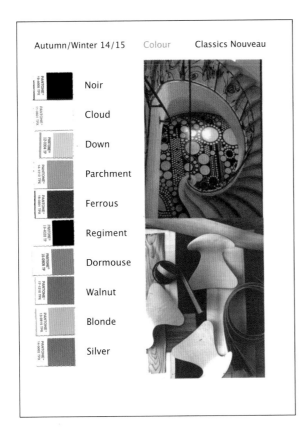

Autumn/Winter 14/15 · Colour · Classics Nouveau

Noir · Cloud · Down · Parchment · Ferrous · Regiment · Dormouse · Walnut · Blonde · Silver

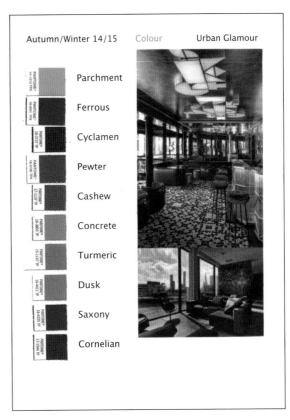

Autumn/Winter 14/15 · Colour · Urban Glamour

Parchment · Ferrous · Cyclamen · Pewter · Cashew · Concrete · Turmeric · Dusk · Saxony · Cornelian

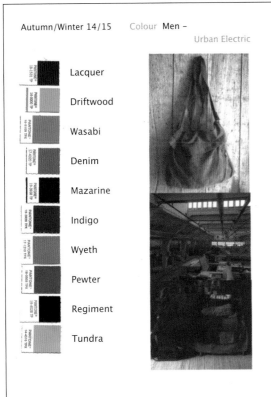

Autumn/Winter 14/15 · Colour Men – Urban Electric

Lacquer · Driftwood · Wasabi · Denim · Mazarine · Indigo · Wyeth · Pewter · Regiment · Tundra

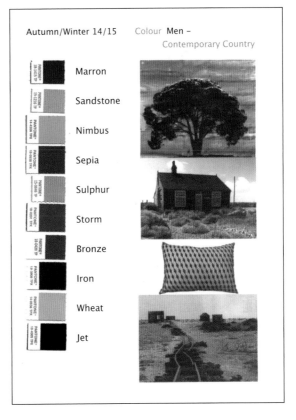

Autumn/Winter 14/15 · Colour Men – Contemporary Country

Marron · Sandstone · Nimbus · Sepia · Sulphur · Storm · Bronze · Iron · Wheat · Jet

ABOVE: *These colour palettes produced for international clients for Autumn/Winter 14/15 efficiently convey the season's colour moods for their market sector and use industry-standard Pantone colour chips to communicate the specific reference codes accurately and effectively.*

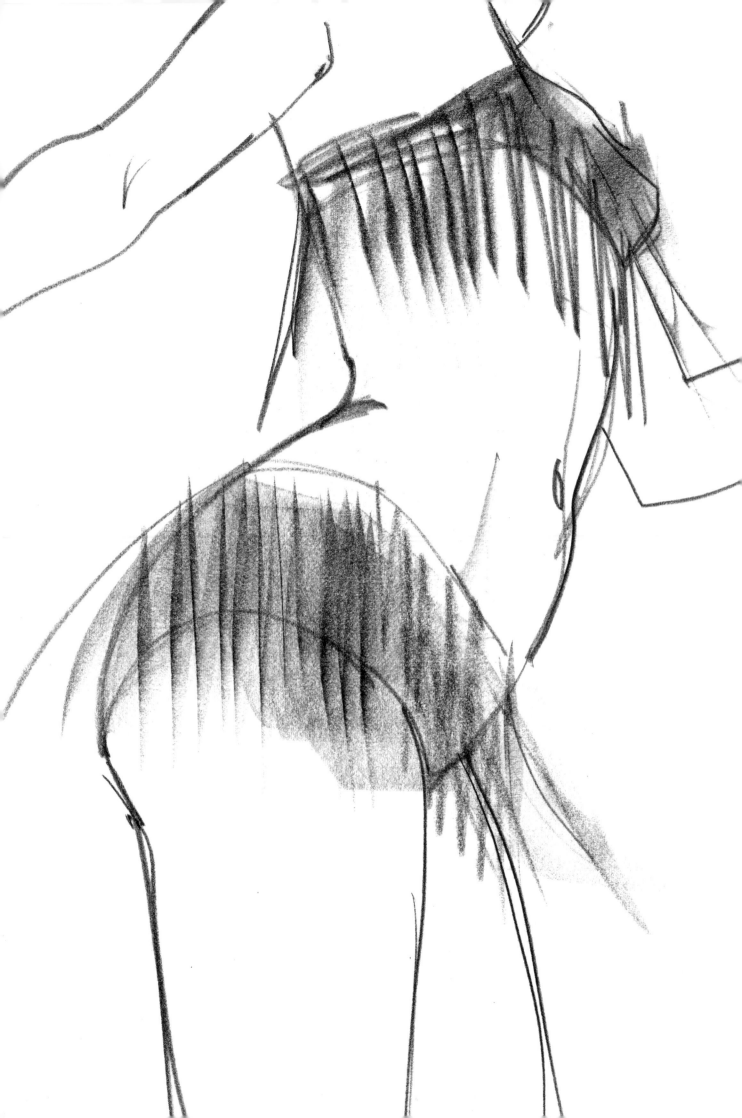

04 DRAWING

*'Drawing is for me the zone of freedom, fertile ground,
out of which all my work comes.'*

ANTONY GORMLEY

The act of drawing is fundamental to the creative process; it is a way of recording, generating and communicating ideas, of refining thoughts and schemes, of resolving and problem solving. At one time, drawing was the only way to record and communicate ideas and discoveries, and was an essential practical skill mastered by the first mapmakers, storytellers, archaeologists, explorers, plant hunters, builders, craftspeople, scientists, physicians, engineers and those involved in ambitious architectural projects. Whether for creative, artistic or practical outcomes, drawing remains the main way of promoting ideas in many fields. It can record the actual, present the unrealized and evoke the intangible. Drawing is thinking visualized; its reach is limitless.

One hears from time to time of designers who cannot or do not draw. Perhaps the most super-successful of these is Marc Jacobs who, memorably, can be witnessed not drawing in Loic Prigent's 2007 documentary film, *Marc Jacobs & Louis Vuitton*. The revered designer is seen cutting and draping fabric on the studio floor and tweaking vintage garments into new life through practical experimentation and discussion with his keen and eagerly compliant team. This may work for the privileged few who are lucky enough to have a close-knit team which is almost capable of mind-reading every nuance of the designers' thoughts and wishes. They have the added advantage that the people making the sample garment are usually sitting in the same room or at least in the same building. For most of us working in the fashion industry, however, a more concrete and transferable form of communication is required. The reality is that our clothes are usually made far away, in a different time zone, by people who may not speak our language. Given that errors from the misinterpretation of ideas and intentions are costly and time-consuming to put right (timing is increasingly a major factor in today's fast-fashion world), the need to communicate in a clear, coherent visual manner is fundamentally apparent.

While it may not be necessary to be an ace illustrator, a designer who cannot or does not draw at least to some level is undoubtedly at a huge disadvantage. Apart from recording and communicating thoughts, drawing is a way of generating, refining and developing ideas. This may involve drawing and redrawing details and proportions until a more pleasing and satisfactory result is achieved. Similarly it is a way of resolving technical, practical and constructional issues, a part of the planning process. Poorly resolved garments are often the result of inadequate drawing and planning; they simply weren't thought through sufficiently at the design stage – in other words, they weren't designed *enough*! Sound drawing skills are one of a designer's prime assets. Computer-aided design can enhance a drawing, it can even camouflage weaknesses, but it cannot compensate completely for the absence of practical skill. In his wonderful book, *Paper: An Elegy*, Ian Sansom makes the point that some of the most successful examples of cutting-edge digital artistic creativity, Pixar films, evolved traditionally by way of hand-drawn storyboards. He notes, ironically, that plain old-fashioned drawing methods were behind such digital marvels as *Toy Story 2* (1999) and *Ratatouille* (2007), for which 28,244 and 72,000 storyboards were used respectively.

*'Any great drawing is a record of a mind and hand moving
at a certain speed, ripping across time and space.'*

ANDREW MARR

DRAWING
FROM LIFE

Drawing from life is an enriching experience derived from using a range of materials and understanding angles, movement, form, poses, light and shade. It is good practice, always – a kind of keep-fit exercise that builds an ongoing appreciation of garments, styling, fabric and flow, behaviour, bulk and volume, proportion and detail, as well as of intangible elements such as atmosphere and mood, attitude and energy.

ALL DRAWINGS: *Rosalyn Kennedy*

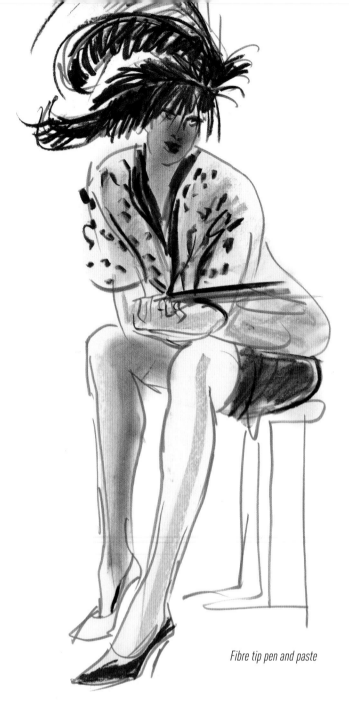

Fibre tip pen and paste

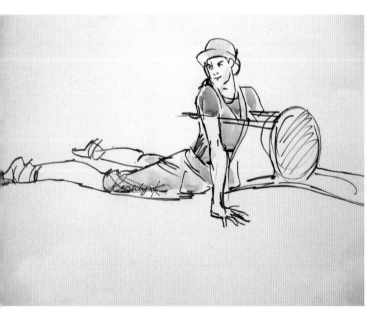

Fibre tip pen and watercolour wash

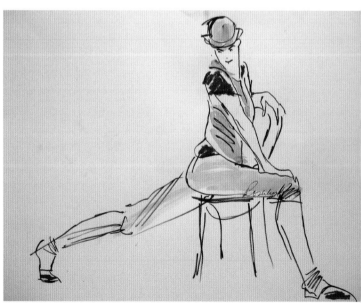

Fibre tip pen, watercolour wash and pastel

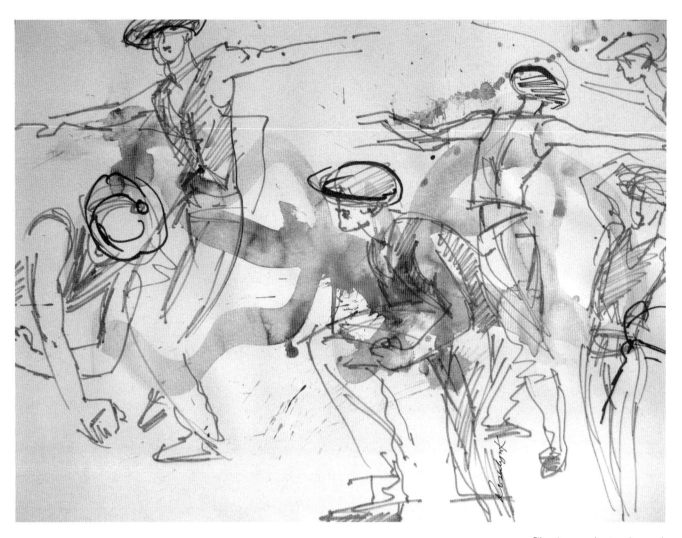

Fibre tip pen and watercolour wash

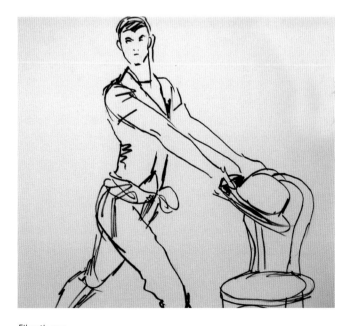

Fibre tip pen

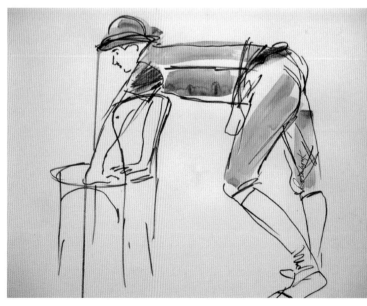

Fibre tip pen, watercolour wash and pastel

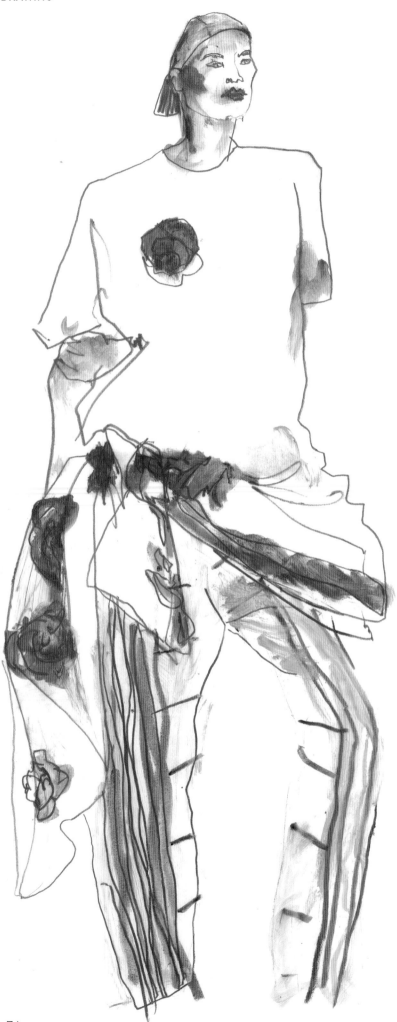

Flora Cadzow is in the final few months of her fashion degree course. Her expressive drawing style is powered by a deep passion for the act of drawing and is vital to her creative processes.

'I have always been interested in drawing, designing and making things. Drawing is extremely important to me – it is the first and foremost important way of capturing and expressing my ideas, and therefore the most effective way of presenting them. The first thing I do when designing is pick up a pencil – it helps me capture my mood, the feeling I want to achieve, the line, the movement, the colour, the shape. It forces me to concentrate on details – a lot of the time your hand does it more instinctively than your head, it shows you what you're thinking and feeling rather than vice versa, if that makes sense.

'It is a form of release for me; if I don't draw for ages I go a little mad. It gives me time to think but also empty my head. The things I see in day-to-day life I imagine turning them into a drawing, especially clothes and people, because for me a pencil captures line, movement and feel the best, but also turns it into something else. A good drawing for me manifests a feeling, the same with design.

'CAD drawings and Illustrator generally don't have any feeling for me, they are too sterile and rigid. There are some illustrators and animators who can do it really well, but personally I love the raw, natural, less precious feel of a hand drawing.'

FLORA CADZOW

LEFT: *Soft pencils and oil pastels*

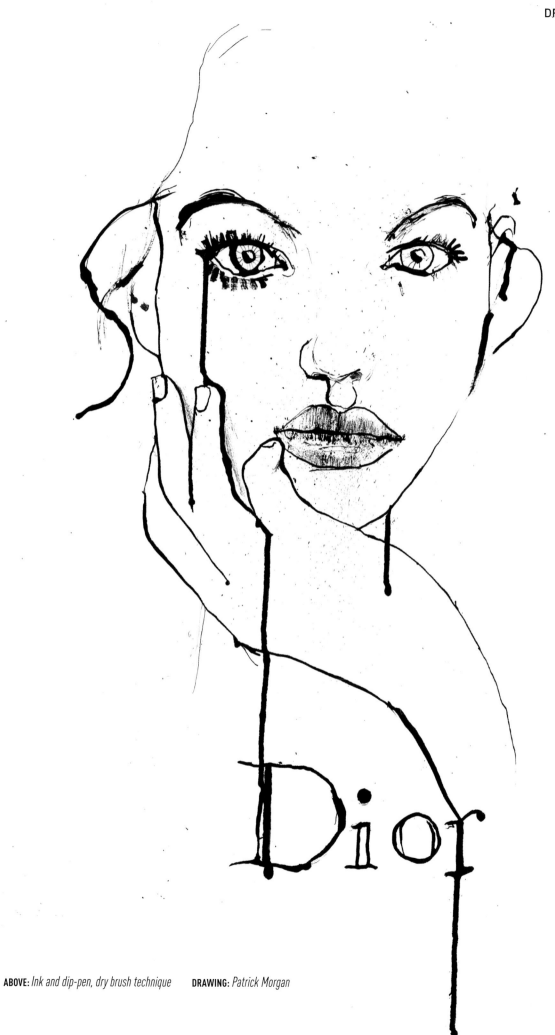

ABOVE: *Ink and dip-pen, dry brush technique*   **DRAWING:** *Patrick Morgan*

DRAWING EXERCISE – FROM A GARMENT

The subtleties of design are what actually matter most, the elements which update and reinvent something otherwise quite familiar or elevate a retro or costume piece to fashion status. Some of our favourite, most interesting garments are not, nor ever were, what we might call fashionable. Utility and workwear clothing comes into this category – functional garments that are almost timeless, their chief and enduring appeal originating from an authentic, inbuilt utility 'fit-for-purpose' logic which underpins much modern design thinking.

The terms 'timeless' and 'classic' are often used in fashion circles, but they may be nothing more than a convenient handle or journalistic hyperbole. To use 'classic' and 'fashion' in the same breath is, in essence, paradoxical, as fashion demands constant change and updating. Italian writer Italo Calvino's definition – 'A classic is a book that has never finished saying what it has to say' – can comfortably be applied to elements of fashion. A true classic is never static, it evolves and adapts to suit each new era in a fresh and relevant way. It may evolve quite drastically in fit and proportion or with subtlety and nuance through fabrication, detail, context or simply colour. 'Appropriation' is a term we frequently hear in connection with contemporary fashion, and many of today's most successful designers are more master-appropriators than truly creative innovators.

Whatever your approach to design, having a good eye for proportion and detail is key and a successful drawing needs to communicate these subtleties accurately and effectively. The following exercise is an excellent way to refine your eye and hone your drawing skills. You can take a garment from your own wardrobe, borrow one, use an exhibit in a fashion museum or even a series of photographs. You may draw from a hanger or find you need to lay the garment on the floor to see the shape truly.

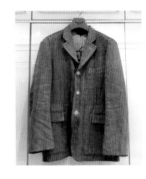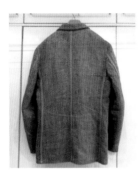

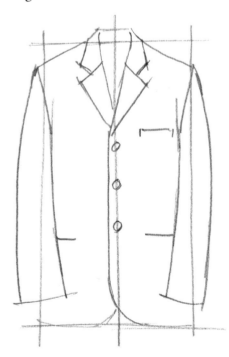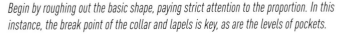

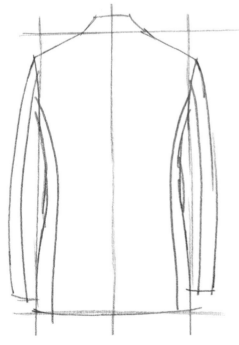

Begin by roughing out the basic shape, paying strict attention to the proportion. In this instance, the break point of the collar and lapels is key, as are the levels of pockets.

Similarly, the back must echo the front and corroborate all proportions.

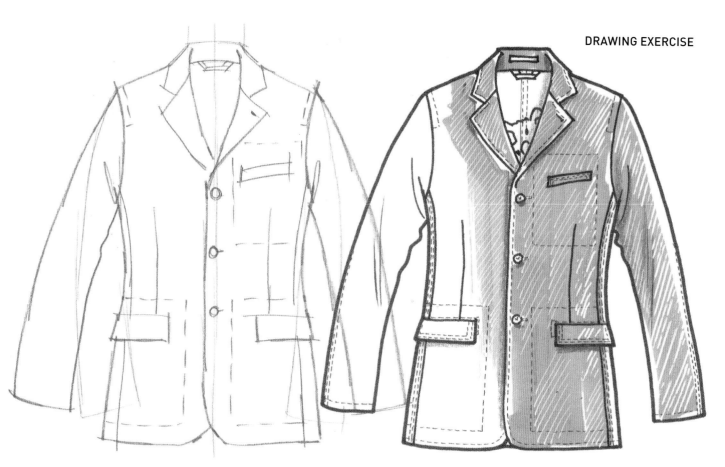

Some adjustment of the garment may be necessary in order to show the clear silhouette and important details. Sleeves can be raised or folded to show quarter seams, cuff details and plackets. The drawing can be folded in half to make sure it is truly symmetrical.

ABOVE: Once you are happy with the roughed-out drawing, you can experiment with choosing appropriate media.

RIGHT: You might draw a swatch of the fabric as further record and reference.

BELOW RIGHT: Important details or areas of special interest can be enlarged and highlighted in close-up.

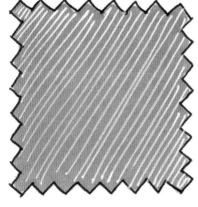

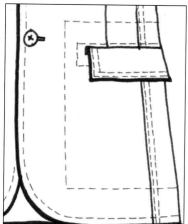

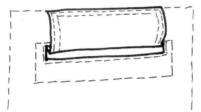

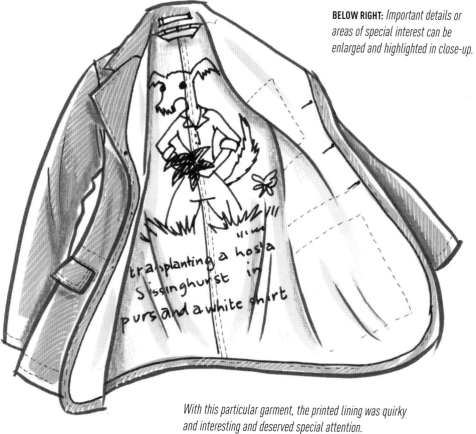

With this particular garment, the printed lining was quirky and interesting and deserved special attention.

SKETCHBOOKS

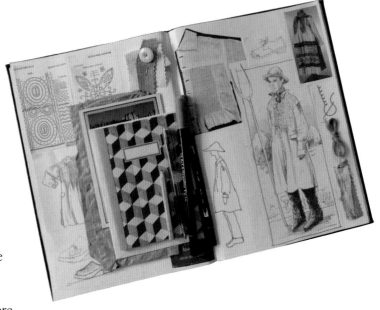

Probably the designer's most important pieces of equipment are a sketchbook and a pencil. Almost all creative people – writers, artists, musicians, filmmakers – keep notebooks, sketchbooks, scrapbooks or journals. Sometimes the sketchbook can be a combination of all these. In her inspirational books, stylist Sibella Court encourages us to be magpies – perhaps, like Autolycus in Shakespeare's *The Winter's Tale*, we should all become snappers up 'of unconsidered trifles'. If you have ever been to an exhibition where the artist or designer's sketchbooks are presented alongside their finished work, you may well have gained much insight into their work by being privileged to view these personal treasure troves.

It is often said that a sketchbook is comparable to a ship's logbook; it is the record of a creative journey where the destination is unknown, the diary of an adventure. For any creative person it can be paralyzing to feel you have no ideas, yet your job requires you to pull something out of a hat. A well-kept sketchbook is a go-anywhere stock of ideas to be tapped into at a moment's notice or reworked for another project at another point in time. It's a receptacle for notes and ideas, awaiting a catalyst or suitable opportunity for development and fruition.

DESIGN, CREATIVITY AND INSPIRATION

Creativity is a gift that can manifest itself in many ways, not least in the ability to draw and paint. As with many things in life, creativity expresses itself according to the talents of each individual. One person may be creative with colour and good at putting things together and arranging them (the skills of a stylist). Another may be marvellous with 3D and at cutting, folding and creating shapes. But it doesn't stop there; indeed, creativity isn't limited to art. Writers and poets are creative with ideas and language. Mathematicians and scientists are creative too, and it's worth remembering that until the late 19th century science was included as one of the arts, alongside music, literature, sculpture and dance. But not to digress, back to fashion and designers – we are a special bunch and should be allowed certain indulgences, not least the right to indulge ourselves! Like many rare things in nature, we need a special environment in which to flourish and we are largely responsible to ourselves for this. Designers need inspiration, our creativity must be fuelled; working designers frequently have to leap from one creative project to another, and must always be inspired with a stock of ideas ready to be developed and launched.

'When I'm walking by myself I like to carry a tiny notebook to make jottings. It turns a walk into an adventure.'

ANDREW MARR

'Authentic inspiration is the emergence of an idea which must be free to flourish and become matter, with form and function, only made real by hard-working hands.'

MERCHANT & MILLS

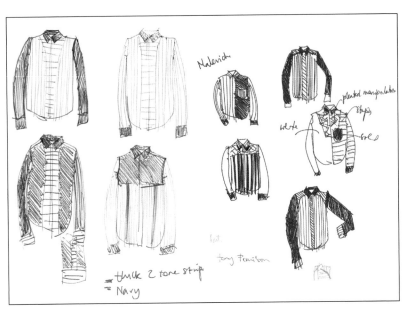

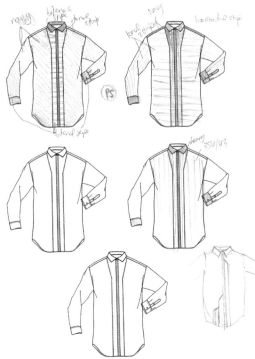

Designer Massimo Casagrande uses his sketchbook to record and generate ideas, work out variations and developments, make notes about fabrics and style numbers and to edit and select when range planning. His sketchbook drawings vary from quick, spontaneous sketches of ideas to refined flats and more finished presentation collages.

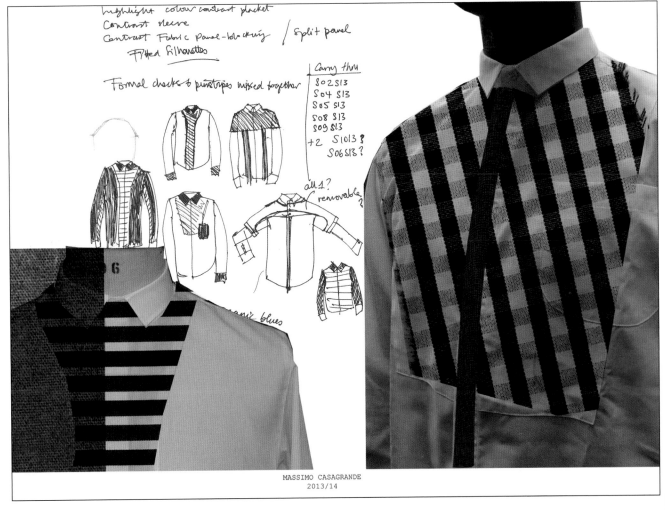

MASSIMO CASAGRANDE
2013/14

NARRATIVES

Many designers find that they work best when creating their own narratives. The story may be simple or otherwise, from their own experience or complete fantasy fed by personal research and investigation, or a combination of all these elements. The narrative doesn't have to be complete nor even necessarily apparent – nothing is more fascinating than enigma. Indeed, many designers are unable fully to explain their work or their inspiration. They often don't even feel the need to; after all, it is the work that must ultimately stand up and be viable in its own right.

JELLY PROJECT – YVONNE DEACON

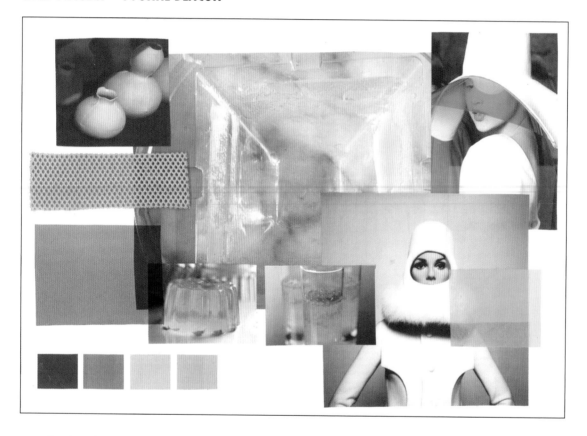

ABOVE: *Starting with ideas about transparency and jelly, Yvonne began this fun design theme by making and photographing jellies in attractive colours. Images of similar structures and the beginnings of a related fabric story form one of a series of lively mood boards.*

RIGHT: *Pencil sketches of silhouettes are laid on to a lightbox to create a quick, spontaneous line-up.*

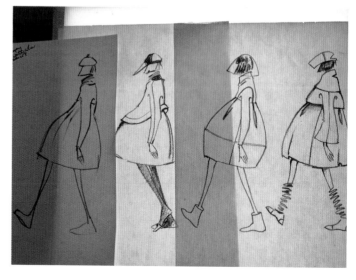

'Drawing is feeling.
Colour is an act of reason.'

PIERRE BONNARD

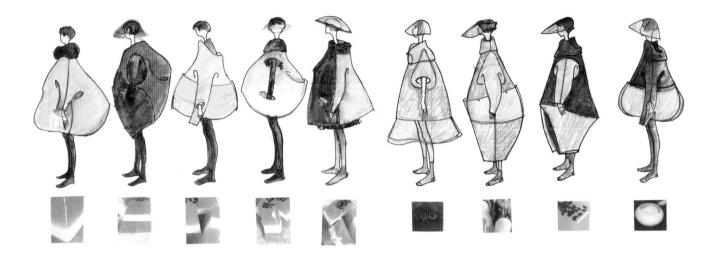

ABOVE: *Silhouettes and styling ideas are developed along with colour stories and combinations using watercolour pencils. The jelly theme is continued alongside the drawings.*

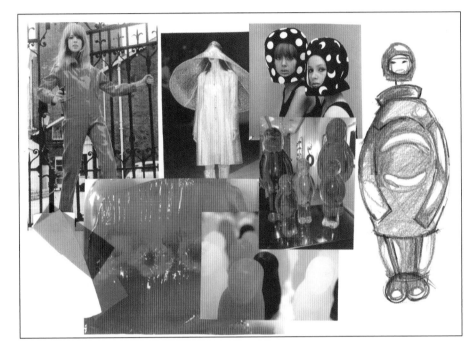

RIGHT: *Vintage fashion images and the jelly baby sculptures of fine artist Mauro Perucchetti build and enhance the theme in this mood board.*

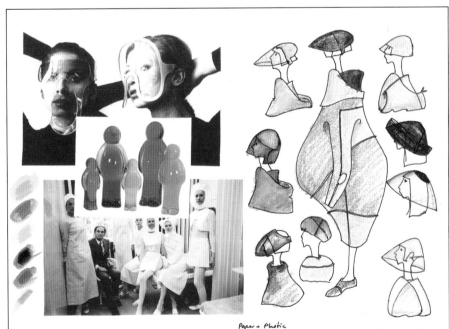

RIGHT: *More vintage fashion images and jelly baby sculptures inspire enquiry into a sculptural silhouette and a range of headwear accessories.*

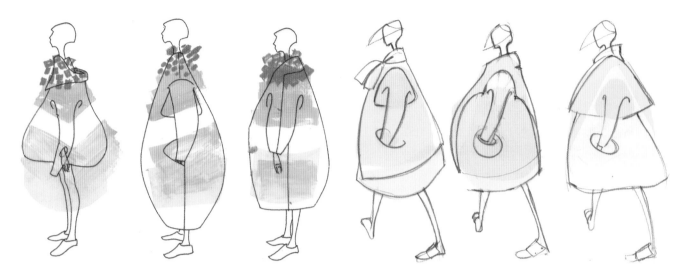

ABOVE LEFT: *Mango jellies inspire a series of fashion silhouettes drawn in fibre pen on tracing paper, cleverly layered over a bold base of scraped paint, oil pastel and coloured acetate collages.*

ABOVE RIGHT: *Another series of fashion silhouettes drawn in soft pencil on tracing paper, layered over cut-out tissue paper and acetate collages.*

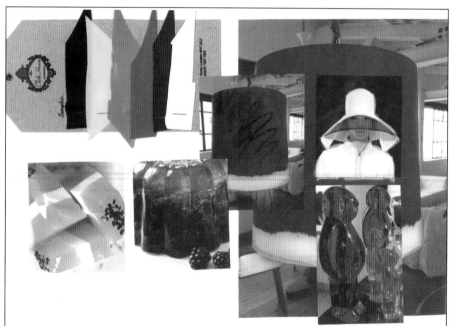

LEFT: *A photograph of an extraordinary, oversized concrete and resin lamp, spotted at the inspirational concept store Merci in Paris, combines with related theme imagery, some of which has been hand coloured. Together with a selection of latex fabrics, these elements create another evocative mood board.*

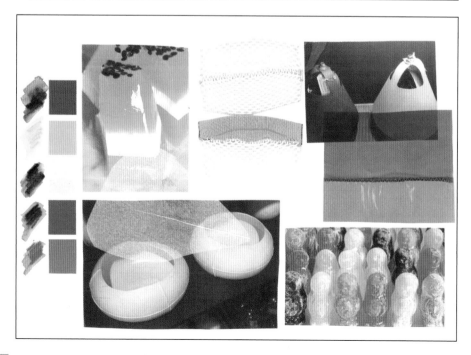

LEFT: *Small constructional experiments using neoprene and sportswear fabrics build upon theme ideas for further design developments.*

MARY RATCLIFFE

Mary Ratcliffe is a designer of fashion textiles who creates garment designs for her fabrics and also upcycles vintage garments in highly creative and original ways, using images taken from drawn references and combining them into the mix. Her exciting, fearless approach is apparent in the lively, energetic drawing style which underpins all her work.

'I continue to draw and sketch from observation things that inspire me. From the everyday – a vase of flowers, objects and textiles I find; shoes, garments, organic forms; shells, stones – the list goes on and on!! I find inspiration from regularly visiting galleries and exhibitions, my enjoyment and understanding is enhanced by sketching and recording.

'The drawing of an antique lace bodice was recorded simply because I loved the item of clothing given to me by a local costume museum because it was worn and not suitable for display (the quality I loved). Many of these fashion sketches were made for a collection shown on the catwalk at Alternative Fashion at Spitalfields, London.'

MARY RATCLIFFE

1 *Pen, collaged photos and painted papers. Religious images juxtaposed with abstract paintings. For the Severina Collection, shown on the catwalk at Alternative Fashion Week*

2 *Drawings of antique bodices given to me by a museum because they were too worn. Inspiration for a collection of garments incorporating lace. Collage with ballpoint pen on old sheet music paper, Indigo 2010*

3 *This illustration was submitted for selection in a catwalk show. Cockerel and Rose Collection, screen printed images, layered fabrics. Collection also shown at Clothes Show Live*

4 *Three vintage garments on hangers. These drawings are taken from reference of garments hanging in my studio. On the middle vintage nightdress I have drawn directly on to the fabric, and then recorded this. The vintage floral dress is in crepe voile and has been one of my treasured possessions, but when it became too fragile to wear I put it on a hanger as display. Line drawing in pen/ballpoint. Many of my ideas for rose prints (see elsewhere on this page) have been inspired by this dress.*

5 *Row of three figures showing strong mood for fashion collection. Line drawing in pen, 2009*

6 *Sketchbook illustration in pen with colour tags in gouache, showing three figures for 2010 collection.*

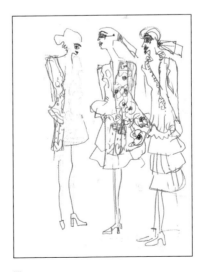

1

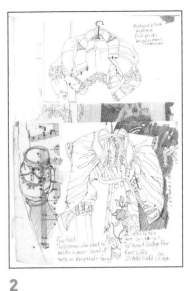

2

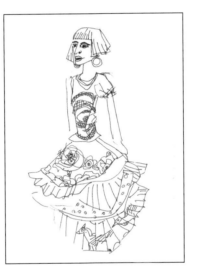

3

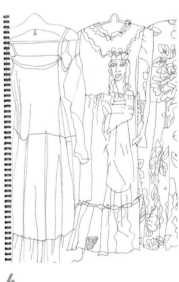

4

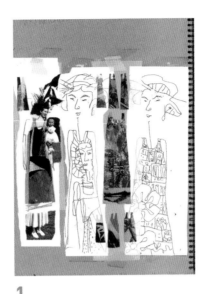

5

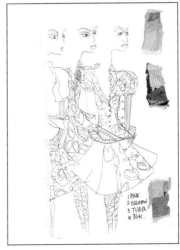

6

RESEARCH & INSPIRATION

'Inspiration is the act of drawing up a chair to the (writing) desk.' ANONYMOUS

Inspiration can be easy when we learn to know ourselves and understand what presses our buttons and stimulates our grey matter. This may be second nature, something that comes naturally and instinctively: a love of art and exhibitions, for example, or period films, visits to museums, learning about history or a personal topic. Travel, theatre and music can be rewarding and effective ways of stimulating the imagination almost automatically. Perhaps most importantly, the research should be actual not simply internet sourced or second-hand from books, but experiential and primary. It should be stuff that is particular to you as an individual (not just the big 'C' cultural experiences): the individual things you are interested in, the quirky objects you collect or the experiences you seek out, the observations you make in the everyday and the humdrum which are particular and personal. These individual characteristics are what are most frequently evident, clearly or otherwise, in the designers and artists we most admire and revere.

Designers have always looked to other creatives for inspiration. Yves Saint Laurent, for instance, created highly original and relevant collections influenced by Matisse, Picasso and others. As we have seen, Jeanne Lanvin was so inspired by the

blue of Fra Angelico's frescoes that she made it her signature colour. But taking inspiration from a contemporary fashion designer is different matter; it can be restrictive and may set you on a narrow path to plagiarism and derivative mediocrity that is best avoided. Many designers have gone down that route, of course, and many have acknowledged it by calling their collection an 'homage'; others, who should have known better, have been less honest about the source of their ideas.

'I always find beauty in things that are odd and imperfect – they are much more interesting.'

MARC JACOBS

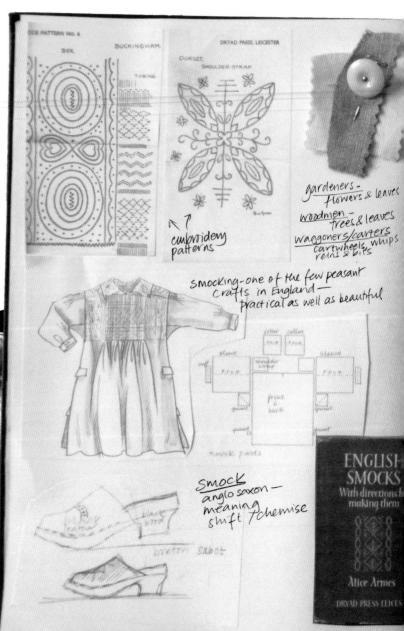

While copying from other designers cannot be described as inspiration, it can be useful to look at fashion eras to keep up with trends, directions and the changing market. But a far more rewarding approach is to look at what has inspired other designers; for instance, from looking at many 1940s fashions it is clear that the designers of this decade were, in turn, looking back to the Edwardian and Victorian eras, to what seemed to be (superficially, at least) idyllic, more appealing times before two successive and devastating world wars. Today a designer can avoid parody by cannoning these eras and influences, fusing elements and ideas for a truly contemporary take. Similarly, if a designer looks at, say, skateboard culture, he or she could examine sources, rather than just the outcomes, adding primary research for a personal, more original result.

Contemporary relevance, though, should be a constant consideration. It is wise to remember that even a collection as revered as Christian Dior's New Look (presented in 1947), which took its inspiration from Victorian dress, drew worldwide criticism at the time for its excessive use of fabric (most of Europe was still under rationing restrictions). It was also criticized for encouraging women back into restrictive, inhibitive clothes. While avoiding the slippery slope of parody, unless your brief is, say, for film or theatre costume where historical authenticity is part of the deal, inspiration can be gained by looking at designers from history and learning about the craft and skills they employed. In this way, in the 1990s John Galliano reinvented the bias cutting techniques pioneered by Madeleine Vionnet in the 1920s, together with a host of other clever cutting tricks from the masters.

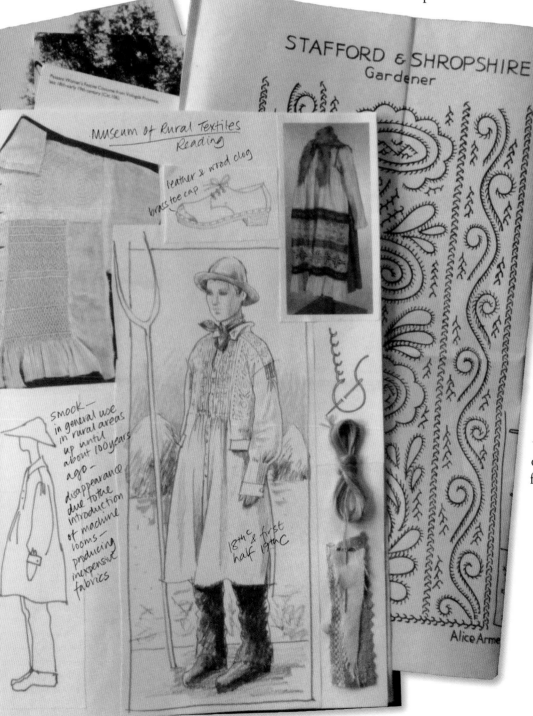

LEFT: *This sketchbook spread shows detailed primary research in the form of museum study drawings of a vintage farmer's smock, with close-ups of features and details, collected vintage reference and photographed back-up. Small but appropriate fabric swatches and comprehensive notes complete the supporting information.*

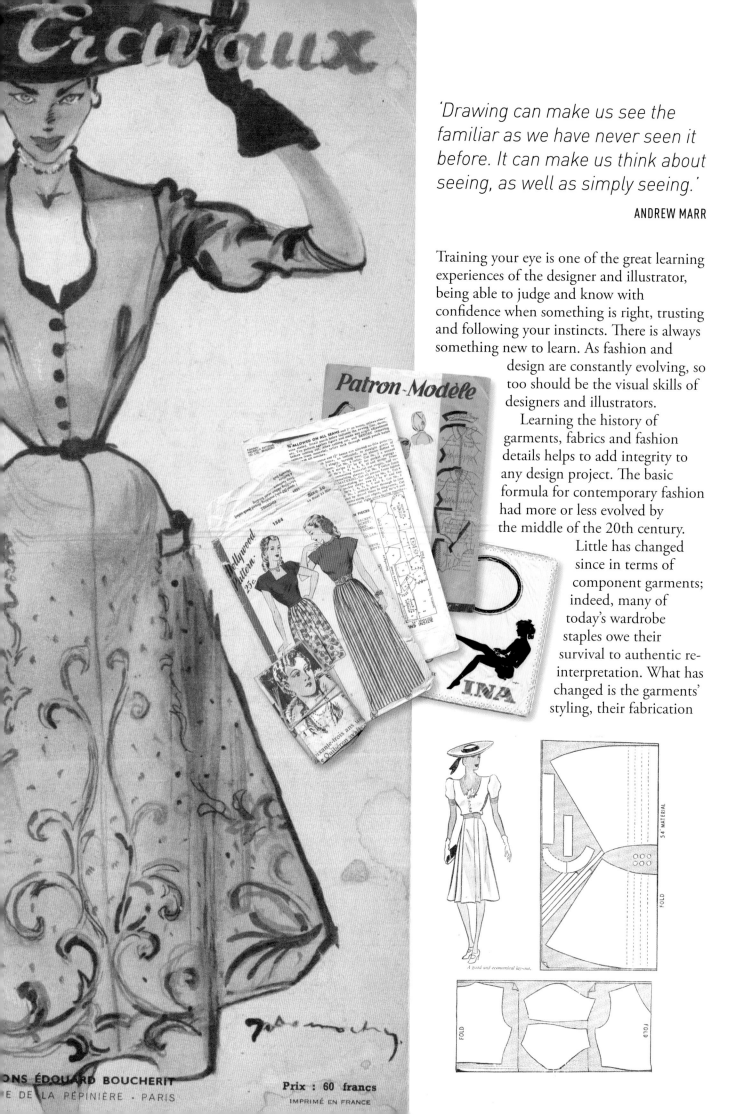

'Drawing can make us see the familiar as we have never seen it before. It can make us think about seeing, as well as simply seeing.'

ANDREW MARR

Training your eye is one of the great learning experiences of the designer and illustrator, being able to judge and know with confidence when something is right, trusting and following your instincts. There is always something new to learn. As fashion and design are constantly evolving, so too should be the visual skills of designers and illustrators.

Learning the history of garments, fabrics and fashion details helps to add integrity to any design project. The basic formula for contemporary fashion had more or less evolved by the middle of the 20th century.

Little has changed since in terms of component garments; indeed, many of today's wardrobe staples owe their survival to authentic re-interpretation. What has changed is the garments' styling, their fabrication

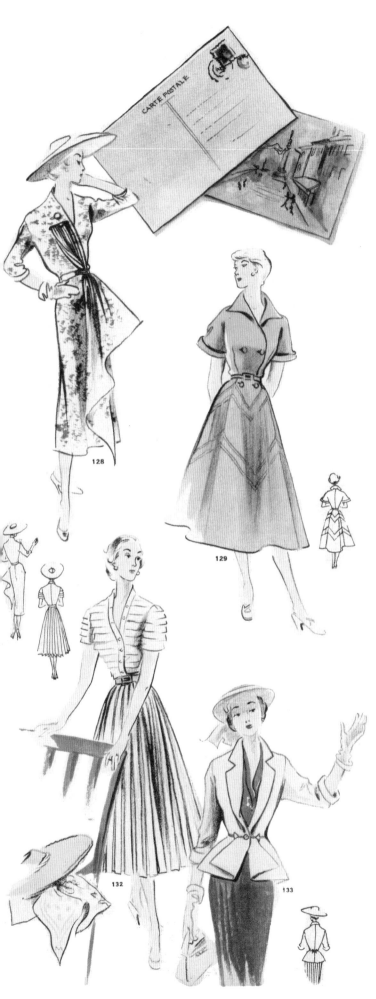

and manufacturing techniques (to some extent) and, most of all, the democratization and globalization of fashion. It is a truism that, despite all the hype, fashion is more about evolution than revolution.

Learning to spot those subtle but significant details of evolution and appropriation, and to be more analytical, is key. When looking at garments or magazine photographs or at a person in the street, try to think beyond the obvious, the superficial, the non-specific meaningless evaluation – 'she/he looks cool'. A mental checklist can help with your analysis:

- Colour
- Proportions
- Fabrication or fabric mixes
- Embellishments or noticeable techniques
- Silhouette
- Details (lapels or shoulders, for example)

Is it a combination of these elements or a less tangible quality that elevates the look to something a little special – an atmosphere, something evocative of an era, culture or nationality? How about the styling, the accessories? Have the garments been put together in a particular or novel way?

As with the exercise on pages 78–9, drawing helps when researching vintage garments. The ability to draw and record well involves analyzing scale and proportion, and questioning: How wide is right for the lapel? How should a collar actually fall? How full should that sleeve/skirt be? How big should the pockets be and where exactly should they be positioned? Similarly, accuracy is crucial to the task of drawing for illustration purposes.

The subtleties of proportion and scale may be the determining factor that updates a look and makes it current and new or tired and old fashioned – the minute amount by which a shirt collar grows or shrinks, for example. Try standing in front of a mirror, holding a piece of paper up in front of you and drawing or folding the paper to just the right size and angle.

Vintage reference is a rich and easily available source of excellent secondary research that can supply detailed information about silhouette, cut, fabrication, construction, garment details and embellishment, styling and accessories for design and illustration inspiration. Aside from the excellent range of fashion history books available, vintage shops and flea markets can be great sources of old fashion magazines, paper patterns and packaging – still at bargain prices – not to mention garments and fabrics for first-hand study.

With special thanks to Niki Zachiadis for the use of her collection of vintage fashion magazines for images.

DRAWING TRICKS

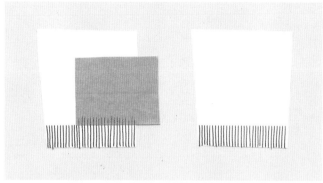
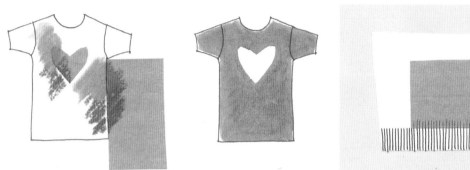

ABOVE: *Use paper masks for adding colour or texture in broad rapid strokes or for bold graphic pattern effects.*

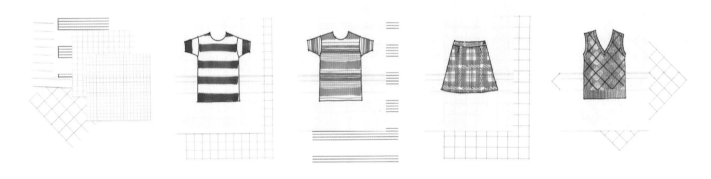

ABOVE: *Use printed papers as guides under layout paper, or on a lightbox, to draw stripes, checks, plaids or argyles. Prints are easy to download in infinite varieties and scale from the internet (see pages 156–9) or can be bought as separate sheets, pads or notebooks. This trick is particularly useful for flats and technical drawings.*

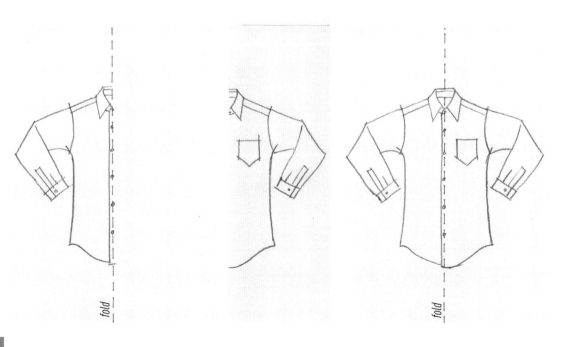

fold

fold

LEFT: *To ensure all hand-drawn flats and technical drawings are completely symmetrical, fold the drawing down the centre line and use a lightbox, layout or transfer paper to trace off the second half.*

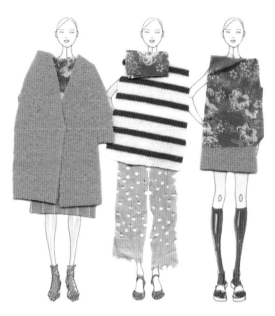

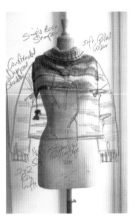

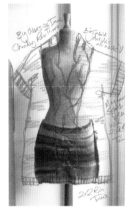

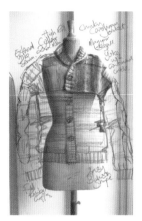

ABOVE: Pin swatches on to a dress stand, how and as you might use them; photograph them using your phone or digital camera; print out and draw the rest of the garment idea on top of the photograph as a quick and easy design tool to extend ideas and possibilities.

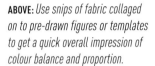

ABOVE: Use snips of fabric collaged on to pre-drawn figures or templates to get a quick overall impression of colour balance and proportion.

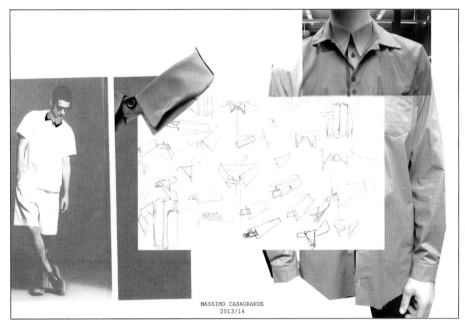

MASSIMO CASAGRANDE
2013/14

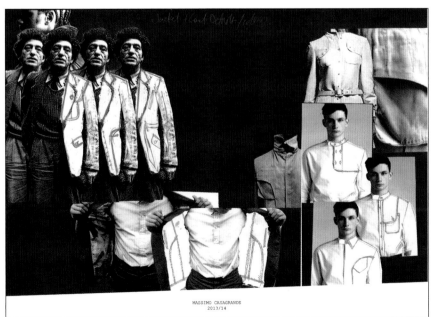

MASSIMO CASAGRANDE
2013/14

ABOVE: Using a similar technique to the above, Massimo Casagrande sometimes manipulates garments on the dress stand, photographs the process and continues to draw ideas and variations on the photographs in his sketchbook.

LEFT: Another technique that is stylish, practical and time efficient – Massimo Casagrande paints white opaque correction fluid on to photocopies or scans of inspirational images in his sketchbook and then draws on top to add his design ideas.

DRAWING STYLES

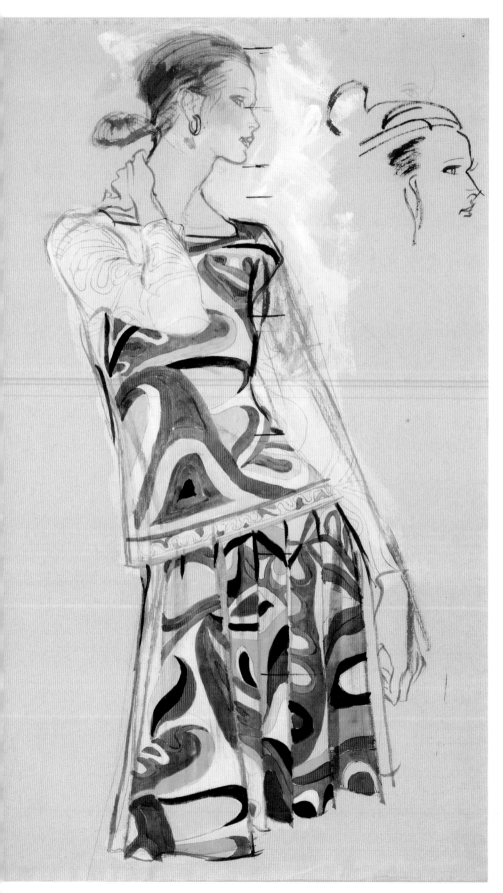

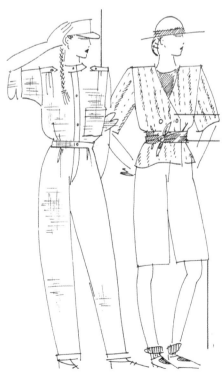

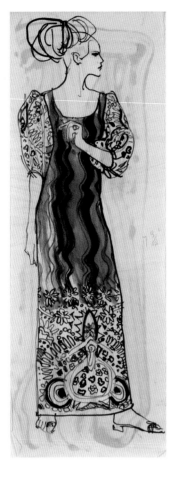

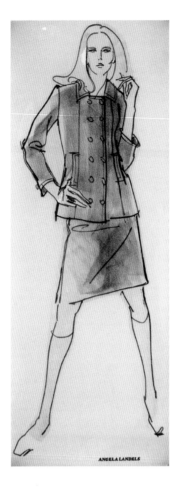

FAR LEFT: *Drawing by Angela Landels (courtesy of Gray Modern & Contemporary Art), Liberty, Princess Lucianna dress circa 1970s, pencil and felt tip, 50 x 18.5cm. Client: Advertisement for Liberty, London*

LEFT: *Drawing by Angela Landels (courtesy of Gray Modern & Contemporary Art), grey suit, 1960s collage, felt tip and charcoal, 68 x 26cm. Client: Liberty, London*

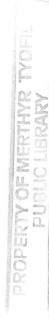

BELOW: *2011 Paul Wearing, digital, adapted from drawing. Created for Neiman Marcus's account holder magazine,* The Book

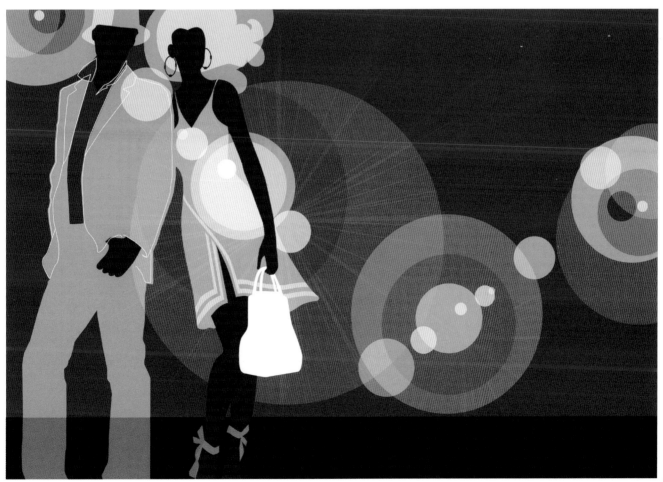

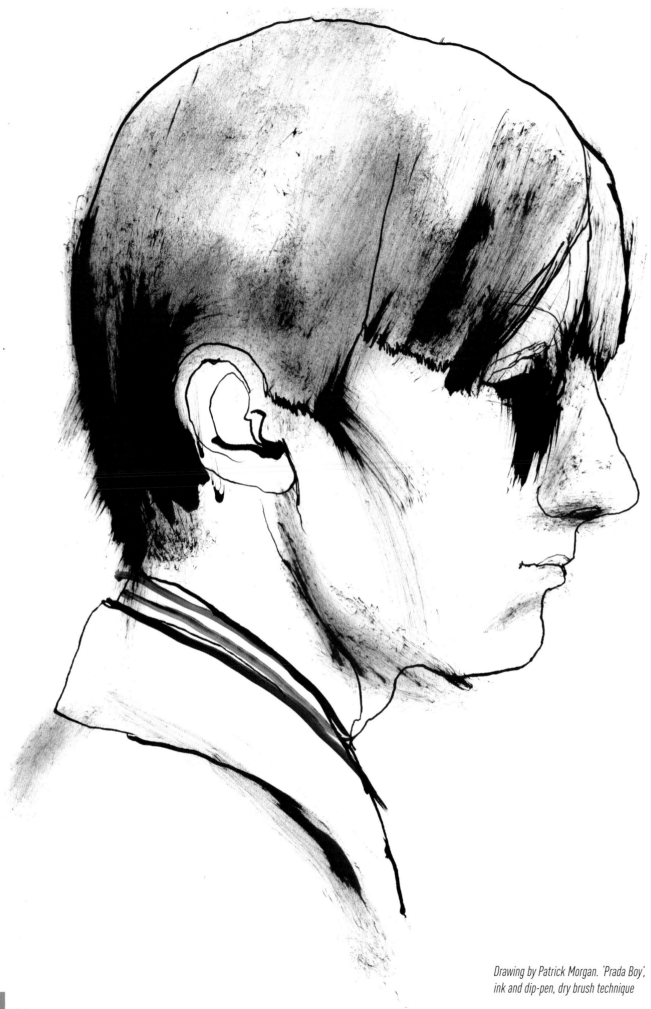

Drawing by Patrick Morgan. 'Prada Boy',
ink and dip-pen, dry brush technique

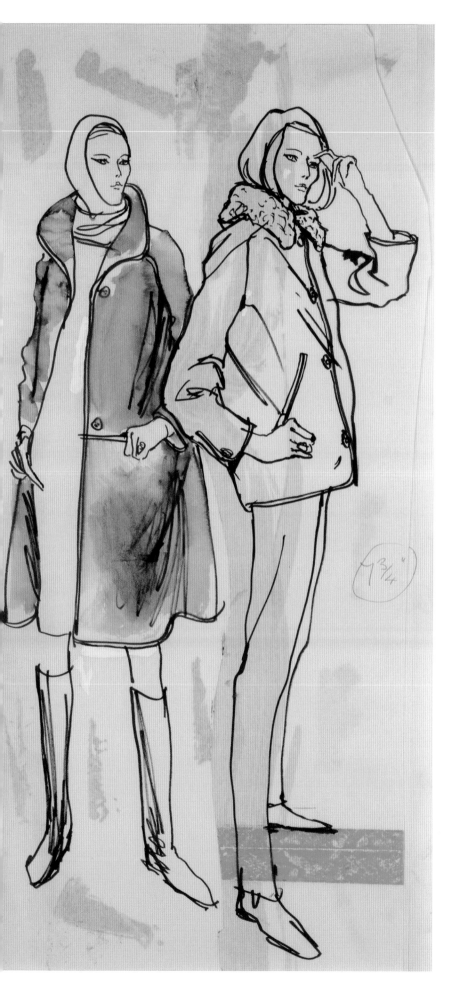

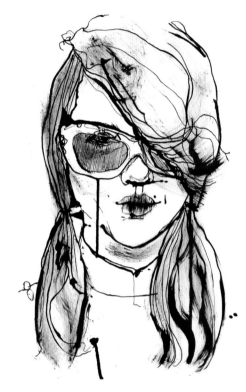

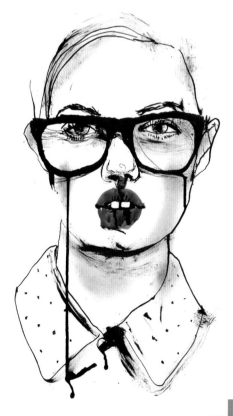

LEFT: *Drawing by Angela Landels (courtesy of Gray Modern & Contemporary Art), winter après-ski wear circa 1960s, featured in the* Sunday Times

BELOW: *Patrick Morgan, 'Prada Girl', ink and dip-pen, dry brush technique*

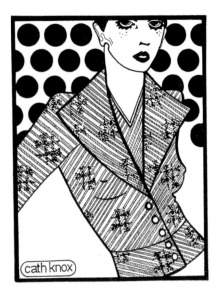

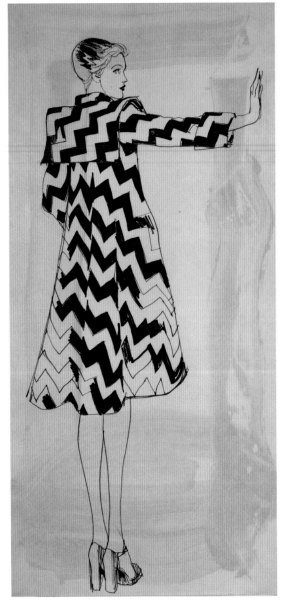

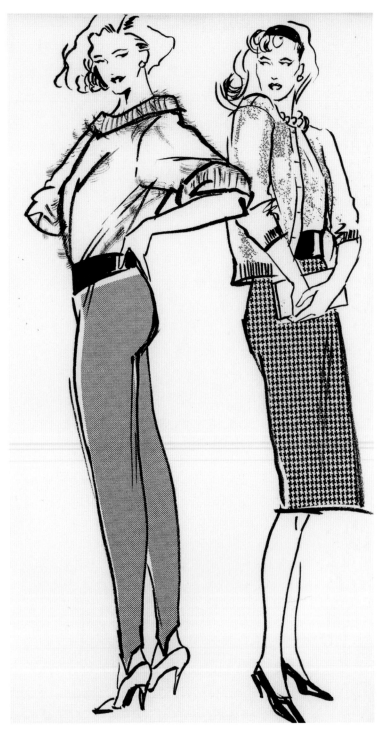

TOP LEFT: *Drawing by Cath Knox, circa 1970s, felt tip (with sticky dots)*

ABOVE: *Drawing by Rosalyn Kennedy, felt tip pen, brush pen and Letratone*

LEFT: *Drawing by Angela Landels (courtesy of Gray Modern & Contemporary Art), circa 1960s, Liberty zig-zag coat, pencil and felt tip pen*

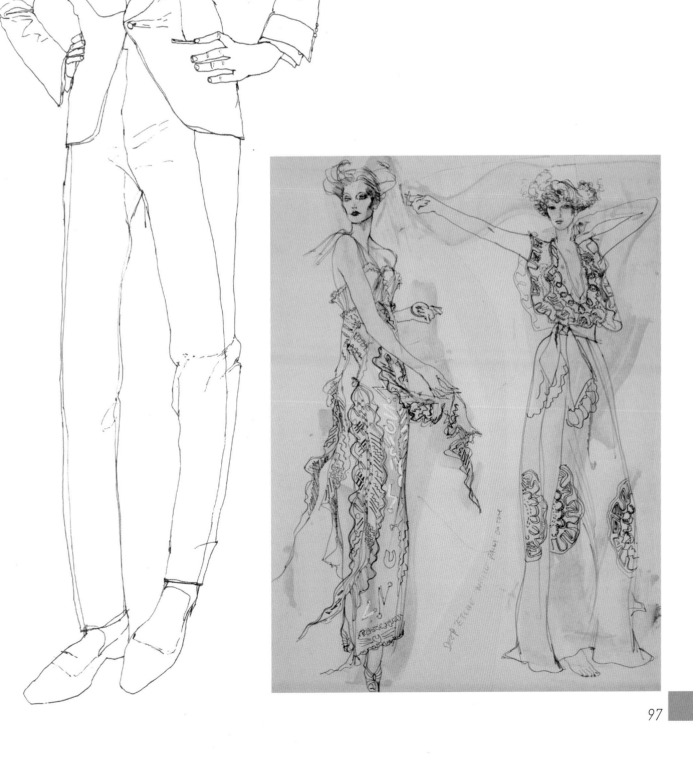

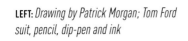

LEFT: *Drawing by Patrick Morgan; Tom Ford suit, pencil, dip-pen and ink*

BELOW: *Drawing by Angela Landels (courtesy of Gray Modern & Contemporary Art), circa 1970s, Zandra Rhodes dresses, pencil, felt tip pen and collage. For* Harpers & Queen *magazine*

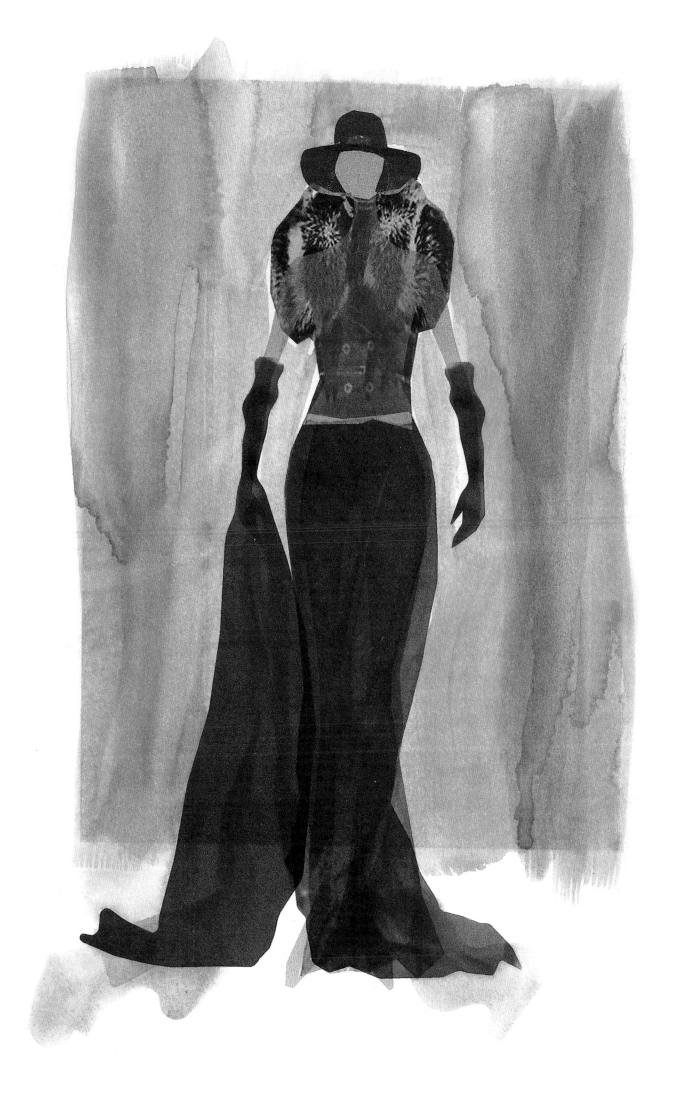

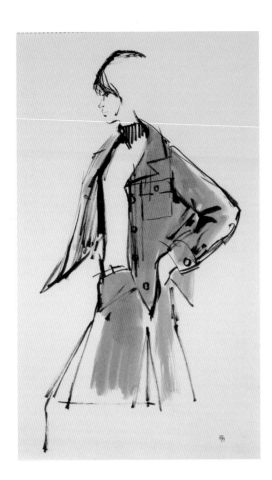

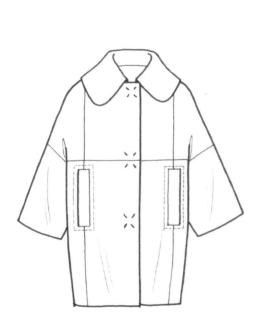

LEFT: *Drawing by Eva Aldbrook (courtesy of Gray Modern & Contemporary Art), circa 1960s, skirt and jacket, watercolour*

BELOW: *Drawing by Brian Stonehouse MBE (courtesy of Gray Modern & Contemporary Art), circa 1950s, winter blouse and gloves, mixed media*

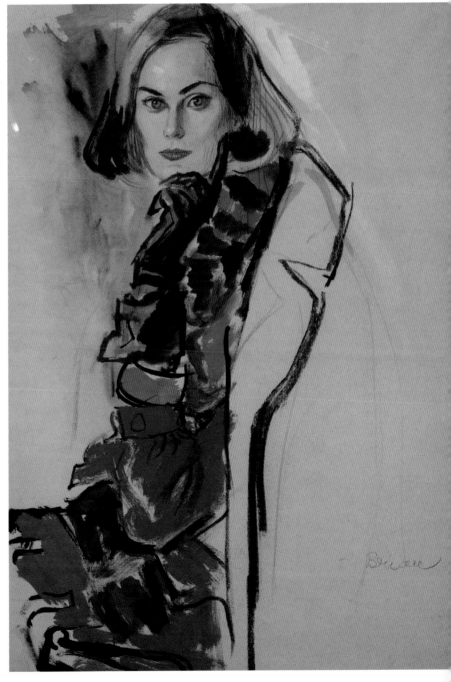

ABOVE: *Drawing by Judith Cheek, fibre tip pen*

FACING PAGE: *Drawing by Leslie Hurst, created using Photoshop, collage and watercolour. Client:* Textile View *magazine*

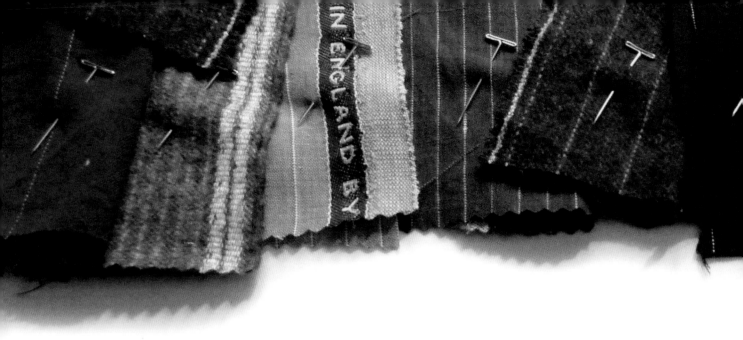

DRAWING FABRIC

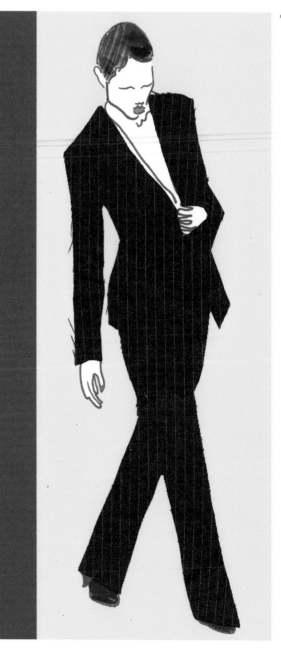

1

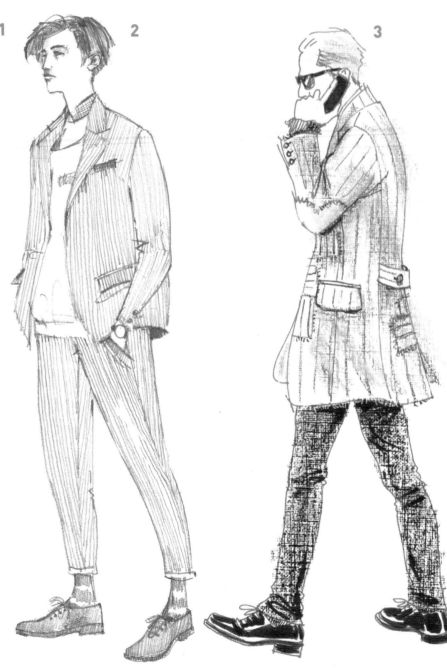

2

3

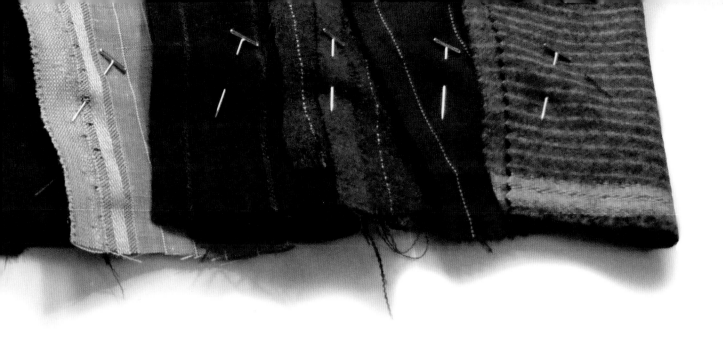

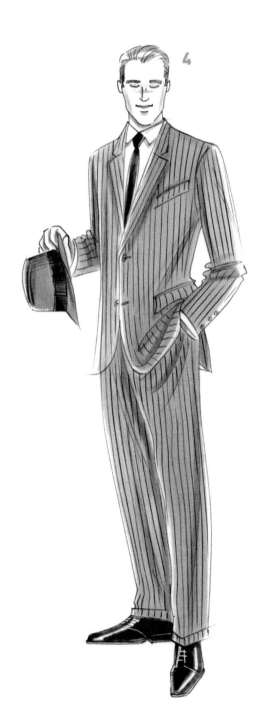

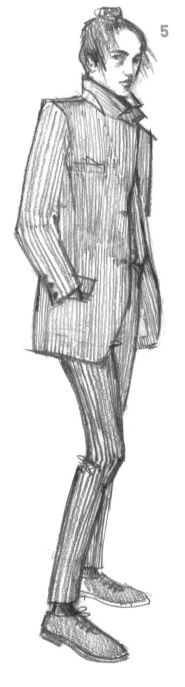

We have selected much-loved pinstripe fabrics to show examples of the scope of design possibilities using a classic and perennial cloth and the opportunities for creative and effective rendering. Over the next few pages, we show a selection of contemporary and vintage drawings and illustrations, presenting a variety of designs and employing some very different media and techniques across a range of styles, markets and end uses.

1 *Hand-drawn image by Alice Fletcher Quinnell, scanned and digitally manipulated*

2 *Drawing by Yvonne Deacon in soft pencil*

3 *Drawing by Judith Cheek in art fountain pen, scanned and printed on to acrylic canvas effect paper, then oil pastel to enhance texture*

4 *Drawing by Hilary Kidd in brush pen, fibre tip pen and marker pen*

5 *Drawing by Yvonne Deacon in soft pencil*

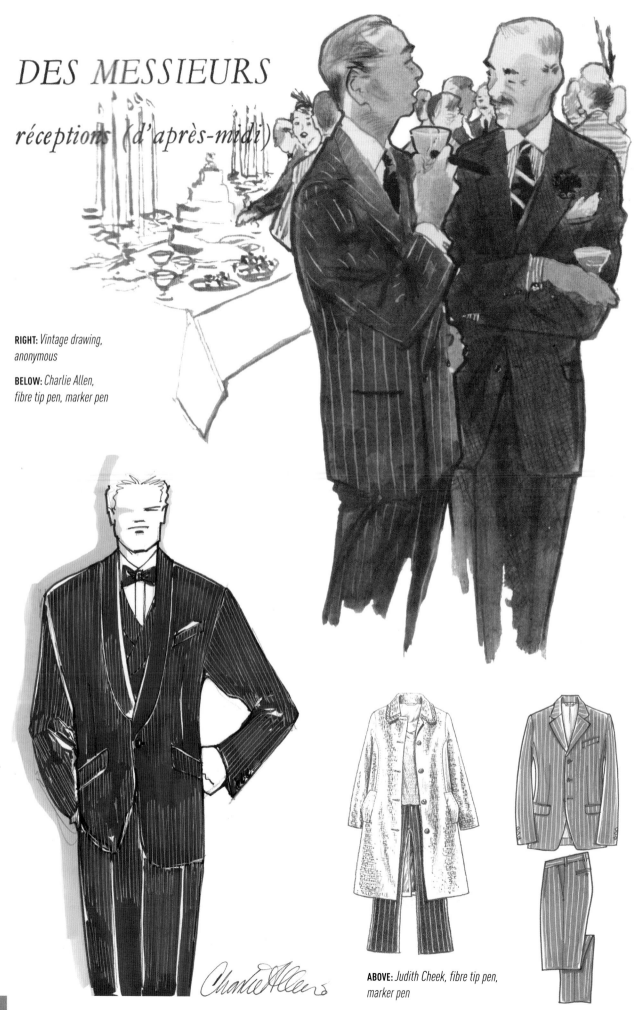

DES MESSIEURS

réceptions (d'après-midi)

RIGHT: *Vintage drawing, anonymous*

BELOW: *Charlie Allen, fibre tip pen, marker pen*

ABOVE: *Judith Cheek, fibre tip pen, marker pen*

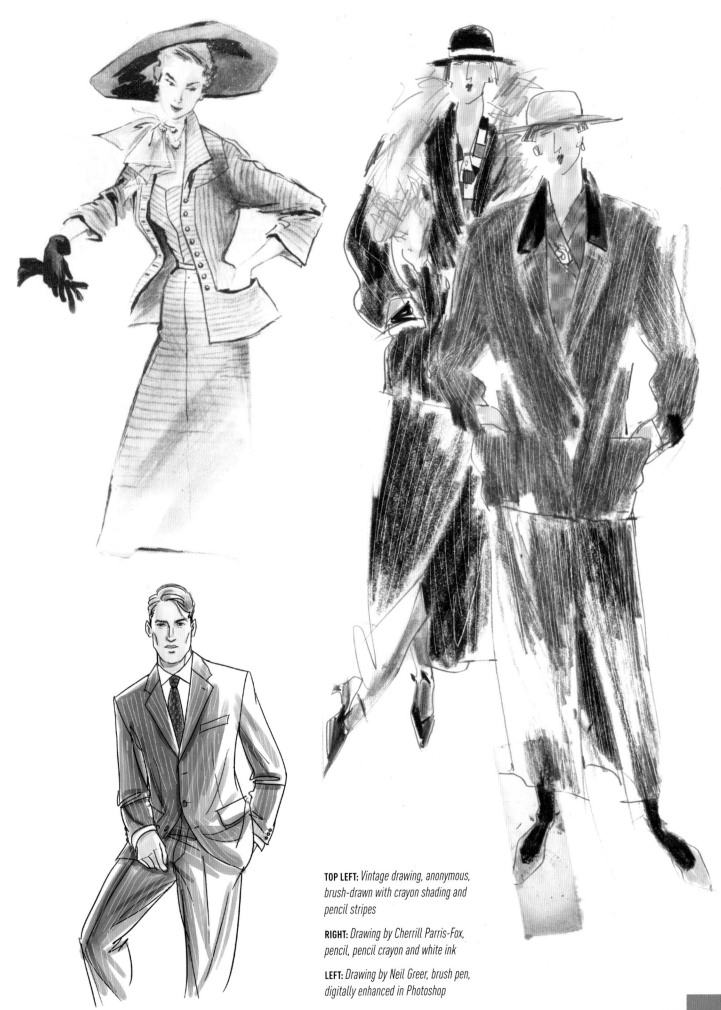

TOP LEFT: *Vintage drawing, anonymous, brush-drawn with crayon shading and pencil stripes*

RIGHT: *Drawing by Cherrill Parris-Fox, pencil, pencil crayon and white ink*

LEFT: *Drawing by Neil Greer, brush pen, digitally enhanced in Photoshop*

DIGITAL DRAWING

In this section, fashion designer and university lecturer Yvonne Deacon sums up the important ongoing relationship between sound traditional hand-drawing skills and up-to-the-minute computer-aided design (CAD) skills and techniques.

USING CAD AS AN AID TO FASHION ILLUSTRATION

To the fashion designer and illustrator, CAD has become an essential means of rendering, recording and instantly sharing fashion ideas and images. But there is an unshakable need to retain the underlying skills that define the individual and feed the creative hunger for expression.

Expressive drawing skills cannot easily be replicated using the computer, although drawing systems are developing quickly. Therefore original artwork, once scanned into the digital system, is usually the basis for further rendering, from hard copy drawing to crisp, clean versions using a specifically designed range of software tools. Systems will allow the raw sketches to be digitally stored, to reuse or rework to process using computer software.

CAD opens up opportunites for creating completed fashion illustrations by the use of layers, in the same way that tracing paper or masking and filling with texture and precise flat colour can be used to create finished, repeatable images. These can then be replicated using cut'n'paste techniques for theme boards, line-ups and the e-portfolio.

In the hands of the skilled CAD artist, strong graphic mark-making and effects will produce exciting and impressive fashion illustrations. It is important to realize that many of the tasks performed by the computer are designed to

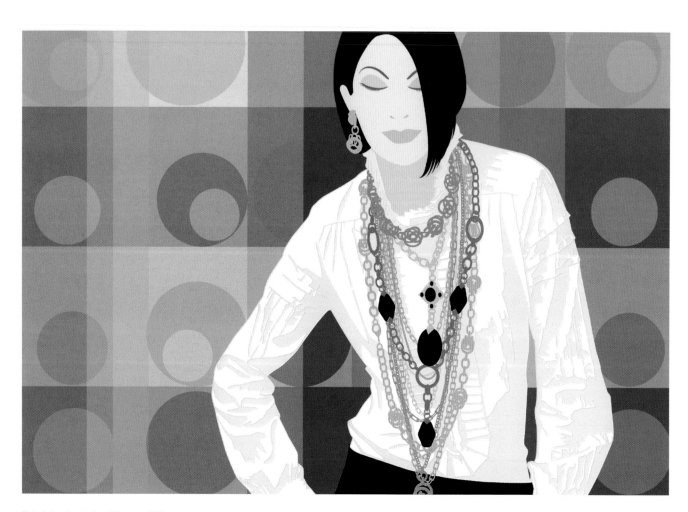

Digital drawing by Paul Wearing, 2011

replicate techniques that were intially developed and performed in the studio as hard copy skills.

Simple observational drawing, used to record and represent images on paper, reveals a capacity to develop the use of media, rendering, mark-making and risk-taking. It develops curiosity in dealing with the unpredictability of real-life imagery, which in turn creates potentials for aspects that excite, please or move. This way, the individual repertoire grows and begins to reveal the creative personality. This learning can then be extended to the digital world.

THE 'MEASURING EYE'

From childhood, we learn the ability to pick up a pencil to communicate our ideas. In the hands of a skilled artist, the ability to express shape, form, texture and idea with fluidity and line inflection becomes a potent tool of expression that flows from eye to hand with skill and competency. This 'measuring eye' of the artist again translates to CAD rendering.

The traditional methods taught in life-drawing classes are still extensively practised in art schools. Drawing can develop perception, which quickly

leads to creative, more personal means of expression. It is then about your own style of drawing and how, as an individual, you are perceived; this applies particularly to the fashion design student. Fashion is about the body, therefore a fundamental understanding of how the body is constructed and the recording of this information through observational drawing and rendering is a large part of the journey for the fashion designer.

The computer is now the medium through which we communicate to the world, taking the hard copy developed by hand then digitally manipulated using the many software tools available to achieve highly polished presentations. Compositional layout techniques can be organized professionally, adding the high-level, clean digital qualities now expected. We can add to our creative repertoire by scanning our renderings, cleaning them up and manipulating them using a vast range of new tools. However, it is important to realize that a lifeless, manufactured rendering will emerge if the basic use of the measuring eye, the fluid line and the messy personality are removed to the point where the creative repertoire is pinioned.

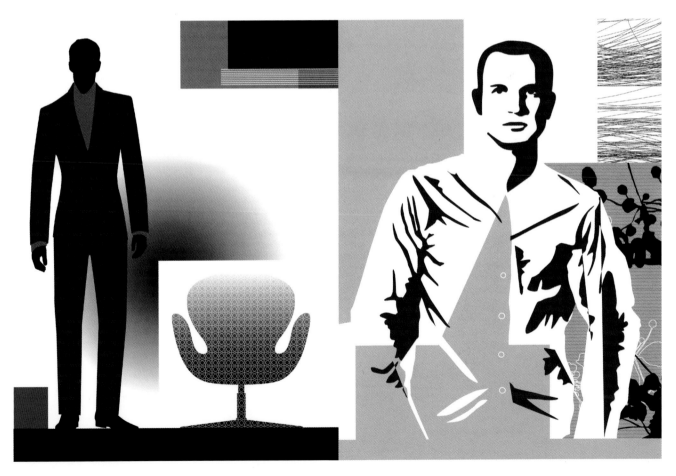

Digital drawings by Paul Wearing

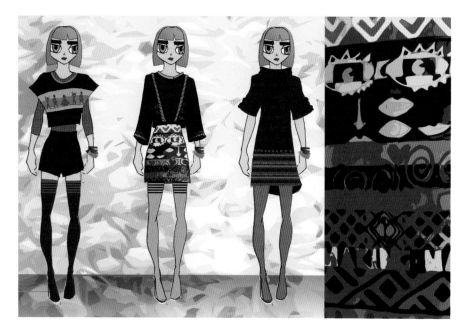

LEFT: *Drawings by Elmina Fors*

'The illustrations are created using Adobe Photoshop CS6 as well as scanned painted patterns and ink sketches of the models. Using CAD can be very creative, especially when using a Wacom Intuos 4 drawing tablet, which enables a more hand-drawn look.

'For the patterned skirt, I first made a repeat pattern, using gouache paints, which I scanned and simplified. There are strong colours in the painted pattern, but to create a very colourful look I increased the contrast and decreased the number of colours used in the original pattern using the Cutout layer in Photoshop.

'The model was first sketched in ink, by hand, and then tidied up and filled in using Photoshop. The clothes were scanned as drawn sketches and traced using the Pen tool in Photoshop. Through using different layers in the program, textures could be added and filled in to shapes. There seem to be endless possibilities with a combined hand-drawn/ painted approach to illustrations in Photoshop, and even more so when combined with Illustrator.'

BELOW: *Both drawings by Paul Wearing, 2011, digital. Adapted from a drawing created for Neiman Marcus' account holder magazine,* The Book

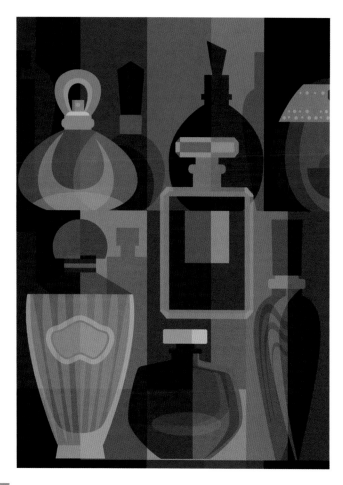

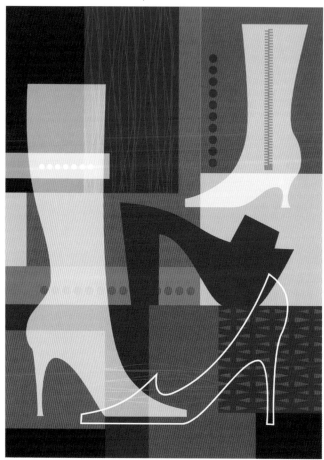

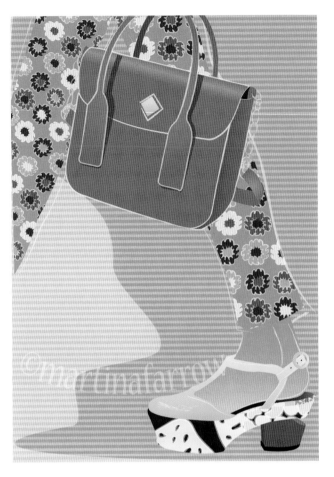

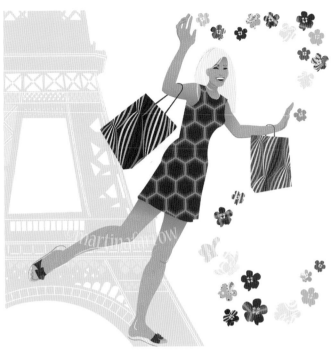

LEFT/ABOVE: *Drawings by Martina Farrow. Agent: New Division. 'Wedge' (left) using Adobe Illustrator CS3, promotional work, 'Spring' (above) using Adobe Illustrator CS3*

BELOW: *Paul Wearing, 2011, digital. Client: a spread for a menswear textile forecast feature in* Textile View *magazine*

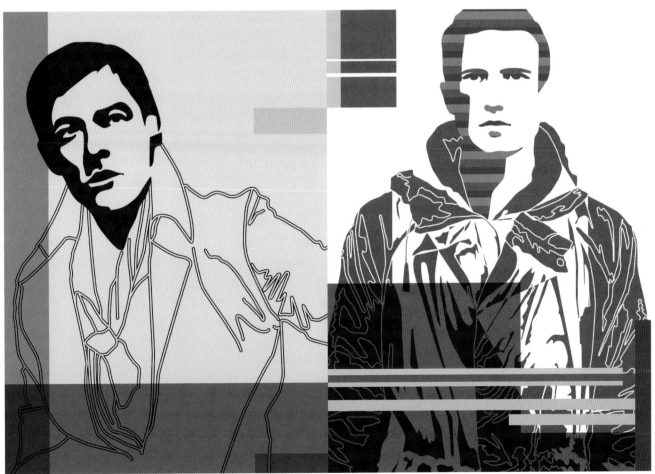

DRAWING THE FUTURE

'Don't worry about what anybody else is going to do. The best way to predict the future is to reinvent it.'

ALAN KEY, COMPUTER SCIENTIST

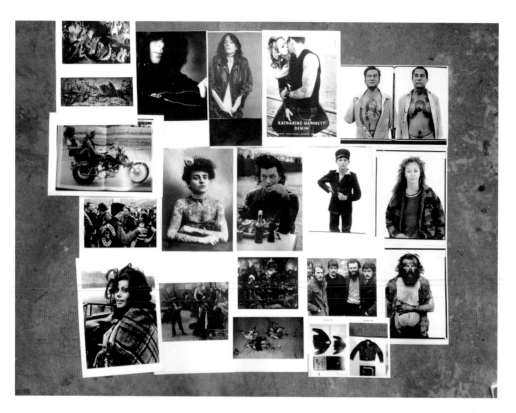

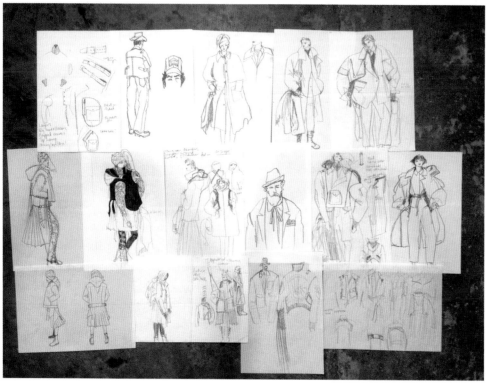

ABOVE LEFT: *'Working Mood Board', collage of magazine tears, photocopies and print-outs*

LEFT: *Research and investigatory sketches, design ideas sketches*

In this section, Flora Cadzow presents an edited version of her final degree collection work. Here is her rationale:

'This collection is inspired by a mood, a feeling, an attitude. I took inspiration from various sources that represented this nonchalant, 'give a damn', seriously cool attitude. These included rockers, bikers, cowboys, the American West, the documentary photographs of Richard Avedon, and films such as The Wild One *and* Django. *The most powerful influence came from everyday people, and the way they naturally wore and styled their outfits in a thrown-on manner – mechanics at work with a rag hanging out of their pocket, builders with a hoodie wrapped around their waist, a jumper thrown over the shoulder, a jacket half on, trousers hanging off, zips undone, belts and buckles hanging off, layers of clothing, hands in pockets, sleeves too long.*

'My aim is to encapsulate this typically masculine and practical attitude in the clothes themselves, and for the wearer to feel *this through them – the point of these clothes is not to be precious, but to be worn.*

Fabrics and elements include leather with metal fastenings, satin twill, cotton flannel, organza, fine wool and silk/linen blends.

Prints and embroideries take inspiration from the Italian Renaissance, baroque, religious art, tattoos and other dark but beautiful pieces of art by Thomas Woodruff, Caravaggio, the Chapman brothers, Hieronymus Bosch, and from the darker side of my imagination. Hand-drawing the prints using a tattoo machine has a more raw and rugged look and echoes some of the references.'

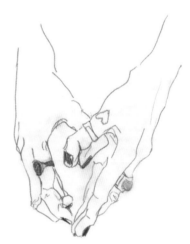

LEFT/BELOW: *'Materials used in all of the drawings and sketches were pencil – I change weights often depending on what it is. Colour was done in oil pastels with white spirit – a tip I learnt from Howard Tangye.'*

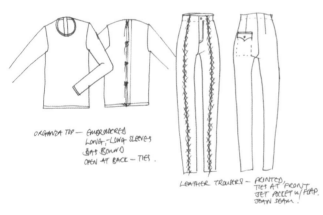

ORGANZA TOP – EMBROIDERED
LONG, LONG SLEEVES
BAT BOUND
OPEN AT BACK – TIES.

LEATHER TROUSERS – PRINTED, TIES AT FRONT
JET POCKET W/ FLAP.
JEAN SEAM.

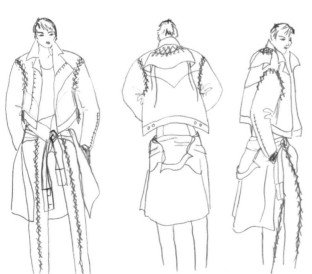

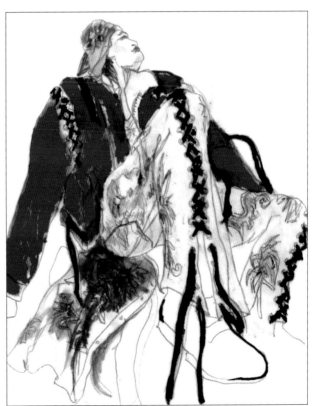

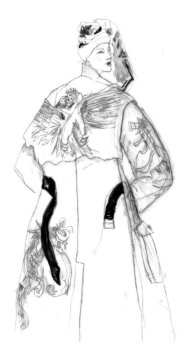

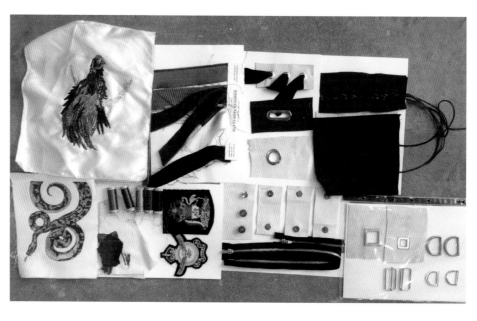

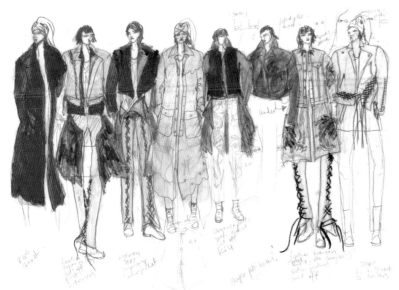

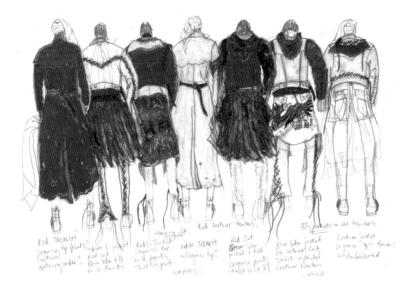

ABOVE: *A selection of fabrics, trims and hardwear used in the designs*

LEFT: *Additional drawing materials include fibre tip pens and marker pens*

'Dream job?! – Erm . . . creative director of the best company! Aim for the top – there is no point in aiming for the middle is there? For me it's not so much about what you do, it's how you do it. What is important to me is that I have a job that allows me to do, see and meet a diverse range of things, places and people. To mix researching, drawing, making, print, textiles, etc. – fuelling my intrigue. I always need to be doing things, I love exploring a diverse range of things, getting excited, learning, I am a curious person, I love adventure.
I love considering how I can use these things and manifest that feeling and make it into clothes. For me, fashion is not just about making pretty dresses – I like design to be relevant, to connect to aspects outside of fashion, to be a reflection of the time and the attitude. Design, it allows me to do all those things – to learn about and explore other cultures, histories and societies. A job that lets me do that is the dream! I am realistic about the corporate reality, but it's nice to hope, and at least try to retain part of that.'

FLORA CADZOW

'I no longer listen to the market – creativity sometimes needs a deaf ear.'

JEAN CLAUDE ELENA

A FUTURE IN FASHION

For students applying to university for degree courses in fashion design and fashion related courses, requirements will vary from establishment to establishment and the specific nature or bias of the course. Yvonne Deacon presents some guidelines:

What we look for in a student applying for a place on a fashion course:

- Personality
- Curiosity
- Observation
- Skill

ONLINE SUBMISSION

Before applicants are called for interview there will be a request for an online sample of their work via Flickr webpage or drop box, so that an initial review of the work can be made. Applicants must ensure that this is original personal work containing most of the attributes required for **portfolio**. Page layout, drawing skills, mark-making and colour will be the first things that interviewers see, therefore they need to be effective. Good quality scanning or photography in the correct resolution and size is essential.

PORTFOLIO

If the potential student is called in for interview, the selection panel will first look at the portfolio and sketchbooks for evidence of creative ability, **personality** and the skills necessary to record images to a good standard that recognizes creative lines of thinking in your research. Each student portfolio should demonstrate individual **curiosity** about wider influences and the creative world in relation to the applicant's work and the specialist subject area of fashion. The interview panel will analyze choices made in activating the variety of media and techniques used to render images. They will also assess the skill and quality of drawing, mark-making and **observation** from the essential skills and developments as evidenced in the portfolio.

SKILLS

Drawing is a fundamental and transferable **skill** that applies throughout the art and design disciplines. It is therefore one of the main criteria by which the qualities in the portfolio are judged. This demonstrates an appetite for the subject of drawing, mark-making and illustration that will reveal the personality of the applicant's work.

Fashion is concerned with the body, therefore confident observational drawings made during clothed life, and in life drawing, are essential components of the portfolio. This demonstrates the development of skill and perception as a personal means of expression.

Compositional skills should reveal the ability, through the 'measuring eye', to judge the position of an image for its impact on the page. Leaving a good space around an image gives it importance and added reverence. Setting out images to connect for theme is a skill where a narrative can be created to lead the eye round a page to induce an understanding of its content and meaning on all levels.

There should be evidence of the careful selection of found or created imagery for size, intensity, depth of colour or tone content, for its juxtapositioning, cluster and spread for rich, intense effects or isolated for clarity and modernity.

The panel is interested in seeing how the work is processed, how research is developed, and to what depth and with what awareness initial ideas are set against a brief, demonstrating how creative problems have been solved and translated into design outcomes and illustrations. It is not always the big, fat sketchbook and portfolio that win the day, but the choices made at all stages for the quality of the work and how it is set out that reveal essential skills for selection.

Careful consideration needs to be given to the order (sequence) of the work in the portfolio. New projects showing best skills should be at the beginning and other skills should be revealed towards the back, usually ending with examples to show off your abilities to good advantage.

INTERVIEW

Once the portfolio and research work have been assessed, group or personal interviews follow. Questions may be asked about the applicant's personal opinion and passions and you will be expected to be able to have an intelligent and informed discussion about your work and the work of others, and to hold opinions about the work of others in the field. You need to be well informed about fashion in general and be able to demonstrate knowledge about contemporary trends and events that are of interest.

WRITTEN WORK

A short essay, rationale or questionnaire concerning the reasons for your application choice may also be requested as you wait for interview.

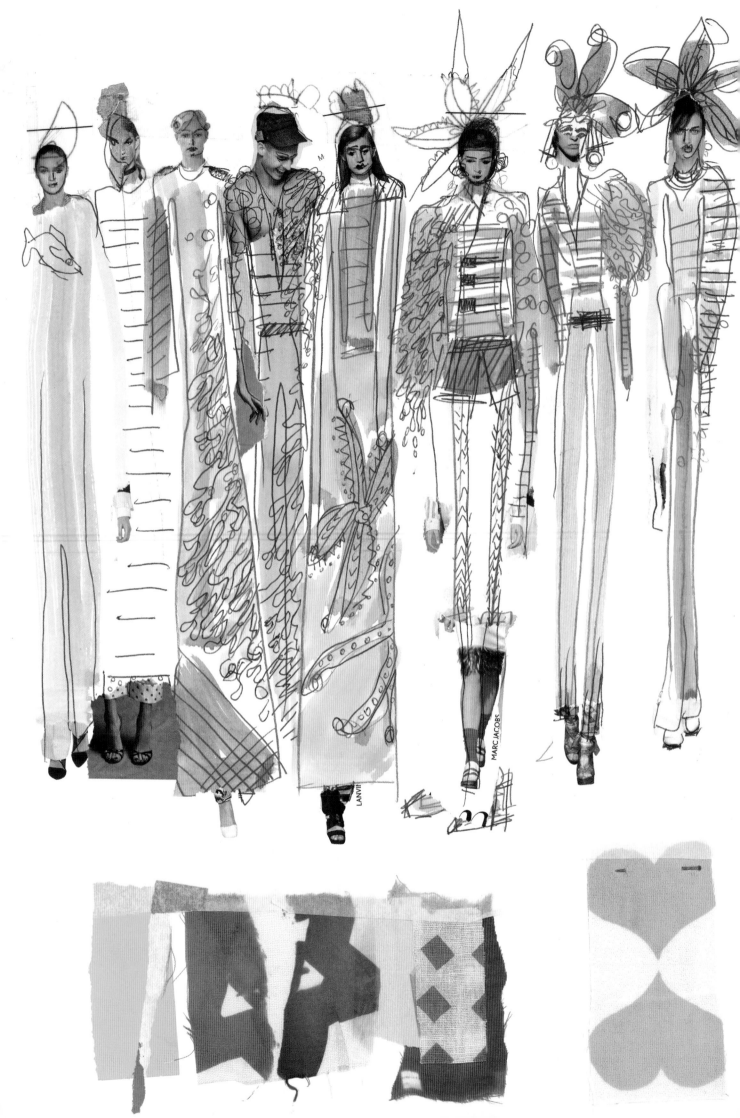

LANVIN

MARC JACOBS

05 LAYOUT & PRESENTATION

'First of all, respect your paper.'

J.M.W. TURNER

The presentation of fashion images and ideas is a mixed affair that brings together many influencing and defining factors; it is never static and is itself affected by fashion trends and the zeitgeist. The presentation work can often be considered a fashion image in its own right. What defines a suitable presentation is governed by the nature of the job, the client's expectations, the target market, whether the work is to be delivered digitally or physically, the time span involved, the budget – and that's just the beginning!

Presentation isn't just something to consider at the end of a project, nor indeed is it something done purely for the approval and benefit of a third party – you are in the process of clarifying and refining for yourself. This method of drawing, illustrating, designing, editing and developing is important and clients may often want to see behind the scenes to get an idea of the work in progress, the way in which ideas are formulated, and how the work has been edited, refined and developed. It is worth remembering that although you may be dealing with someone who is design-literate, they won't necessarily be a designer themselves and may have a limited appreciation of certain design aspects. Seeing an idea explored and developed from conception to finish can often give the client confidence and insight into the validity of your work. So sketchbooks and design developments are frequently a part of presentation. Sometimes it may be appropriate to produce an edited and polished version of your sketchbook – a kind of fast-forward glimpse into your design process – for the client to view as an introduction to the finished work.

SIMPLICITY AND CLARITY

The brief dictates the elements to be included. While the visual style of the presentation should be sympathetic to and evocative of the theme of the project, it should not confuse or overshadow the content of the work itself. It should not be overcomplicated and should generally be in keeping with current trends for simplicity and clarity. Any text or instructions should be well laid out (it is good practice to get into the habit of noticing and analyzing quality fashion magazine layouts and such). Hand written titles and text are not acceptable – computers enable the printing of professional standard graphics cheaply, quickly and easily. Novelty and over-decorative typefaces should generally be avoided; the simple, timeless logos of many high-fashion brands provide a good example of the use of stylish graphics.

It is worth developing a simple style for your name that can be unobtrusively incorporated into the presentation. It is useful and practical to create a label with your name and contact details, which can be readily printed out to stick to the reverse of all physical work submitted. Your work may have a long afterlife in a plans chest or such, and may be rediscovered and appreciated in the light of a follow-up project. We've all left work behind at a meeting or interview; if clearly labelled on the reverse, it can easily be traced and returned to you.

FACING PAGE: *This lively, vibrant illustration by Mary Ratcliffe presents a collection line-up for Alternative Fashion Week at Spitalfields, London. It shows the 'Starfish and Periwinkle Collection' (menswear and womenswear). Ratcliffe says: 'Drawings for digital and screen prints [are] taken from underwater forms. This illustration was worked to show the coordinated colour and overall print mood, to plan styling prior to the catwalk presentation.'*

LAYOUT

Planning and organization are key factors in the successful completion of any project, not least design-driven ones. One of the biggest errors is not to allow enough time at the end to bring a project to conclusion, so it's important to plan for that as you go. Use drawings and sketches to rough out and try different layouts, and allow time for experimentation with different styles, alternative media and techniques so you're not simply ploughing on with your fingers crossed in the final hours.

Components for presentation may typically include: project title; season; client/brand drawings (designs) on a figure and/or as flats or technical drawings; colour palette; fabric swatches; mood/theme or inspiration images; and a brief description of garments or theme-story/legend. Juggling this array of imagery and information while allowing for breathing space and clarity is a skill to be learned and continually honed and refined. The techniques and formats for layout and presentation of design work, mood boards and

colour palettes are constantly evolving as trends and technologies themselves progress. Where a number of presentation sheets or boards are necessary, it is important that they all follow the same layout and format as a cohesive whole.

In the tutorial on the following pages Yvonne Deacon simplifies some the possible approaches to a stylish formula, which allows plenty of scope for personality and individuality to shine while conforming to contemporary standards of good design presentation. She shows how traditional methods of layout use negative space, deploy narratives on the page and lead the eye as directed by the artist, using classical compositional rules from fine art. The significance of images is prioritized by their scale and positioning. But how we read images is changing. Through social media, we are becoming more familiar with images presented in new ways. Flickr, Pinterest, Google Images and Instagram all present multiple images in grids or scroll-down formats. Their

Layout Planning

- Composition

- Juxtaposition

- Meaning

- Narrative

- Cluster and group

- Colour palette

Planning your portfolio for direction content and page layout aiming to show your work to its best advantage, to achieve the best read

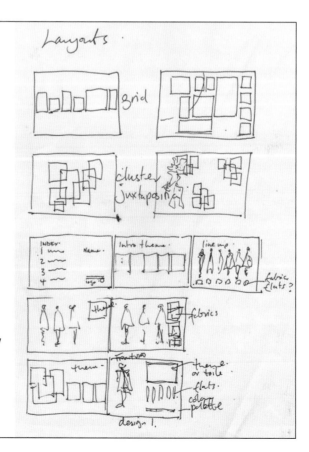

Once you know what material and information you need to include, you can sketch out plans for alternative layouts.

prioritizing is done in different ways – by impact, by our own interests, by trails, by 'best people' and 'most popular', by similar associations and related connections – evidence indeed that change and design influences can come from all directions. As designers we need to engage with this technology, remaining open to newness and continually refreshing our views.

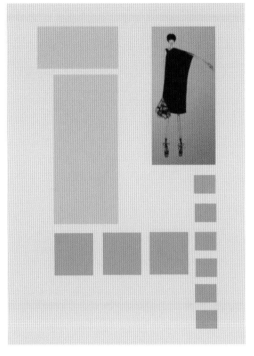

Portrait grid

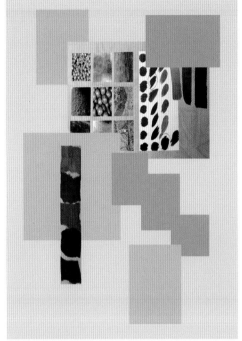

Portrait tiled grid

These two alternatives for a portrait layout show something of the scope and options open for creative presentation. The positioning of images is crucial to how the board is read; composition itself can help create elements of mood.

The portrait grid (far left) is clear and simple; the eye is led around in a circular direction that is quite calm.

In the portrait tiled grid (near left), energy and rhythm are created by the overlapping images and their strong diagonal direction. The eye criss-crosses around the board, generating a certain visual excitement.

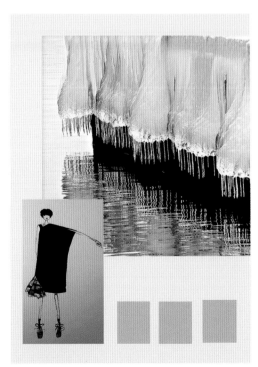

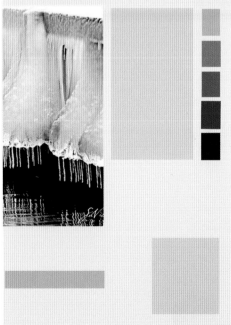

Double page spread, fashion and theme – colour trend

This double page spread opens up yet more scope and opportunities. The partial repeat of the central image provides a dramatic focus and a connecting visual link between the two boards.

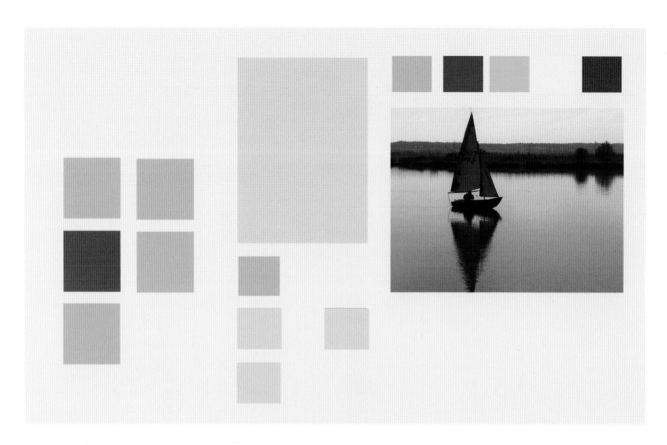

The grid format here is split between uniform and regular groups that balance and contrast in scale and direction. Larger images grab priority, smaller ones take supporting roles and create directional rhythms, leading the eye around the board.

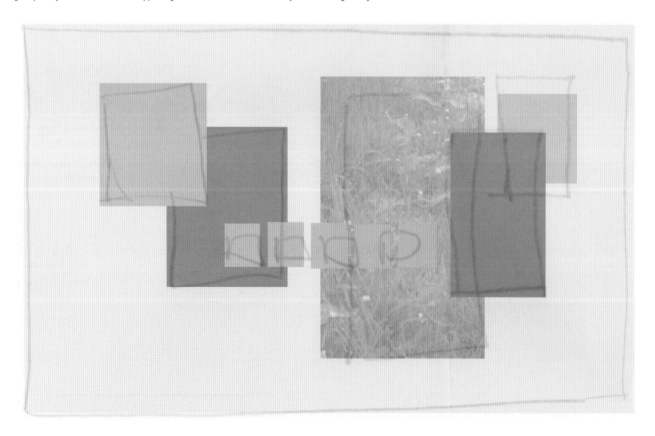

This landscape layout uses tiling to plan where themes, colours and ideas connect. The tiling technique makes strong visual connections that can reinforce narrative and thematic links between images. Variations of scale and proportion add interest.

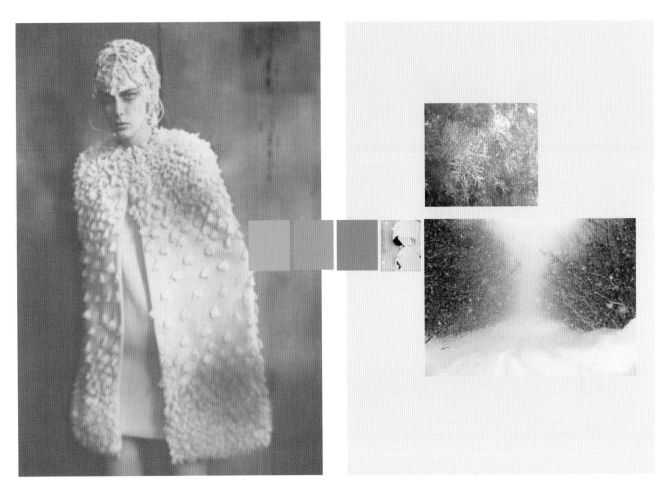

Portrait and landscape combined: the clever use of a large portrait image adds impact and importance to a significant visual. Colours taken from the main photo are used to connect it across the landscape format to its supporting research imagery.

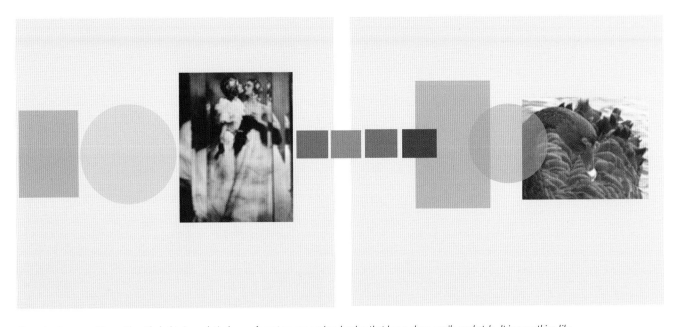

Linear landscape – either grid or tiled: this is a relatively new format we are seeing develop that has a clean, easily read style. It is something like a visual sentence, but can be read left to right and right to left or from any point outwards as though along a horizon.

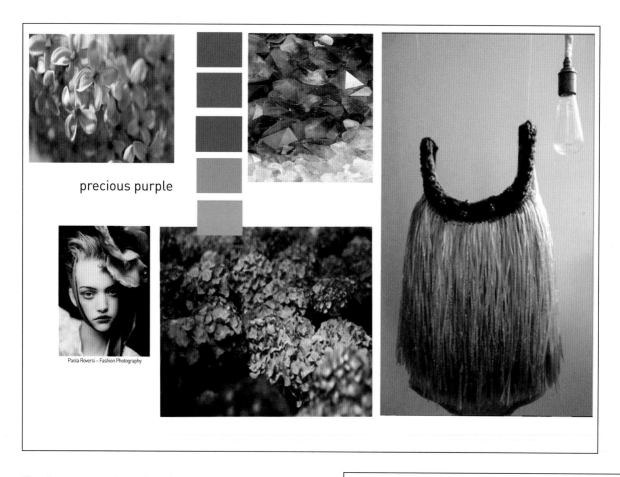

precious purple

Paola Roversi – Fashion Photography

These formats present almost identical information, but each prioritizes different aspects, with quite different visual results. The eye is drawn to different images and prioritizes attention because of variants in scale and positioning.

Grass skirt by Heather Ridley-Moran

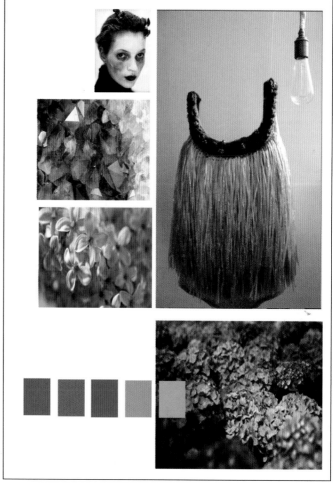

Layout

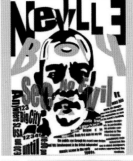

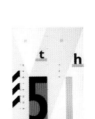

- Use the invisible grid (Neville Brody for The Face, Peter Saville for Factory Records) for original 80s layout technique
- Cluster and group to connect images and juxtapose
- Negative space to lead the eye through
- Rich and confusing
- Isolated and clear
- Ordered
- Not a scrapbook
- What is the page saying? Are you communicating the evocative content and main intent?

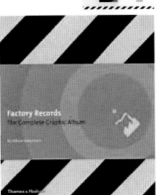

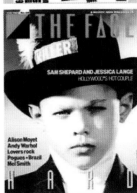

Remembering the key rules of presentation does not prohibit you from experimenting with some unlikely but exciting elements. Here a strong grid and subtle visual links with diagonals contribute to the balance and success of this bold, energetic layout. The text continually leads the eye back to the images.

119

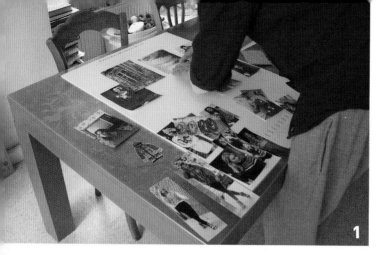

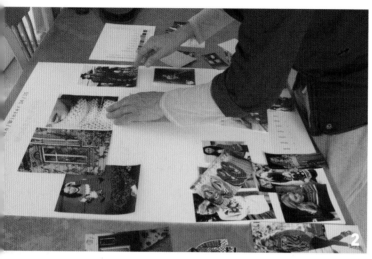

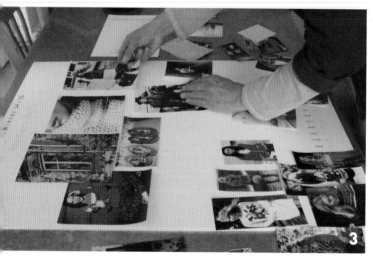

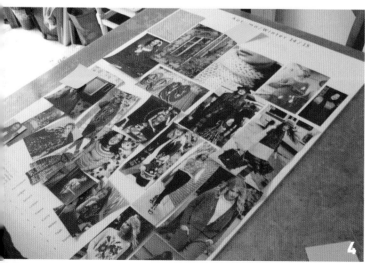

PRESENTATION BOARDS

I am by nature an advocate of simpler, sparer boards – with just perhaps four key images – but the brief for this project for a very commercially driven client required masses of clear, precise information for their buying and design teams.

I assembled one board for each of six themes identifying trends appropriate to their private label brands. Each board included a colour palette, with a short written synopsis of the colour story; comprehensive selections of images identifying a range of key garment types; and all elements and possibilities for each theme. Consequently the boards became image-heavy and needed clever organizing to be clearly defined and as readable and self-explanatory as possible.

The images had to be new, not US originated (to minimize the risk that the customer would already be familiar with them), style-right, and colour-right to reflect the colour palette. So as not to send out confusing messages, they had to be modelled by an appropriate image model (age, demographic, etc). Once all the images were found, I printed them to approximately the right scale, then trimmed and cropped them using a paper trimmer/cutter for speed and accuracy.

I usually have 'working titles' when researching themes until, gradually, final versions of titles are decided. I always use the same typeface every season and each of my clients has a different version of my format – this simplifies the decision-making process and so saves time and ensures continuity. By adhering to my formula, which includes a specific layout, point size for type, title positioning and all measurements kept on record, I stamp the boards with a style recognizable as my own as a kind of subtle branding. Titles, the season and all information required are printed on to Safmat, a printer-friendly transparent adhesive film that can be trimmed and applied to the foam boards I use for such presentations. When working on a set such as this, I will break the tasks down and print and trim all titles and text at once, then stick them to the boards. As all the pictures have already been printed and trimmed, along with a few spares or alternatives, I can arrange them for each theme one board at a time.

1 Start with the strongest or preferred images placed more or less centrally in prime position (although nothing is fixed at this stage).

2 Shift the images around and give some of them an extra trim to get them to fit or read better.

3 Juggle and shift the images as necessary (some will get edited out).

4 Use removable sticky notes to hold some of the images in position or to mark levels and right angles when they are lifted off to apply adhesive spray.

5 Stick down the images, taking care to maintain the exact positions and sequence of any layering.

6 A rubber roller reserved solely for this task (to keep it pristine) is used to flatten all images.

7 Once the images have been stuck in place, it is sometimes necessary to make tiny final trims using a craft knife and a cutting-edge rule.

8 Tiny slivers are trimmed away as some of the images are overlapped to fit or to cover any random text in a photograph. The last stage involves attaching the Pantone chips to the Safmat printed and placed colour palette at the foot of the board.

HEALTH AND SAFETY NOTE!

Adhesive spray is really useful and gives highly professional results, but it is proven to have health risks if inhaled so always use it outside or in a vacuum-pumped spray booth. Alternatively, disposable masks are available cheaply at good art and graphics suppliers and at all DIY stores.

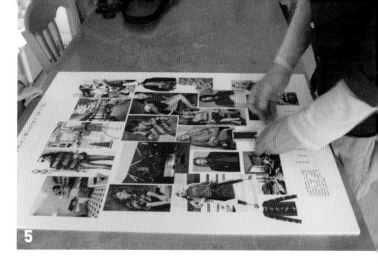

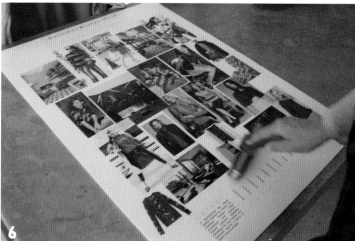

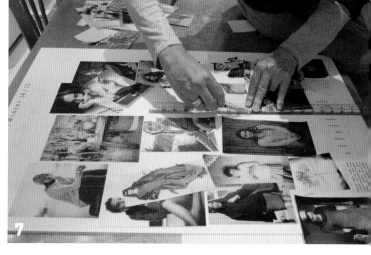

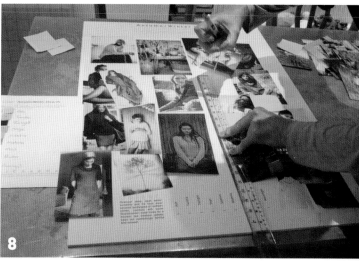

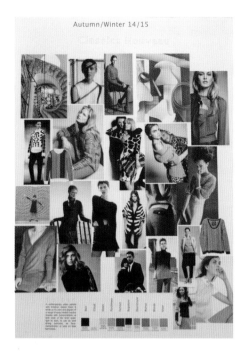

The six A1 boards are finished. While each displays its individual thematic differences, the six present a matching professional set and are ready to pack off to the client. Smaller less image-dense boards are sometimes produced using Photoshop and can be sent electronically or printed out. But for large format presentations such as this, actual boards with accurate colour references are still – for the moment, at least – required by clients for presentations to teams and meetings.

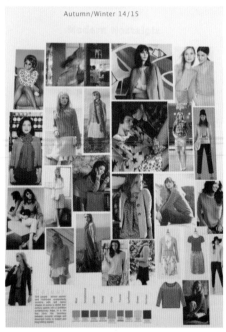

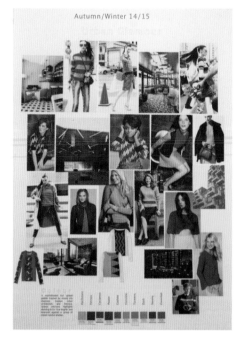

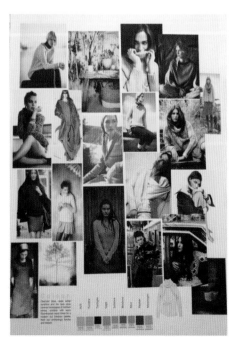

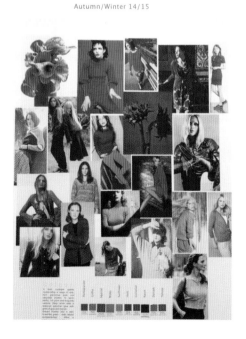

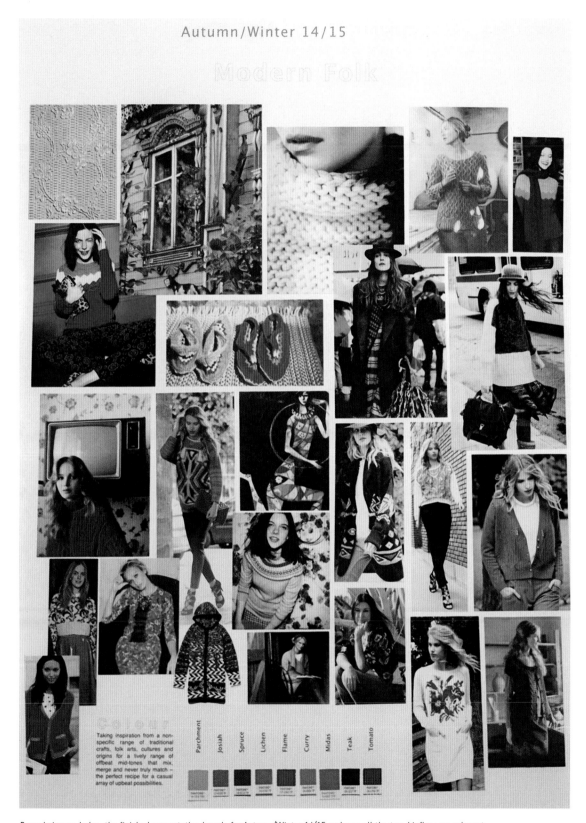

Autumn/Winter 14/15

Densely image-laden, the finished presentation boards for Autumn/Winter 14/15 embrace all the trend influences relevant for each look, while successfully consolidating them under an umbrella theme that covers colour, yarn, pattern, texture, silhouette, detail and styling. The customer is presented with a complete overview of opportunities for trend-driven design ideas for each theme as appropriate for their market levels.

'Great stories happen to those who can tell them.'

IRA GLASS

MASSIMO CASAGRANDE

Massimo Casagrande is a London based menswear designer. Here selected sketchbook images and collages of reference and inspirational images are reconfigured and annotated for a kind of polished edited highlights approach to a lookbook/sketchbook.

The design narrative is told via images of contemporary style icon Nick Cave and late 1950s/early 1960s photographs of Paul Newman as muses, combined and enforced with strong atmospheric elements conjured up by images of Giacometti and related Rebecca Warren sculptures. Fabric swatches and a moody shot of a model wearing a final design bring the concept to completion.

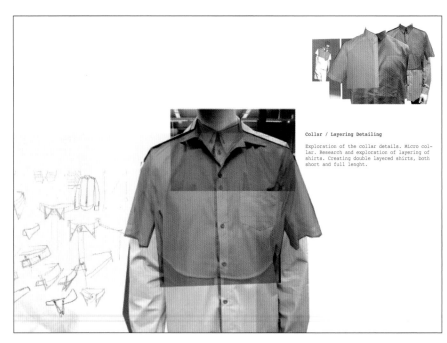

Collar / Layering Detailing

Exploration of the collar details. Micro collar. Research and exploration of layering of shirts. Creating double layered shirts, both short and full lenght.

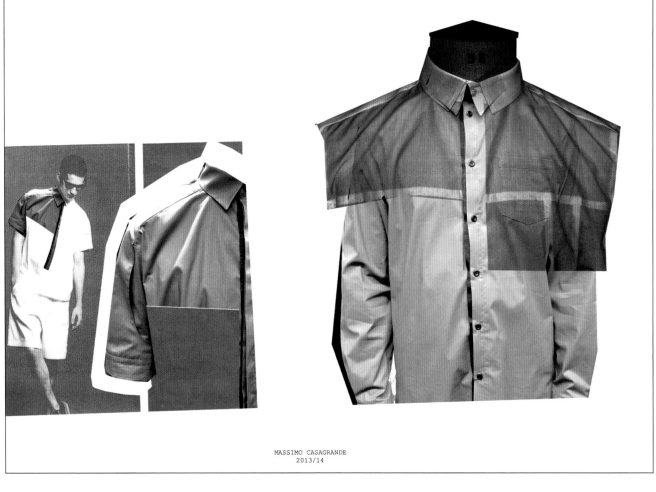

MASSIMO CASAGRANDE
2013/14

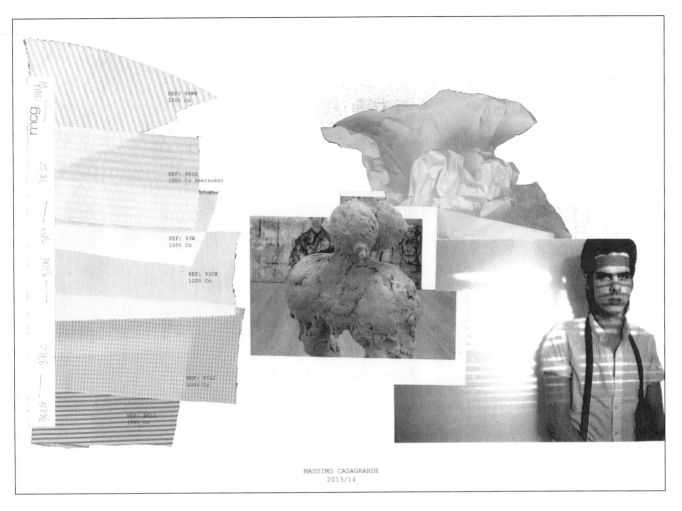

MASSIMO CASAGRANDE
2013/14

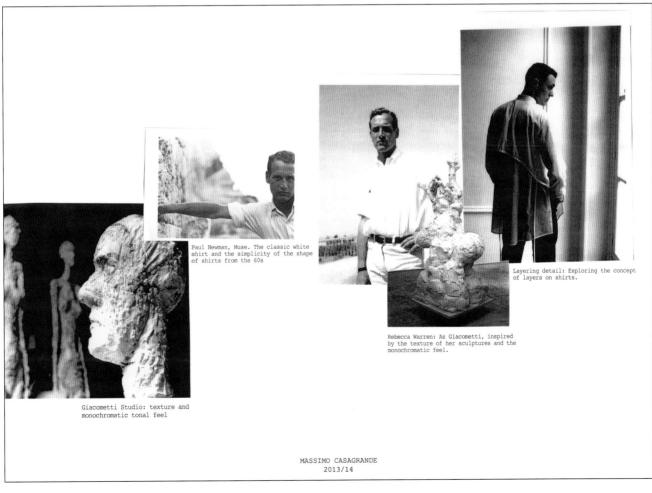

Paul Newman, Muse. The classic white
shirt and the simplicity of the shape
of shirts from the 60s

Layering detail: Exploring the concept
of layers on shirts.

Rebecca Warren: As Giacometti, inspired
by the texture of her sculptures and the
monochromatic feel.

Giacometti Studio: texture and
monochromatic tonal feel

MASSIMO CASAGRANDE
2013/14

ILLUSTRATION

In these images for a commercial client, the illustrators use different techniques to achieve a loose, free approach to convey moods that are appropriately young and casual.

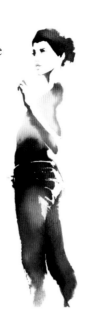
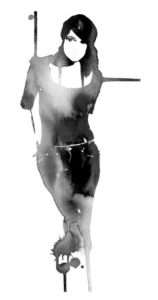
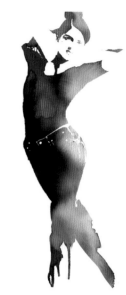

RIGHT: *Three figures, hand-drawn with inks and digitally manipulated, make for strong image and impact. Stina Persson*

BELOW: *In these two lively illustrations hand-drawn figures and loose mark-making are boldly combined through digital enhancement to achieve strong impact. Patrick Morgan*

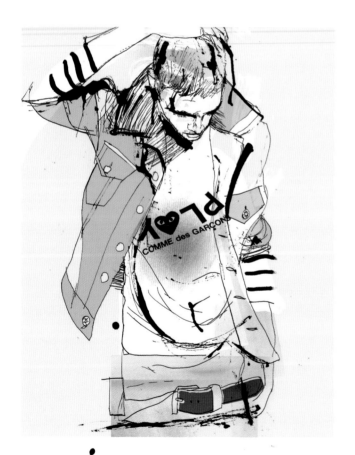

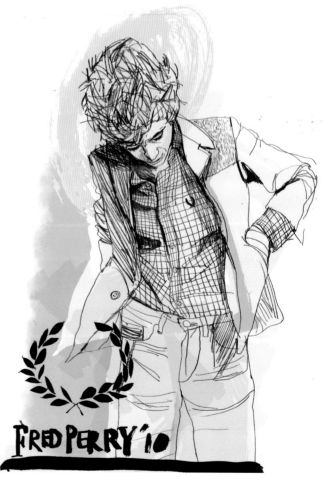

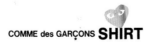

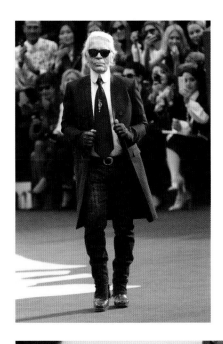

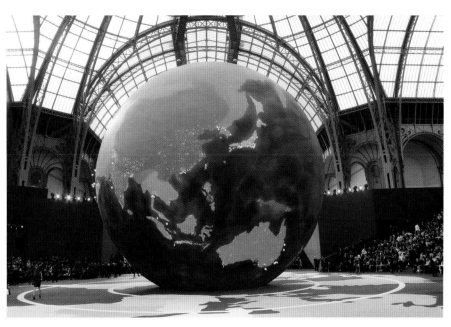

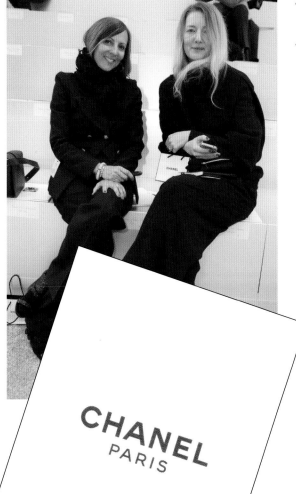

A fashion show, perhaps viewed as the ultimate presentation, is often supported by illustrations or designers' drawings in press packs and on invitations and promotional material.

At Chanel, creative director Karl Largerfeld recently used his own illustration skills to create an image of Madame Coco Chanel herself which was printed on the front-row goody bags.

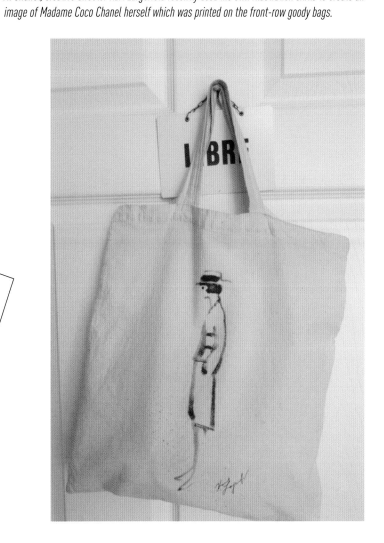

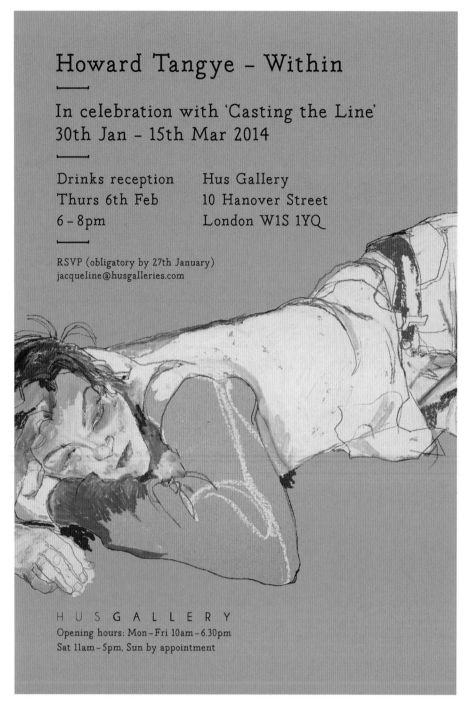

Howard Tangye – Within
———
In celebration with 'Casting the Line'
30th Jan – 15th Mar 2014

———

Drinks reception   Hus Gallery
Thurs 6th Feb   10 Hanover Street
6 – 8pm   London W1S 1YQ

———

RSVP (obligatory by 27th January)
jacqueline@husgalleries.com

H U S G A L L E R Y
Opening hours: Mon – Fri 10am – 6.30pm
Sat 11am – 5pm, Sun by appointment

HOWARD TANGYE

Howard Tangye is an artist, fashion designer and lecturer (or, as he prefers, educator). He has worked with many of the biggest names in fashion and is known and respected for his distinctive and individual style.

LEFT: *Howard Tangye's boldly cropped drawing is combined with simple but complementary graphics to create a powerful and arresting poster. Designed by Stinsensqueeze © 2014 for his exhibition at the Hus Gallery, London*

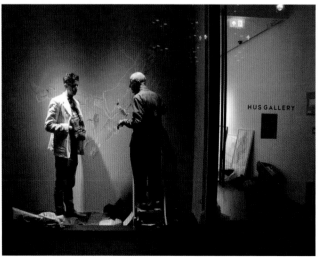

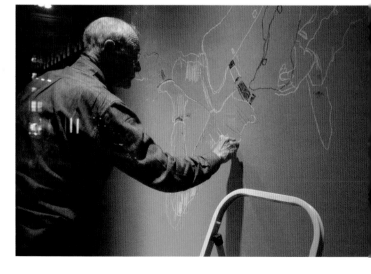

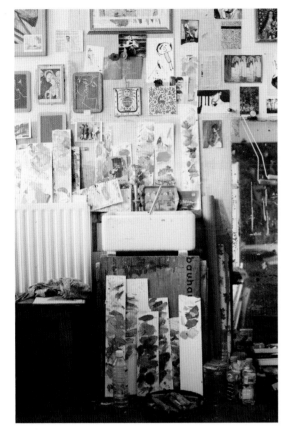

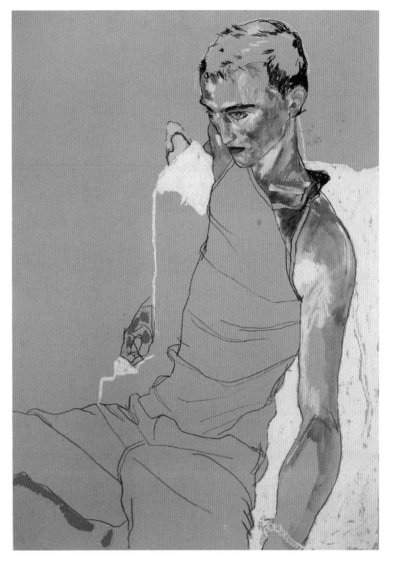

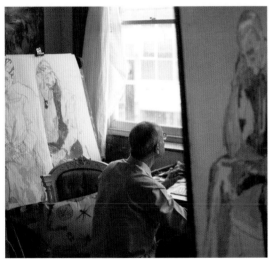

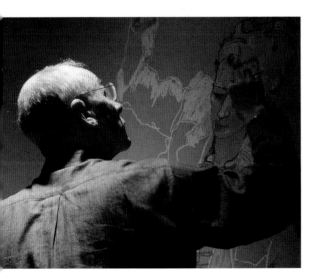

ABOVE: *Portrait of Richard Nicoll, 2000, mixed media on card*

ABOVE LEFT: *A corner of Howard's studio. Photo: Kasia Bobula © 2014*

LEFT: *Studio photo: Sidekick Creatives © 2013*

FACING PAGE AND BELOW LEFT: *Howard is seen drawing a stunning life-size portrait in readiness for his exhibition opening. He works through the night, drawing from life in the cramped window of the Hus Gallery.*
Photos: Anna-Nicole Ziesche

JONATHAN KYLE FARMER

In some instances, designs and concept ideas are so entwined with the presentation of those ideas that they are visually inseparable, one and the same. Jonathan KYLE Farmer's work explores the relationship between 2D and 3D design processes, how the body interacts with a garment and how both analogue and digital 3D modeling techniques can be used to design, pattern-cut, illustrate, style and present clothes from multiple views simultaneously.

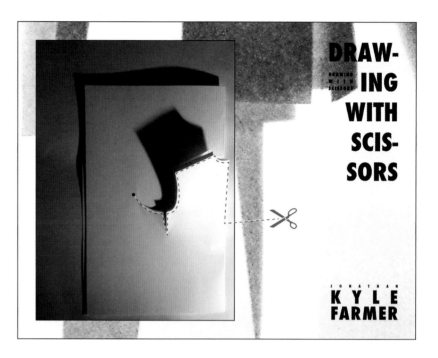

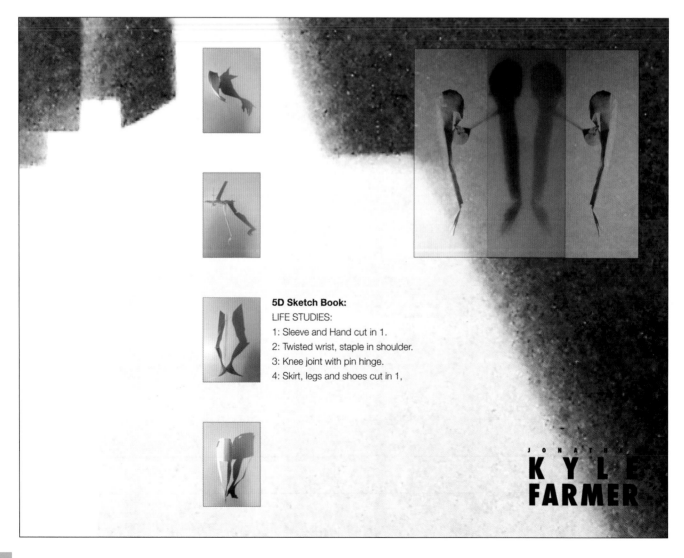

5D Sketch Book:
LIFE STUDIES:
1: Sleeve and Hand cut in 1.
2: Twisted wrist, staple in shoulder.
3: Knee joint with pin hinge.
4: Skirt, legs and shoes cut in 1,

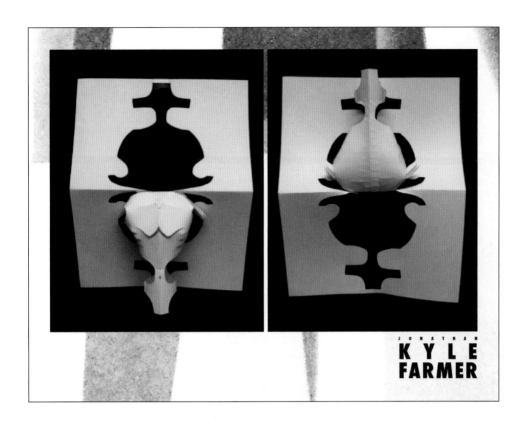

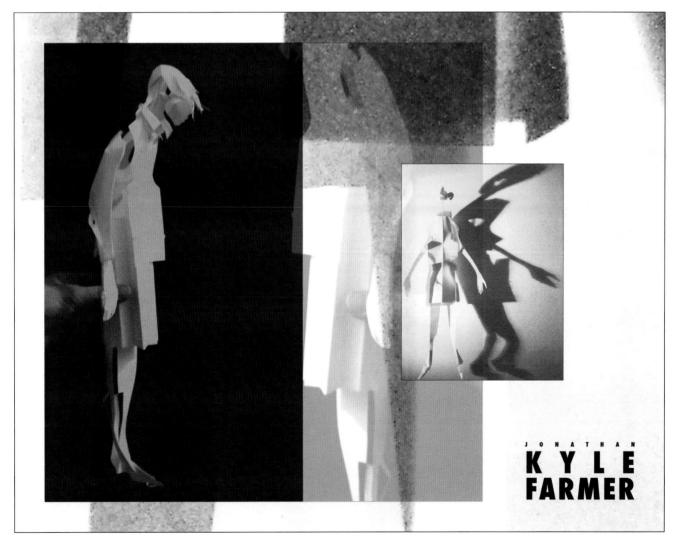

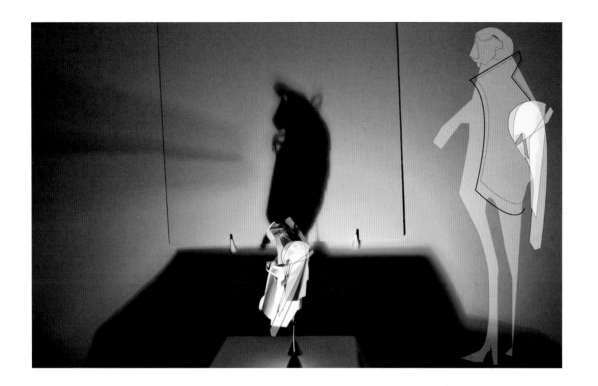

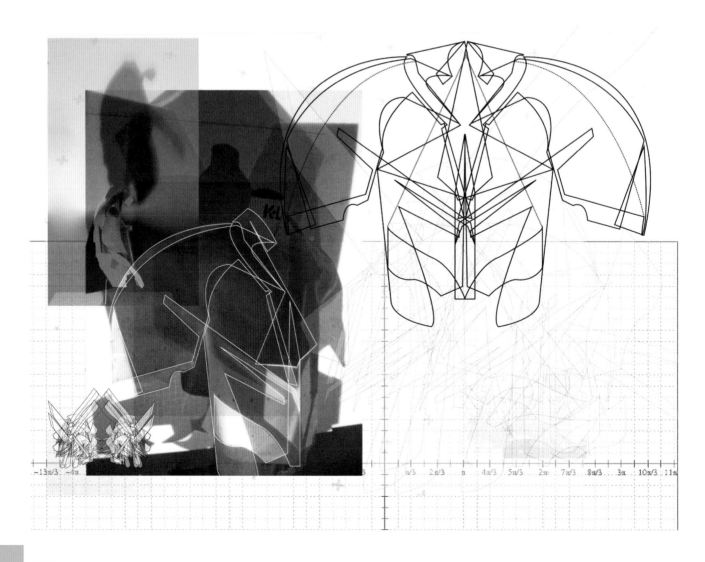

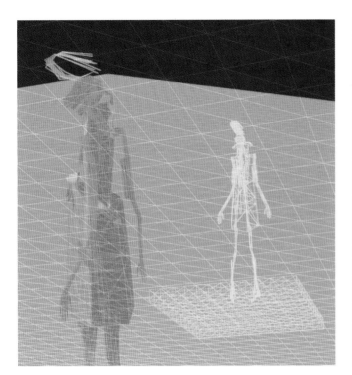

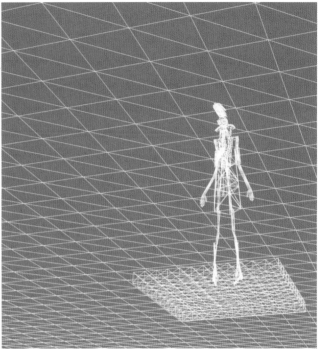

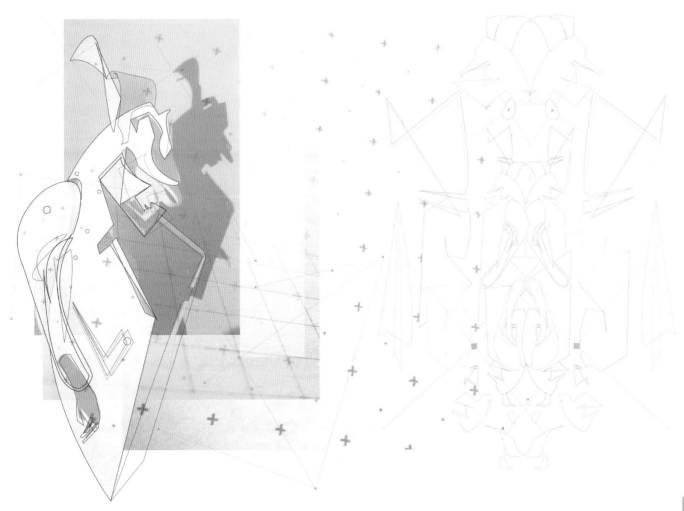

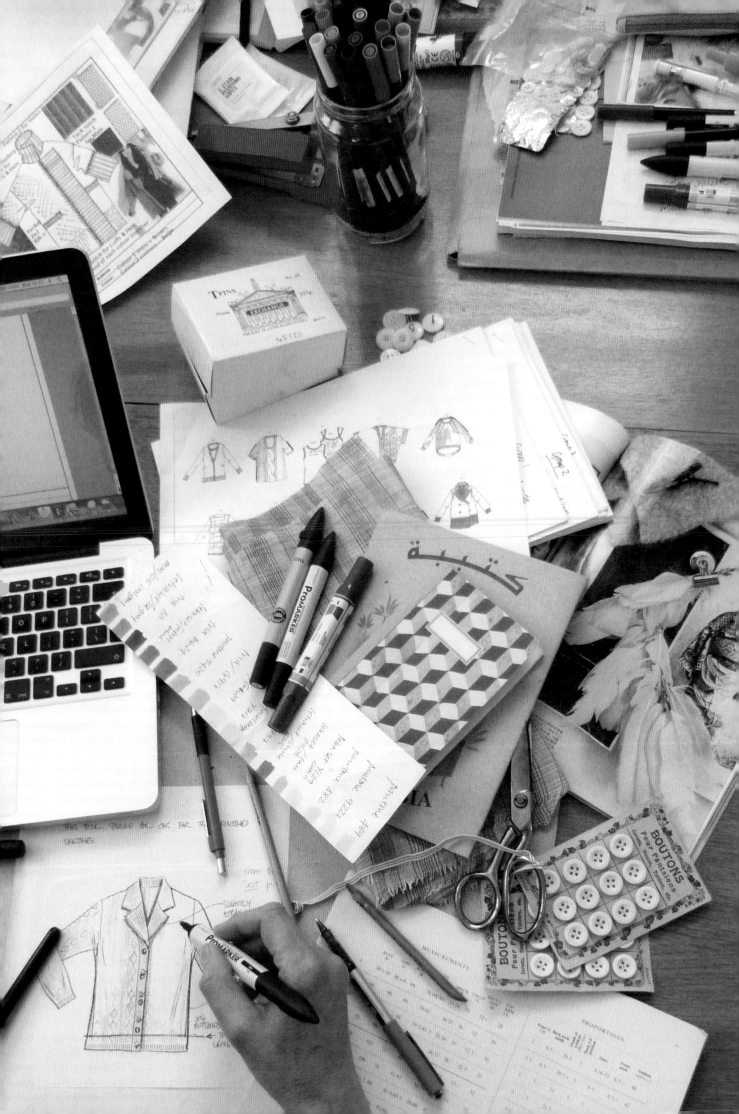

06 WORKING IN INDUSTRY

'I have three muscles (of seeing) without which I couldn't do my work. The first is curiosity; the second . . . appreciation; the third . . . imagination.'

MICHAEL WOLFF

Whether employed by a company or self-employed, as most illustrators and many designers are, it is important to be able to follow and adhere to a brief. Industry briefs, like any other, may be well planned and presented, straightforward and clear; but they are not always – your boss or your client may not fully know what they want, be vague about their requests or they may be fickle and change their mind without realizing they have shifted. Perhaps they have asked you to undertake a project without fully grasping its scope or the amount of work involved. The request may be unreasonable or impossible to achieve within the budget or time-span. You may even be briefed 'secondhand' by someone 'down the line' who is passing on requests without fully understanding the task themselves. Always try to get a written brief and don't be afraid to amend it; both parties need to clarify any grey areas and gather together all possible information. If anything is unclear or unspecified, remember it is important to ask questions and get the answers in writing.

AGREEING TERMS

Always get your fee and payment terms agreed and try to secure an advance, particularly if the project is long-running or will involve expenditure on your part. If your client is based overseas, make sure you are paid in your own currency at the agreed rate, not in their currency, as you may lose money in conversion; the client should also cover the cost of any payment transfer fees. Agree in advance how the work will be delivered; if electronically, check the

digital resolution needed and ensure that your client is able to receive the right size files, etc. If you have physical (hard copy) to deliver, make sure it is clear who pays for the postage or courier, how long it will take to reach the client, and how much of your time will be involved, as that too should be allowed for in the budget.

When agreeing terms don't forget to take into consideration any other projects you are working on or engagements that may collide. If you think there may be a conflict between projects, alert your client to this and assure them of your discretion and professionalism – and be sure to follow that through! If you are not sure about a new client, check them out online, ask around – has anyone you know done work for them? Before beginning any work always understand your client's business, their market and customers. Check out their product and their stores; ask them how they perceive themselves and their brands they aspire to. It does not make you look silly to ask questions, but you are silly not to.

CAREER PATHWAYS

Career pathways are seldom clear and direct; careers segue along, offers are seized and undertaken. If we are lucky, someone may see talent and potential within us and we might end up in the most undreamt of places – frequently quite happily! The career pathways of the super-successful are familiar to us via the media; but other less prominent people have followed equally creative and rewarding careers and left their significant mark on fashion history.

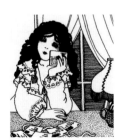 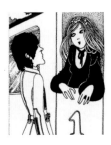 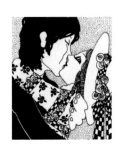 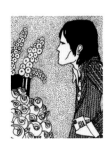

Malcolm Bird – four illustrations – 'Love through the letterbox', for Honey magazine, circa 1970

MALCOLM BIRD

After studying Art Foundation at Rochdale Art College, Malcolm Bird studied fashion design at Manchester and gained an MA in Fashion Design at the Royal College of Art. He went on to be a key figure in the graphic and visual style of some of the most influential magazines and worked for Biba, the iconic fashion brand of the 1960s and 1970s.

Malcolm's illustrations presented here show his characteristic wit and distinctive personal handwriting, while reflecting a strong 1920s and 1930s influence very much in vogue at the time.

'Whilst still studying at Manchester, Honey magazine did an audition from the North and I took my portfolio of fashion drawings, but it was the humorous little drawings I'd added around the edges that they liked. I did illustrations for that issue, and others followed.

'Whilst at the Royal College, I also became a regular contributor to Petticoat, *the weekly 'sister' magazine of* Honey, *and subsequently several other*

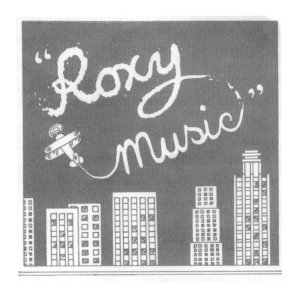

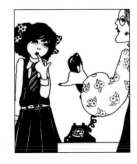

ABOVE: *The first artwork designed for the band Roxy Music in 1971 by Malcolm Bird. It was used, printed on satin, as backstage passes and, in repeat, as a paper poster.*

LEFT: *One of a series of illustrations 'Love through the Letterbox' by Malcolm Bird for* Honey *magazine, circa 1970*

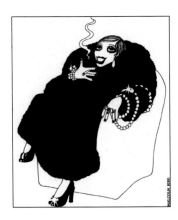

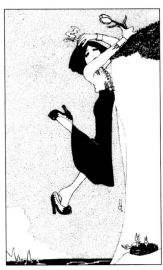

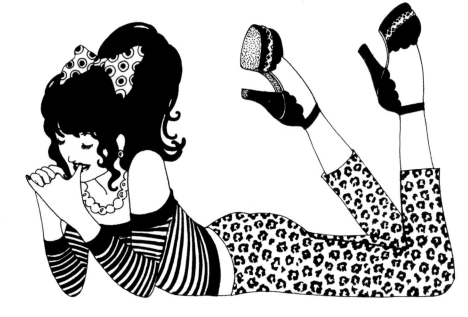

CALENDAR 1972

magazines. *After leaving college I continued the magazine work, whilst taking a fashion design job three days a week.*

'*After that – being a huge Barbara Hulanicki fan – I went to work as one of her pattern cutters, and later was a colourist. I also did several interior drawings to promote the store, designed the children's department in the third of her four successive shops, and designed a huge reclining Biba lady cake for a party there. The illustration work continued and I worked regularly for a range of magazines and publications including:* Jackie, Fashion Forecast, Vanity Fair, Mother, Woman's Realm, Woman, The Times, Sunday Times, *and the* Daily Mail, *and designed greeting cards for Gallery Five.*

'*Many of my early magazine drawings were done freehand with a Rapidograph pen. Later, for both magazine and children's book illustration, I used Daler fine surface line and wash card, pencilled in first (tracing off a preliminary rough on a layout pad), using a Rapidograph for the black line and then watercolour for the colour. For black and white work I always use an A4 Bristol Board pad.*'

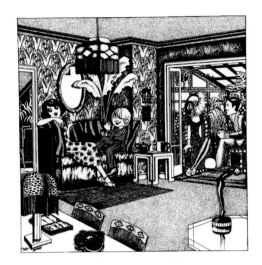

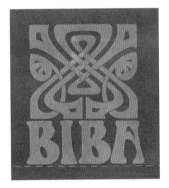

ABOVE: *Malcolm Bird, lounge drawing to promote the Biba brand, 1974*

LEFT: *The iconic, Art Nouveau inspired Biba logo*

BELOW: *Bedroom drawing to promote Biba, 1974*

FAR LEFT CENTRE: *Woman smoking in an armchair by Malcolm Bird,* Petticoat *magazine, 1969*

FAR LEFT BOTTOM: *Malcolm Bird, 'How possessed are you?' – a quiz illustration for* Vanity Fair, *1970*

LEFT: *The cover of a calendar to promote Malcolm Bird's work*

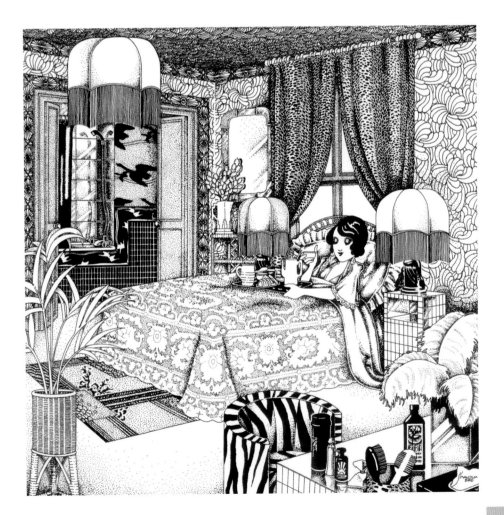

MASSIMO CASAGRANDE

Massimo Casagrande runs his own line of self-designed shirts, consequently he has multiple roles to perform and different styles of illustration that fulfill different tasks. On pages 124–5, a selection of his roughs show his first ideas sketches, combined with mood and inspiration collages. Below Massimo combines sketches, found images, scans of fabric swatches, technical drawings (specs) and commissioned photography to fulfil the various presentation and communication roles his work requires.

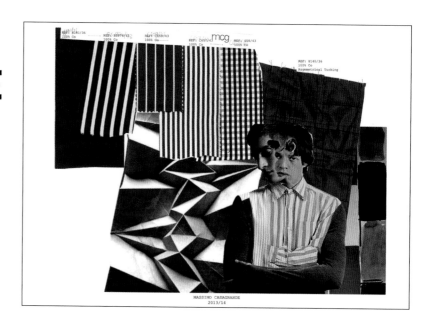

ABOVE: *Here we see a mix of fabric reference information combined with mood/inspiration in his look book.*

BELOW: *The mood is set and explained via a short piece of written copy and additional supporting imagery. An element of repetition is echoed both in a repeated image motif, in design elements such as pleats, layering and double sleeves, and in the very nature of the stripe itself.*

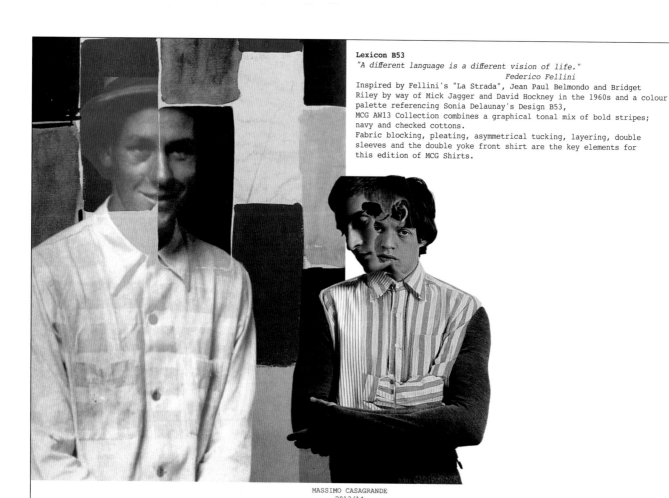

Lexicon B53
"A different language is a different vision of life."
Federico Fellini
Inspired by Fellini's "La Strada", Jean Paul Belmondo and Bridget Riley by way of Mick Jagger and David Hockney in the 1960s and a colour palette referencing Sonia Delaunay's Design B53,
MCG AW13 Collection combines a graphical tonal mix of bold stripes; navy and checked cottons.
Fabric blocking, pleating, asymmetrical tucking, layering, double sleeves and the double yoke front shirt are the key elements for this edition of MCG Shirts.

MASSIMO CASAGRANDE
2013/14

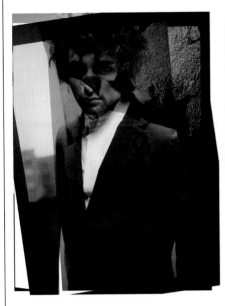
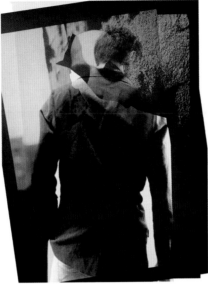
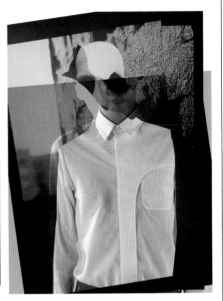

MASSIMO CASAGRANDE
2013/14

ABOVE: *A teasing set of photographic imagery aims enigmatically to suggest collection designs and stimulate curiosity to pursue further enquiry, rather than to completely illustrate and reveal.*

BELOW: *Crisp, clean flats, with fully supporting information, clearly illustrate specific designs, suitable for sales team/showroom guidance and internet sales.*

mcg

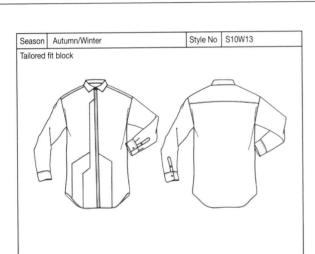

Season	Autumn/Winter		Style No	S10W13
Tailored fit block				

Patchwork Detail Long Sleeve Shirt

Bold Stripe Cotton Shirting B5 974/43
Blue Navy Cotton Shirting H140/36
Blue Stripe Cotton Shirting C657/43

Price £116.00   €139,38

Fine light stripe cotton shirting (96LG)
Seersucker White on White shirting (9655)
White on white stripe cotton shirting (94WW)
Fine light check cotton shirting (97LC)

Price £106.30   €127,72

Size: 38, 40, 42, 44

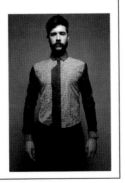

Season	Autumn/Winter		Style No	S11W13
Tailored fit block				

A-Front Long Sleeve Shirt

Bold Stripe Cotton Shirting B5 974/43
Blue Navy Cotton Shirting H140/36
Blue Stripe Cotton Shirting C657/43
Blue Check Cotton Shirting C658/43

Price £126.84   €138,00

White poplin cotton (93W)
Fine light stripe cotton shirting (96LG)
Fine light check cotton shirting (97LC)

Price £94.35   €113,37

Size: 38, 40, 42, 44

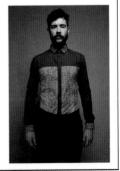

www.massimo-casagrande.com
info@massimo-casagrande.com

MASSIMO CASAGRANDE
2013/14

HILARY KIDD

Hilary is a freelance illustrator working for a wide range of clients that include womenswear, menswear and childrenswear. She also does beauty and accessories illustrations, working through agents and with design studios, trend bureaus and directly with brands and magazines.

1 *Insight women's trend forecast artwork, 2005/06. Brush pen, Pantone marker and crayon*

2 *Beauty advertisement, 1980s. Pencil and crayon*

3 *Trade magazine, 1990s. Brush pen, marker and crayon*

4 *Christmas card, 1980s. Brush pen and marker*

5 *Promotional drawing, 2011. Pencil and grey marker*

6 *Insight women's trend forecast, artwork 2008/09. Brush pen, marker and crayon*

7 *Insight women's trend forecast, artwork 2008/09. Brush pen, marker and crayon*

8a and b
International Wool Secretariat, 1996–7, womenswear styling directions. Brush pen, marker and crayon

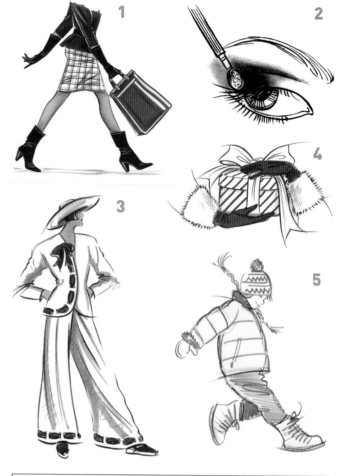

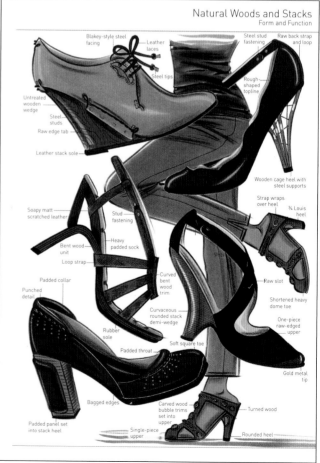

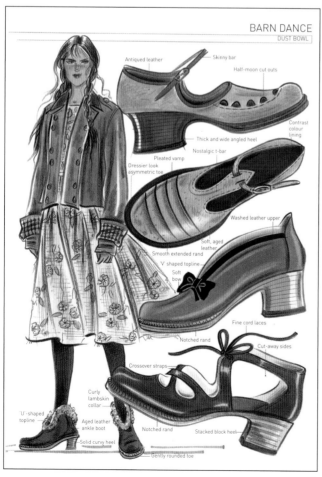

6

7

8a

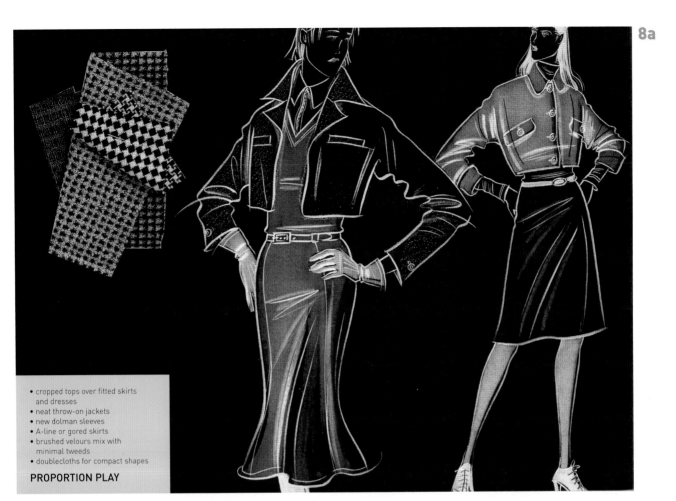

- cropped tops over fitted skirts and dresses
- neat throw-on jackets
- new dolman sleeves
- A-line or gored skirts
- brushed velours mix with minimal tweeds
- doublecloths for compact shapes

PROPORTION PLAY

8b

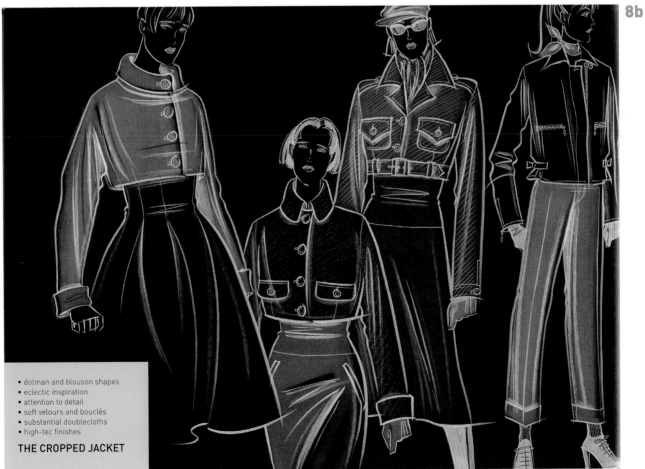

- dolman and blouson shapes
- eclectic inspiration
- attention to detail
- soft velours and bouclés
- substantial doublecloths
- high-tec finishes

THE CROPPED JACKET

CHRISTOPHER BROWN

'I consider myself as an illustrator who records fashion rather than a "fashion illustrator", a slightly different approach which has been popular. I try to create a mood, a feeling or "fantasy" of the collection rather than simply recording the clothes.'

'When visiting the collections, I always sketched, using a camera simply as an aide-mémoire. At first I was rather slow at getting details down but I soon sped up. I feel that unless I draw something I won't remember it.'

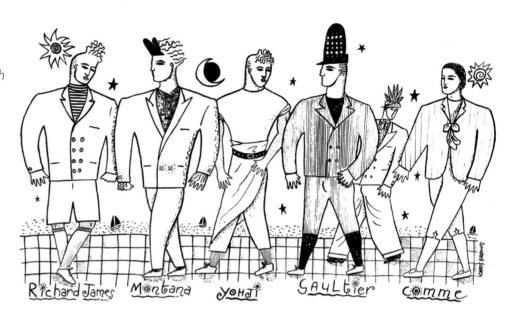

ABOVE: The Times, *double page spread, black and white illustration, ink with brush and dip pen, late 1980s*

BELOW: Sunday Times, *late 1980s, double page spread*

BOTTOM OF FACING PAGE: *'Les Hommes Like It Hot',* Sunday Times, *1988–9. Cerruti (left) and Yves St Laurent (right). 'For this article I used my sketches done both in the show and afterwards in the showroom, and I also took photographs to use as additional reference back in my studio for the finished illustrations, which used collage of found and hand-painted papers.'*

'I suggested the article after seeing an YSL show and meeting with Bernard Sanz who became designer in 1987. I was interested in how designers working for famous houses design not for "themselves" but in the spirit of the designer . . . After the article was published Bernard Sanz asked me to design ties for his next collection.'

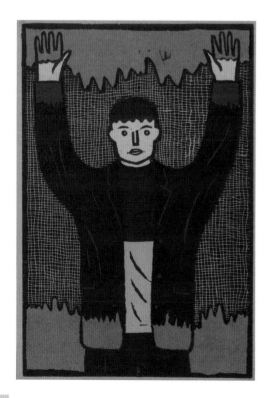

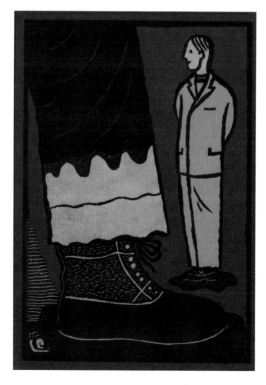

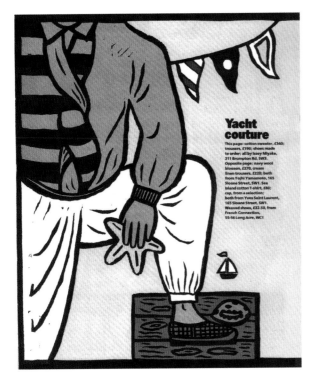

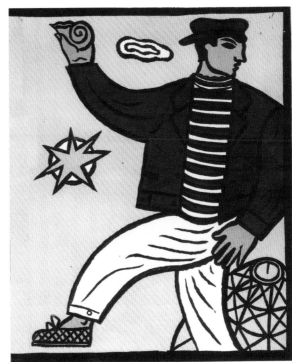

ABOVE: *'This large linocut was one of three spreads for the* Sunday Times. *It was the first of my "fashion" illustrations for a newspaper although I had previously done work for designers such as Artwork, Jasper Conran, Betty Jackson and Paul Howie.*

'It came about because Pedro Silmon, the art director (with whom I had been at the RCA), asked if I was interested in contributing to the men's supplement. I, of course, jumped at the chance and went in and met with him and Caroline Baker the fashion editor.

'I then arranged to get invitations to the shows in Paris sketching. On my return I put together a story based around a summer in my imagination in the south of France. Once I decided which clothes to use, I contacted the designers and borrowed the items to draw using a model to pose for me. Then I transferred the drawings to lino and printed and collaged the final artwork.

'The illustrations won the W.H. Smith Illustration Award.'

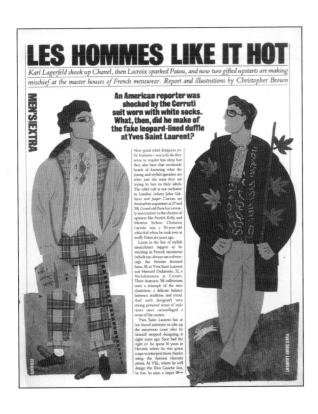

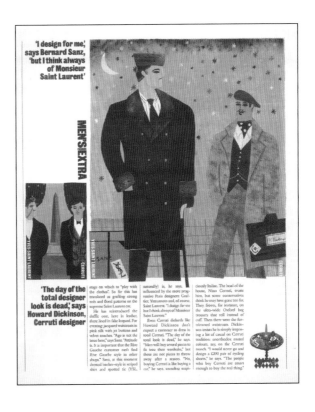

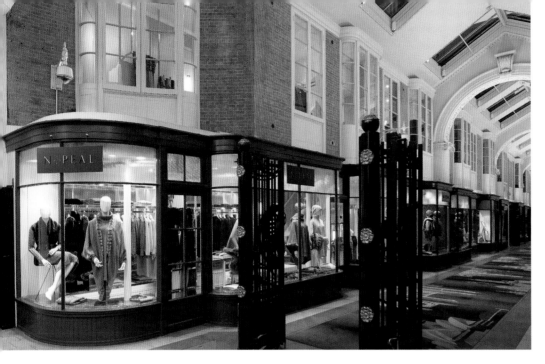

LEFT: *The window of N Peal in Burlington Arcade, London*

BOTTOM LEFT: *Mobile phone camera photographs, quick roughs and notes record the essential details and information while on site with the client's range.*

CATALOGUING AND RECORDING

N¹⁹³⁶ PEAL

Founded in 1936 by Nat Peal, this company has traded in luxurious cashmere knitwear from its Burlington Arcade shop for over 75 years. This assignment is an example typical of some of the many 'behind the scenes' roles for a freelance fashion illustrator, which are part of the rich and sprawling support system of the fashion industry.

'For this project, the brief was to sketch the client's knitwear range in a clear and readable style for the purpose of making a complete range plan. This plan was to be used by sales and merchandising teams when organizing, planning and tracking stock.

'I had just a day to work from the samples in the limited space of the company's stockroom to rough out the range. I could then do the final drawings at home in my workroom, a total of 126 pieces. The whole project needed to be completed in just a few days.

'So I arrived armed with layout pads, post-it notes, pens, pencils, a men's and a women's template, bulldog clips and pegs to hold garments in a good shape and my camera-phone to make additional records. A bottle of water and a sandwich completed my kit – it was a busy day!

'I began by making quick roughs, keeping an eye on the time to pace myself. I knew how many pieces I had to record in the available time – so to speed up I took photos of stitches, patterns and details – for accurately checking of proportions when refining my sketches later – all the time keeping a record of the style numbers too.

'The drawings later became an aide mémoire for staff teams to view against the sales figures when designing and range-building the following seasons.'

JUDITH CHEEK

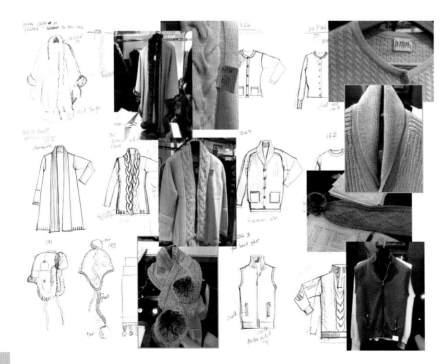

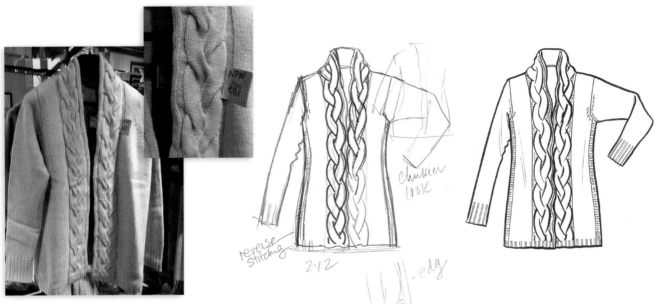

ABOVE: *Photographs, rough sketches and notes made on site help with detail and accuracy when redrawing roughs. The final clear drawings are completed and inked in using a fine fibre-tip and a brush pen.*

BELOW: *The finished drawings provide a clear and readable overview of styles in the range. Simple, precise drawings like this have all manner of end-uses including websites and e-commerce.*

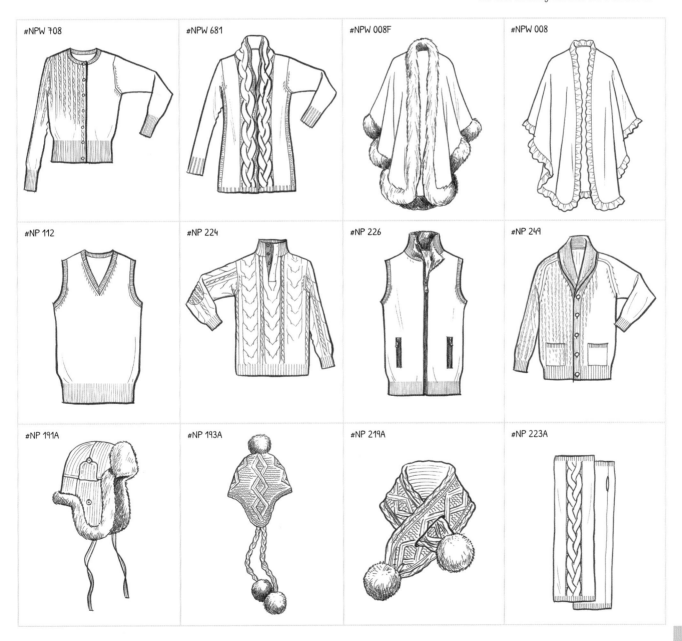

#NPW 708

#NPW 681

#NPW 008F

#NPW 008

#NP 112

#NP 224

#NP 226

#NP 249

#NP 191A

#NP 193A

#NP 219A

#NP 223A

IAN BATTEN

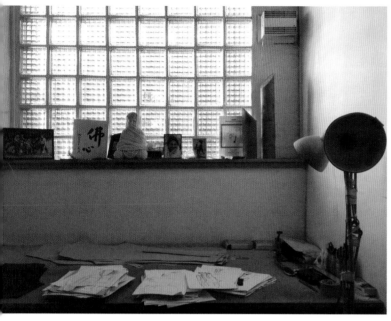

Ian Batten runs his label from a London studio, designing two collections a year for men and women. He works largely with traditional quality British and European cloth mills and he manufactures in the UK. The Ian Batten range sells to selective stores worldwide and directly to an exclusive range of personal clients.

Ian draws initially for himself, to generate and develop ideas. His drawings help him refine and select ideas to go forward into sampling, range planning and, later, production.

LEFT: *Greatly influenced by Japanese design aesthetics, the studio is spare, compact, well-planned and organized.*

BELOW: *Menswear design sketches demonstrate traditional influences and Batten's flair for strong tailoring. The sketches also show fabric allocations and designer's notes for variations.*

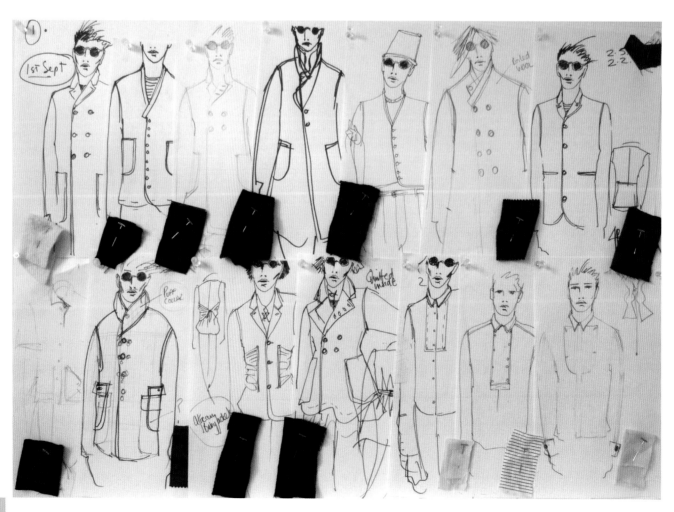

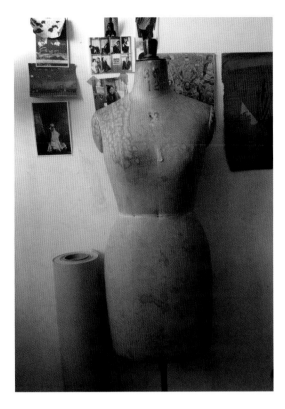

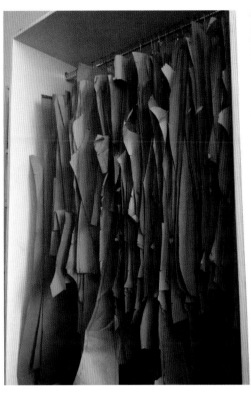

ABOVE: *In a corner of the studio, a tailor's mannequin stands next to selected images and inspirational tearsheets on the wall, creating an unpretentious but stylish still life.*

ABOVE: *Original patterns and blocks are stored away neatly for easy access.*

BELOW: *Womenswear designs reveal a wealth of ideas and share the same strong aesthetic as Batten's menswear sketches.*

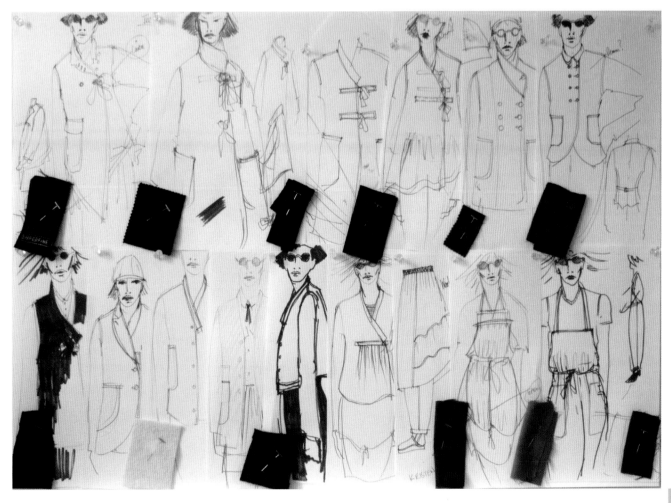

PROMOTIONAL

In this section we look at some of the ways in which drawing may be employed in the promotion of a designer brand, an actual design or a collection. In the process, a number of styles of drawing may be used to communicate different information.

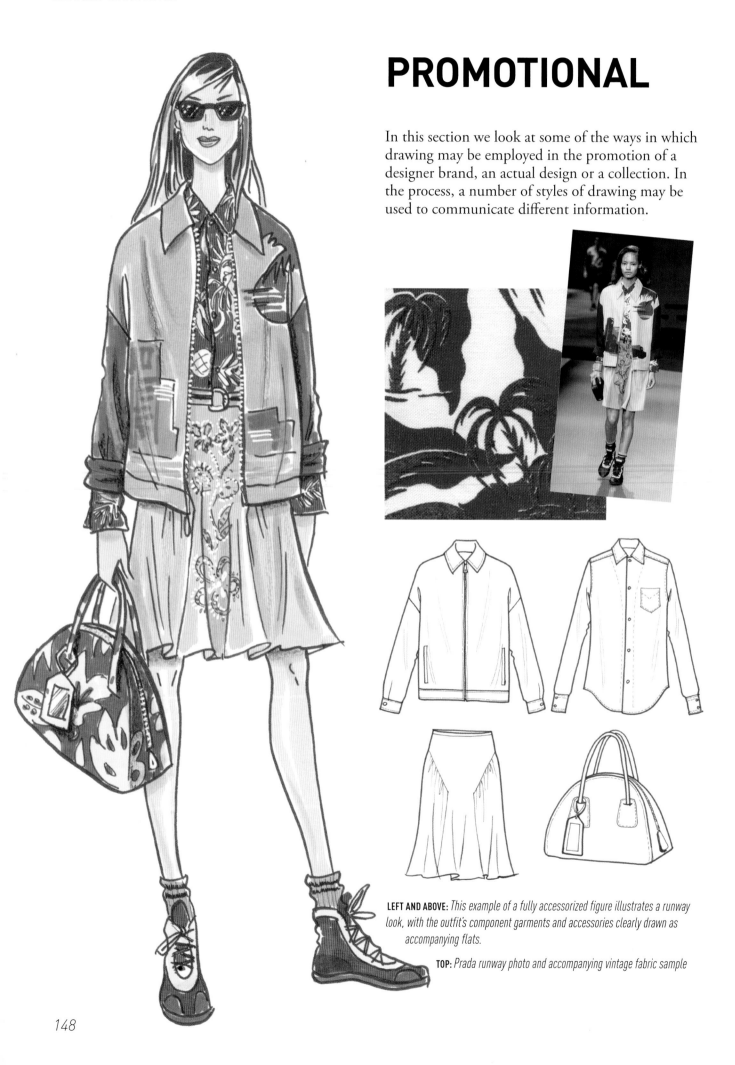

LEFT AND ABOVE: *This example of a fully accessorized figure illustrates a runway look, with the outfit's component garments and accessories clearly drawn as accompanying flats.*

TOP: *Prada runway photo and accompanying vintage fabric sample*

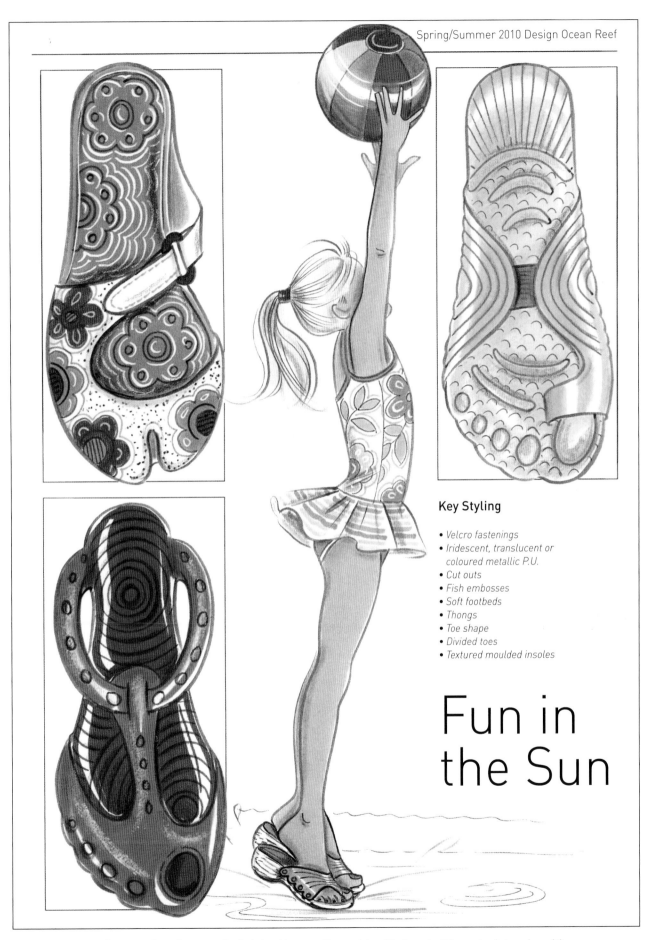

Spring/Summer 2010 Design Ocean Reef

Key Styling

- *Velcro fastenings*
- *Iridescent, translucent or coloured metallic P.U.*
- *Cut outs*
- *Fish embosses*
- *Soft footbeds*
- *Thongs*
- *Toe shape*
- *Divided toes*
- *Textured moulded insoles*

Fun in the Sun

This drawing is less an illustration of actual garments, but is designed to convey the more intangible elements of the mood and atmosphere of the collection. It could be compared to a film poster that tries not to reveal specific details of the movie, but evokes a sense of the story and ambience.

COMMUNICATING DESIGN IDEAS

These pages show two cashmere knitwear projects, womens and mens, for a China-based company. The collections were designed separately, but consecutively, with each following the same work pattern. All communication was done via email. Timing was tight, so drawings and instructions had to be as clear, precise, self-explanatory and foolproof as possible.

'A typical design process would be as follows: to research the customer thoroughly, together with the customer's competitors and the brands to which they aspire; to research colour, yarn, stitches, patterns, styling and silhouette trends. The designer generally works about a year ahead of the season. Ideas are sketched in pencil with appropriate reference information gathered together to inform and inspire. I then select designs to draw in detail with fibre-tip pen, marker pen and crayon. I add a brief

description and carefully selected images of related looks and styles – sometimes vintage, sometimes contemporary – to further explain the look. The designs – approximately 60 – are scanned and sent digitally to the client for selection.'

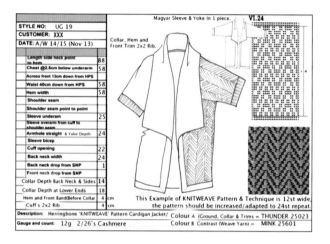

BELOW: *A composite image of part of the womenswear collection shows how the first design sketches are presented alongside images of related styles to assist in explaining and contextualizing the designs into a fashion look/theme.*

ABOVE: *Womenswear – a patterned cardigan jacket with magyar sleeves. The hand-drawn design sketch is scanned into an A4 spec sheet using Photoshop, along with details of the stitch and pattern techniques. All necessary measurements are included for manufacturing.*

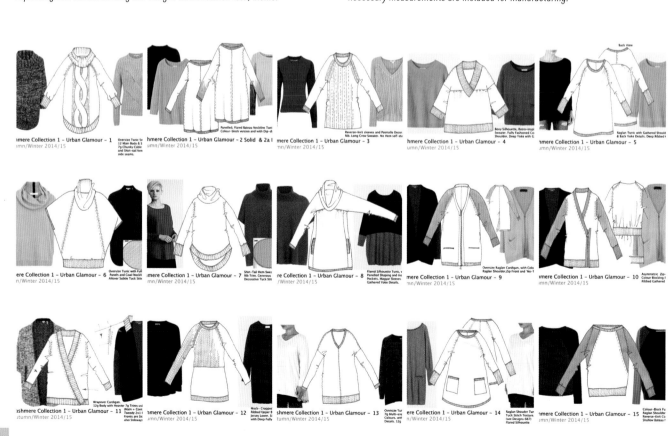

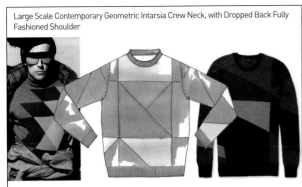

Large Scale Contemporary Geometric Intarsia Crew Neck, with Dropped Back Fully Fashioned Shoulder

Cashmere Collection – Men – Contemporary Country **– 69**
Autumn/Winter 2014/2015

'The selected designs are then scanned into a spec sheet and sent off with key measurements and information, sometimes with additional sheets of information, including close-up or detailed construction sketches and swatches, to ensure accurate interpretation by the sample room. Additional designs are requested and added at this stage, where the client feels they are needed. The timespan would typically be between six to eight weeks from initial briefing to send-off of final designs and specs.'

NOEL CHAPMAN

STYLE NO:	66
CUSTOMER:	XXX
DATE: December 2013 A/W 14/15	
Length side neck point to hem	68
Chest @2.5cm below underarm	55
Across front 13cm down from HPS	
Waist 40cm down from HPS	
Hem width	
Shoulder seam	
Shoulder Width	45
Sleeve underarm	
Sleeve overarm from cuff to shoulder seam	59
Armhole straight	24.5
Sleeve /Width	20
Cuff opening	9.5
Back neck width	16
Back neck drop from SNP	1
Front neck drop from SNP	17
Shoulder slope	
Cuff Trim 1x1 Rib	6
Hem Trim 1x1 Rib	7
Neckline Trim 1x1 Rib	1.5

* See Accompanying Sheet with Colour/Stripe Sequence. Sleeves are same sequences in Reverse (ie Top to Bottom).

<----33.5cm ----> <-21.5cm->

1.5cm Single Rib NOT Double

Description: V Neck Sweater with Asymmetric Split Engineered Stripe. **Colours; Trims & D:** Indigo 25893, B. Thunder 25023 C: Foggy 25251, D Charcoal 25082
Gauge and count: 2/26's Cashmere

ABOVE: Design sketches are scanned into spec sheets and completed in Photoshop with all key information and instructions added.

TOP: Menswear for Autumn/Winter 14/15 – first finished design drawing presented for the client with supporting and contextualizing fashion images on A4 sheets.

BELOW: As with the womenswear image on the facing page, an A4 composite image of part of the menswear collection shows first design sketches alongside images of related styles. The sketches must be clear so that they can be read very small, when they are amalgamated on to range pans and the like.

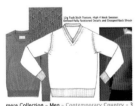
mere Collection – Men – Contemporary Country – 3
mn/Winter 2014/15

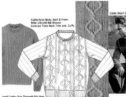
mere Collection – Men – Contemporary Country – 3
umn/Winter 2014/15

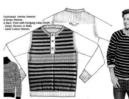
nere Collection – Men – Contemporary Country – 1
nn/Winter 2014/15

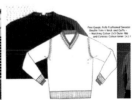
mere Collection – Men – Contemporary Country –
mn/Winter 2014/15

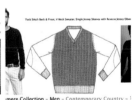
mere Collection – Men – Contemporary Country – 3
mn/Winter 2014/15

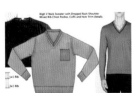
re Collection – Men – Contemporary Country – 33
Winter 2014/15

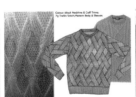
mere Collection – Men – Contemporary Country – 3
umn/Winter 2014/15

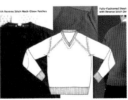
e Collection – Men – Contemporary Country – 35
/Winter 2014/15

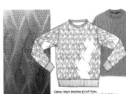
ere Collection – Men – Contemporary Country – 3
mn/Winter 2014/15

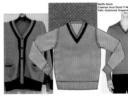
mere Collection – Men – Contemporary Country – 3

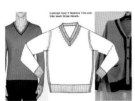
shmere Collection – Men – Contemporary Country –
tumn/Winter 2014/15

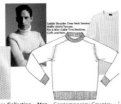
imere Collection – Men – Contemporary Country – 3
mn/Winter 2014/15

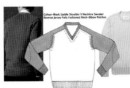
hmere Collection – Men – Contemporary Country –
umn/Winter 2014/15

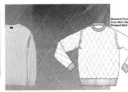
ere Collection – Men – Contemporary Country – 41
/Winter 2014/15

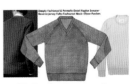
mere Collection – Men – Contemporary Country –
mn/Winter 2014/15

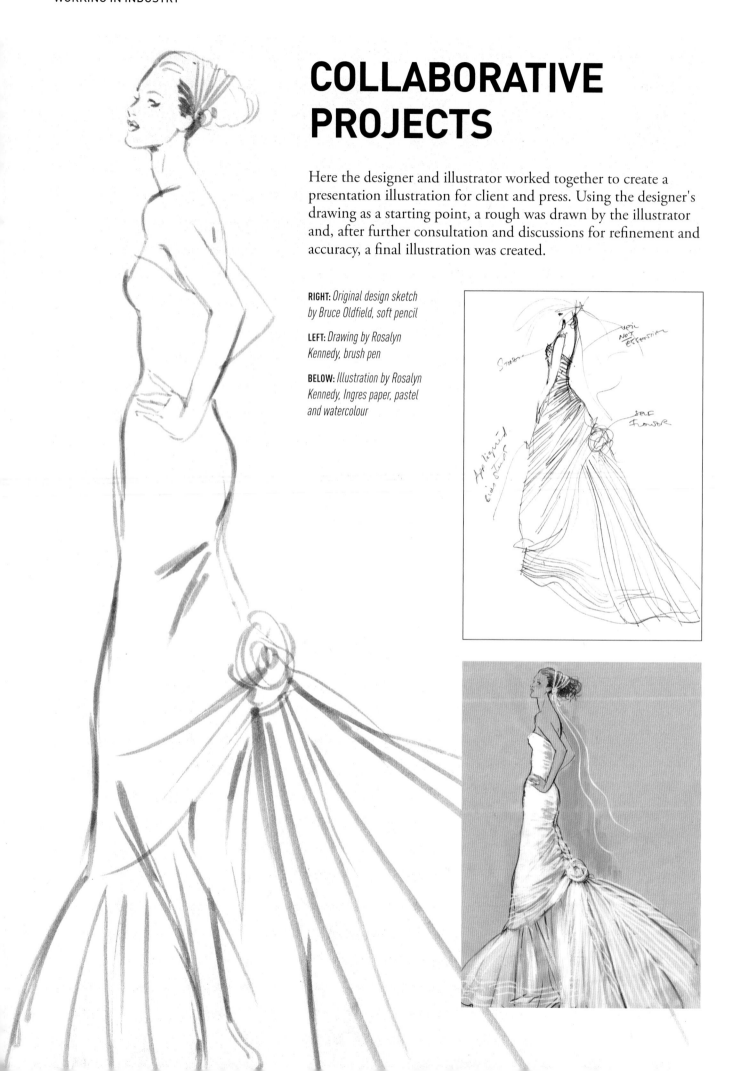

COLLABORATIVE PROJECTS

Here the designer and illustrator worked together to create a presentation illustration for client and press. Using the designer's drawing as a starting point, a rough was drawn by the illustrator and, after further consultation and discussions for refinement and accuracy, a final illustration was created.

RIGHT: *Original design sketch by Bruce Oldfield, soft pencil*

LEFT: *Drawing by Rosalyn Kennedy, brush pen*

BELOW: *Illustration by Rosalyn Kennedy, Ingres paper, pastel and watercolour*

Cherrill Parris-Fox works as an illustrator in the fashion and advertising industries for a variety of high-profile international companies. Most recently she has directed her creativity into fine art projects and become more or less a full-time painter. In a recent collaboration with her fashion and textile designer daughter, Louisa Parris, she produced a witty, delightful series of illustrations to promote Louisa's range of marvellous graphically printed silk scarves and accessories. Louisa sent her mum a 1940s Dick Whittington comic, suggesting the old cartoon sketches typical of *Punch* magazine as an inspiration source.

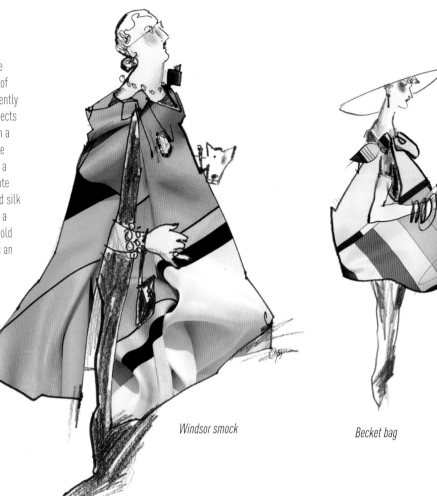

Windsor smock

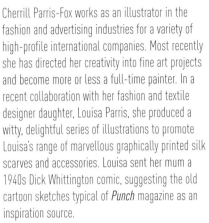

Becket bag

'I thought of my grandmother's good friend, Aunt Lee – she wore bright voluminous tops, anchored to her chest with strands of pearls and always carried a large silk hankie to dab the occasional facial glistening!'
Cherrill Parris-Fox

'Although we have quite different aesthetics within our work, we trust each other's eye implicitly and this unspoken truth allows us to take risks when we work together – and to be surprised by the outcomes.'
Louisa Parris

Savoy cocktail

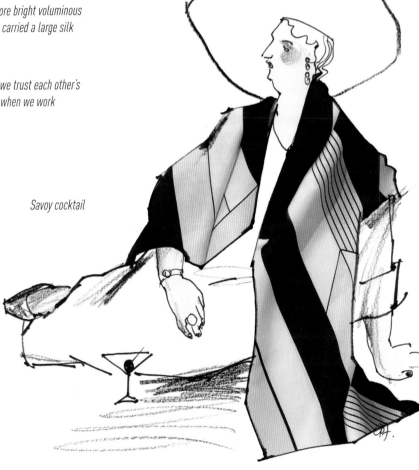

LOUISA PARRIS

DESIGN: *Louisa Parris*

DRAWINGS: *Cherrill Parris Fox*

DIVERSITY

The drawings and illustrations on these pages show something of the range and diversity of roles that drawing can play in contemporary fashion – from communicator of strict and precise instruction to image promotion, echo of attitude and creator of ambience and aspiration.

NEAR RIGHT: *Clare Dudley Hart – women's ski jacket, working sketch in pencil, fibre tip pen, marker pen*

FAR RIGHT: *The presentation drawing of the design, digitally generated using Adobe Illustrator*

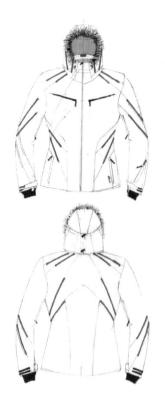

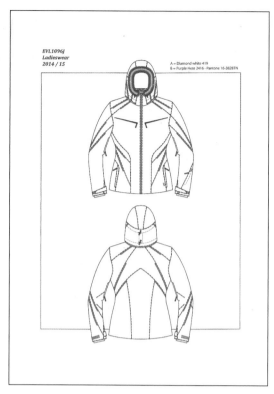

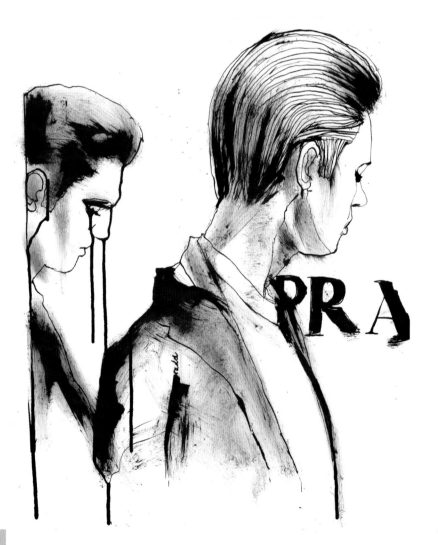

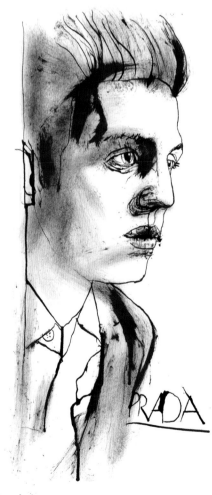

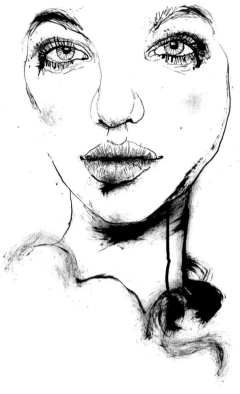

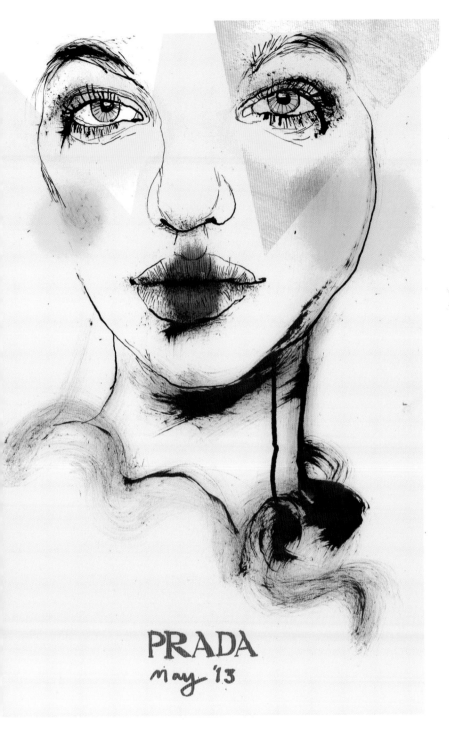

PRADA
may '13

LEFT: *Patrick Morgan – Prada girl, ink and dip-pen, dry brush technique, digitally manipulated*

ABOVE: *The first version of the drawing without added colour*

BELOW: *Patrick Morgan – Chanel. An example in simple mark-making using sponged and masked colour*

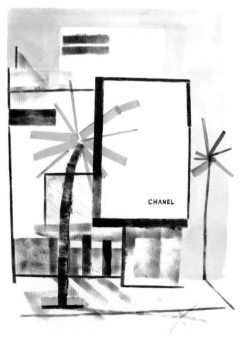

OUR ADDRESS BOOK

A few highlights from our favourite, most useful and inspirational places around the world, with special thanks to friends who shared their address books with us for this information.

BEIJING

The Bookworm
Building 4
Sanlitan Nan Lu
Chauyang
Beijing
Probably the most interesting place for international books and magazines, with talks by writers

Chaterhouse Booktrader
B107 The Place
9 Guanghua Lu
Chaoyang
Beijing
International books and magazine selection

China Central Academy of Fine Arts
8 Hua Jia Di Nan Lu
Chao Yang District

Beijing 100102
B1 Block A
Wangjiing International Business Centre
9 Wangjing Lu
Beijing

The Academy of Arts & Design of Tsinghua University
Haidian District
Beijing
Library bookshop; three stores in Beijing

Muxiyuan Fabric Market
For fabrics, haberdashery and trims head straight for the area south of Muxiyuan Qiao, the oldest store being Jingdu Qingfangcheng

Page One
Chian World Trade Centre
Chaoyang District
Beijing
A branch of the renowned book and magazine store that began in Singapore; for a huge range of international fashion, design and lifestyle magazines and books

HONG KONG

Hong Kong Museum of Art
10 Salisbury Road
Hong Kong Island
Permanent collection and exhibitions

Hollywood Road
Hong Kong Island
The area for private galleries

I.T.
Shop 401. Times Square
Causeway Bay
Hong Kong Island
For the most cutting edge domestic and international fashion labels. With nine stores in Hong Kong at the last count, branches of this exciting store are now springing up all over in China's most progressive cities

I.T.
Shop 2219 Harbour City
Tsimshatsui
Kowloon
Hong Kong

Page One
Times Square
Causeway Bay
Hong Kong Island
See Beijing entry for info

Sham Shi Po
The area for fabric and haberdashery buying; start around Nam Cheong Street and explore . . .

LONDON

Beyond Retro
58-59 Great Marlborough Street
London W1 7JY

92–100 Stoke Newington Road
London N16 7XB

110–112 Cheshire Street
London E2 6EJ
The vintage store that started in Brick Lane and has extended to central London, Brighton, Gothenburg and Stockholm

The Cloth Shop
290 Portobello Road
London W10 5TE
A great selection of fabrics, terrific 'ends of lines' and vintage haberdashery too

Condé Nast Worldwide News
20 St George Street
London W1
Beautiful minimal state-of-the-art store designed by Ab Rogers for all the international Condé Nast publications

Daunt Books
83 Marylebone High Street
London W1 4QW
www.dauntbooks.co.uk
In our opinion, probably the nicest bookshop in London ever

Dover Street Market
17-18 Dover Street
London W1S 4LT
Flagship store for Comme des Garcons and a host of international fashion brands

Hostem
41 Redchurch Street
London E2 7DZ
The most interesting menswear store to open in London for ages

Hunterian Museum
Royal College of Surgeons
35-43 Lincoln's Inn Fields
London WC2A 3PE
*Once you get over the gory stuff, it's one
of our favourite places to draw and study
anatomy*

Ian Batten
201 Archway Road
London N6 5BN
*Great menswear with a Japanese
aesthetic*

Magma Books
117–119 Clerkenwell Road
London EC1R 5BY

8 Earlham Street
London WC2H 9RY
*The best cutting-edge contemporary
niche graphic art and fashion books
and journals*

McCulloch & Wallis
25-26 Dering Street
London W1S 1AT
*The best central London shop for
haberdashery and notions*

The Wallace Collection
Hertford House
Manchester Square
London W1
*World-famous range of fine and
decorative arts from the 15th–19th
centuries; with outstanding 18th century
French paintings*

The Wellcome Collection
183 Euston Road
London NW1 2BE
*'The free destination for the incurably
curious'*

Berwick Street
Poland Street
Soho
London W1
*The main areas to visit for fabric and
haberdashery stores*

MILAN

10 Corso Como
Corso Como 10
20124 Milan
*The home of the concept store that changed
concept stores and became a brand*

Fondazione Prada
Via Spartaco 8
20135 Milan
*For some of the most talked about art
exhibitions and events in Milan*

Galleria d'Arte Moderna
Via Palestro 16
20121 Milan
Permanent collection and exhibitions

Spazio Rossana Orlandi
Via Matteo Bandello 14-16
20123 Milan
*Concept store by the former fashion
editor of Italian Vogue, located in an old
tie factory*

Pellegrini
Via Brera 16
20121 Milan
For a good selection of art supplies

NEW YORK

**Anna-Maria and Stephen Kellen
Archives**
Parsons the New School for Design
66th Fifth Avenue, lobby level
New York, NYC 10011
Specialist fashion-related archives

Bookmarc
400 Bleeker St
New York, NYC 10014
*The first of Mr Jacobs' small global chain
of really cool book and stationery stores*

Habu
135 W 29th #804
New York, NYC 10001
www.habutextiles.com
Natural fabrics and haberdashery

Hyman Hendler & Sons
21 W 38th Street
New York, NYC 10018
Haberdashery

JAM Paper & Envelope
135 3rd Avenue
New York, NYC 10003
A huge selection of papers

Jeffrey
449 W 14th St
New York, NYC 10014
*The concept store that changed the
Meatpacking District to Fashion Central*

Metropolitan Museum of Art
1000 Fifth Avenue
New York. NYC 10028-0198
*Fabulous collections and regularly some
of the best fashion exhibitions we've seen*

Muji
455 Broadway
New York, NYC 10003
*New York outpost of this fantastic shop
for all stationery and storage*

New York Central Art Supply
62 3rd Avenue
New York, NYC 100003
Good for art materials

Purl
459 Broome St
New York, NYC 10013
Craft supplies

Taschen
107 Green Street
New York, NYC
Books and magazines

Urban Jungle
118 Knickerbocker Street
Brooklyn, NYC
*Another reason to go to supercool
Williamsburg – to visit this great
vintage store*

PARIS

Bookmarc
17 Place du Marché St-Honoré
75001 Paris
*Mark Jacobs' book store – music,
stationery, accessories and special items*

Centre Commercial
2 Rue de Marseille
75010 Paris
*The socially and ecologically conscious
store that proves ethics and fashion can
co-exist*

Didier Ludot
24 Galerie de Montpensier
Jardin du Palais Royal
75001 Paris
*Only the very best of vintage haute
couture and high-end fashion labels by
everyone you've ever read about. It's a treat
just to look, and you get to walk round the
beautiful gardens of the Palais Royal too!*

Fondation Pierre Bergé-Yves Saint Laurent
5 Avenue Marceau
75116 Paris
Established by Pierre Bergé to celebrate and perpetuate the art and craft of Yves Saint Laurent, with exhibitions of his work and those artists and designers whose work he loved, collected and was inspired by – no more encouragement needed to make you go there on your next trip

Galignani
224 Rue de Rivoli
75001 Paris
www.galignani.com
The first English language bookshop in mainland Europe, opened in 1802

Kiliwatch
64 Rue Tiquetonne
75002 Paris
The 'go to' shop for affordable vintage clothes and accessories

La Droguerie
11 Rue du Jour
75001 Paris
A Pandora's box of wonderful haberdashery and notions

Marche aux Puces de la Porte de Vanves
Avenue Marc Sangnier / Avenue George Lafenestre
75001 Paris
This flea market is the best place to spend Sunday morning

Merci
111 Boulevard Beaumarchais
75003 Paris
Inspirational concept store for fashion and lifestyle, from the people behind Bonpoint

Musée les Arts Decoratifs – Mode et Textile
107 Rue de Rivoli
75001 Paris
One or two must-see major fashion exhibitions every year with exhibits from arguably the world's best fashion archives and more . . .

Palais Galliera – Musée de la mode
10 Avenue Pierre 1er de Serbie
Rue Galliera
75016 Paris
Seasonal exhibitions themed around fashion

SHANGHAI

Ken Fine Papers
337 Fuzhou Lu
near Shanxi Lu
Shanghai
A wide range of artists' papers including beautiful Japanese washi papers

Shanghai Foreign Language Bookstore
390 Fuzhou Lu, near Fujian Zhong Lu
Huangpu District
Shanghai
Books and magazines

Shanghai Tan Mall
388 Renming Lu
Huang Pu District
Shanghai
A whole multi-storey building full of every kind of haberdashery and trimmings you could ever want

Tian Zi Fan
An area of the French Concession, rapidly turning into the new Brooklyn

TOKYO

Asagaya Animation Street
2-40-1 Asagaya Minami
Suginami-ku
Tokyo
Manga museum, stores and animation college, all situated under the elevated railway

Bookmarc
4-26-14 Jingumae
Shibuya –ku
Tokyo
Mark Jacobs' bookstore – magazines, stationery, music, accessories and special items

Bunka Gakuen Costume Museum
Quint Building
3-22-7 Yoyogi
Shibuya-ku
Tokyo 151-8529
Everything a study centre for costume and fashion history should be; in conjunction with the university, this museum also has a great library

Cow Books Nakameguro
1-14-11 Aobadai
Meguro
Tokyo Prefecture 153-0042
Vintage and new books in the Dragonfly Café – there's no reason not to go!

Daikanyama
17 Sarugakucho
Shibuya-ku
Tokyo
Books, music, café and a whole lot more. Located in an award-winning building by Klein Dytham Architecture

Fabric Street and Fabric Town
Nippori Station
Tokyo
A whole area of fabric and haberdashery stores, a favourite haunt of many Japanese fashion students. Tomato and Lemmon are two shops that have been recommended. Take cash as only a few shops accept cards

Ome Kimono Museum
4-617, Baigo, Ome-shi,
Tokyo, 198-0063
Outside of central Tokyo, about one hour or so from Shinjuku

SOME OF OUR FAVOURITE WEBSITES & BLOGS

http://incompetech.com
For free downloadable graph paper, etc.

www.bryanboy.com
A fashion blog featuring pics, pictures, photos, images, videos and commentary on trends and pop culture

www.theyallhateus.com
Pics, champagne culture, Instagram, Pinterest, fiveseventeen, fashion-gone-rouge, coffeebags-n-shoes

www.whoworewhatwear.com
Celebrity style and fashion trend coverage

http://le-21eme.com/
A photo-journalistic view into the daily world of fashion from cities and fashion weeks around the world

www.facehunter.org
Fashion and trend spotting – 'eye candy for the style hungry'

http://streetpeeper.com/
Street style snapped

http://www.parkandcube.com/
Shini Park's fashion blog, featuring her photography and thoughts

www.filterlife.blogspot.com
Street style

http://www.vogue.co.uk/
Fashion news daily, backstage photos, fashion trends, catwalk videos, supermodel interviews, beauty trends and celebrity party photos

http://www.style.com
Covering the world of fashion, designers, models, celebrities, beauty and shopping

www.garycardiology.blogspot.co.uk
Photos, illustrations and ideas

SOME OF OUR FAVOURITE BOOKS

100 Years of Fashion Illustration, Cally Blackman (Lawrence King, 2009)

100 Years of Fashion, Cally Blackman (Lawrence King, 2012)

100 Years of Menswear, Cally Blackman (Lawrence King, 2012)

The New Drawing on the Right Side of the Brain, Betty Edwards (HarperCollins, 2001)

Ways of Seeing, John Berger (Penguin Modern Classics 1972, new edition 2008)

A Short Book About Drawing, Andrew Marr (Quadrille Publishing, 2013)

Colour and Meaning: Art, Science and Symbolism, John Gage (Thames & Hudson, 2000)

A History of Colors, Manlio Brusatin (Shambhala Publications, 1992)

Colour: Travels Through the Paintbox, Victoria Finlay (Sceptre, 2003)

Colors: What They Mean and How To Make Them, Anne Vachiron (Harry N. Abrams, 2007)

Colour: A Journey, Victoria Alexander (Murdoch Books, 2012)

Mauve, Simon Garfield (Faber & Faber, 2000)

Bright Earth: The Invention Of Colour, Philip Ball (Vintage, 2008)

Colourful World, Amandine Guisez Gallienne (Thames & Hudson, 2005)

CONTRIBUTORS

Charlie Allen
www.charlieallen.co.uk

Ian Batten
www.ianbatten.com

Malcolm Bird
www.malcolm-bird.co.uk

Christopher Brown
chrissbrown@btinternet.com
Agent: Central Illustration Agency
www.centralillustration.com

Flora Cadzow
fcadzow@gmail.com

Massimo Casagrande
www.massimo-casagrande.com

Noel Chapman
nbcassociates@btinternet.com
bleuanglais@btinternet.com
noelchapman.co.uk
www.bleuanglais.co.uk

Judith Cheek
judith.cheek@btinternet.com

Yvonne Deacon
Regents University London
Regents Marylebone Campus
deacony@regents.ac.uk
ydeacon@aiulondon.ac.uk

Mary Edyvean
mary.wilson2010@hotmail.co.uk

Martina Farrow
Agent: New Division
www.newdivision.com
www.martinafarrow.com

Jonathan KYLE Farmer
Associate Professor of Fashion
Parsons the New School
farmerk@newschool.edu
www.newschool.edu/parsons

Elmina Fors
www.elminafors.uk

Gray Modern & Contemporary Art
www.graymca.co.uk

Neil Greer
neiltendenz@aol.com

Clare Dudley Hart
claredhart@btinternet.com

Christopher Heeney
www.christopherheeney.com

Hus Gallery
Jessica Warren
Artist Liaison & Exhibitions Director
jessica@husgalleries.com
www.husgalleries.com

Lesley Hurst
lesley.hurst@virgin.net

Rosalyn Kennedy
rosalynkennedey@hotmail.com

Hilary Kidd
www.hilarykidd.co.uk

Patrick Morgan
www.patrickmorgan.co.uk

Bruce Oldfield
www.bruceoldfield.com

Louisa Parris
www.louisaparris.com

Cherrill Parris-Fox
www.parrisfox.com

N Peal
www.npeal.com

Stina Persson
Agent : CWC-i
www.cwc-i.com
www.stinapersson.com

Mary Ratcliffe
maryratcliffe8@gmail.com

Heather Ridley-Moran
www.hridleymoran.co.uk

Mitchell Sams
m@mitchellsams.com

Anthea Simms
www.antheasimms.com

Howard Tangye
www.howardtangye.com
Central Saint Martin's
Senior Lecturer Womenswear
www.csm.arts.ac.uk

Paul Wearing
www.paulwearing.co.uk

Textile View
www.view-publications.com

Alice Fletcher Quinnell
fletcherquinnellalice@googlemail.com

Niki Zachiardis
for her vintage magazine collection

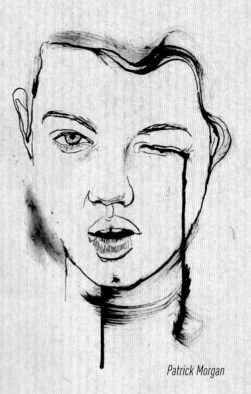
Patrick Morgan

FABRIC AND STILL LIFE CONTRIBUTORS

Butlers Emporium
70 George Street
Hastings
TN34 3EE

Wayward
www.wayward.co

The Cloth Shop
www.theclothshop.net

We would also like to extend our gratitude and send a very special thank you to Dick Knox for permission to use Catch Knox's lovely illustrations.

PICTURE CREDITS

Christopher Brown: page 24, Oscar Wilde linoprint
Noel Chapman: page 11, 38, 122, 123, 146, 147
Judith Cheek: page 78, 144, 145
Lynn Goldsmith: page 108, Patti Smith portrait as part of collage © Lynn Goldsmith 1976
Christopher Heeney: page 70, 120, 121
Mitchell Sams: page 28, 148
Anthea Simms: page 32, 127
Ann-Marie Ward: page 40, 45, 47, 49, 51, 53, 55, 57, 59, 61, 63, 65, 87 and page 127 (bottom right)